AN IRISH EXPERIENCE

An Irish Experience

Travel Tales Flowing from History, Humor & the Search for Home

by

Howard G. Franklin

INKWATER PRESS

PORTLAND • OREGON

INKWATERPRESS.COM

Cover and interior design by Masha Shubin
Edited by Linda Weinerman

Blackstairs Mountain Co. Kilkenny Ireland © 2007 Brian Kelly. Image from iStockPhoto.com
Author photo (back cover, from behind on front cover) by Image Express, Beaverton, Oregon
Map by Jim Miller/fennana design

www.inkwaterpress.com

ISBN-13 978-1-59299-313-0
ISBN-10 1-59299-313-3

Publisher: Inkwater Press

Franklin, Howard G. (Howard Grant), 1940-
  An Irish experience : travel tales flowing from history, humor & the search for home / by
Howard G. Franklin.
      224 p. cm.
  Summary: "Chronicles the author's three-week journey through the Emerald Isle in 2001,
where he was when the terror attacks of 9/11 occurred. Weaves humor and Irish history,
literature, and culture with his travels around the country, relating the author's own search for
home, love, and belonging"--Provided by publisher.
  ISBN-13: 978-1-59299-313-0 (pbk. : acid-free paper)
  ISBN-10: 1-59299-313-3 (pbk. : acid-free paper) 1. Franklin, Howard G. (Howard Grant),
1940---Travel--Ireland. 2. Ireland--Description and travel. I. Title.
  DA978.2.F73 2008
  914.1704'824--dc22

Printed in the U.S.A.
All paper is acid free and meets all ANSI standards for archival quality paper.

For Amy, Matt, and Nick,
that they might find such joy

TABLE OF CONTENTS

FOREWORD

Howard first entered my life in a letter, one filled with earnest praise for my memoir, *Are You Somebody?* Soon, he materialized off the page as a dinner guest during his eagerly anticipated second visit to Ireland. And over wine and seafood, I was introduced to the empathy, humor, and passion for Ireland which are idiosyncratically embodied in his writing.

Uniquely, Howard isn't Irish, nor even the possessor of Irish roots. Yet his love for the Irish way of life is so genuine that it allows him to belong here. And his energy and enthusiasm for sharing his observations and insights into Irish history and culture not only complements the natural pull that Ireland exerts on so many, but makes him a warm-hearted spokesperson for the sights, sounds, and smells that form its magic.

Nuala O'Faolain
County Clare, Ireland
August, 2007

May the road rise to meet you.

May the wind be always at your back...

May the blessing of light be upon you,

light without and light within...

And in all your comings and goings,

may you ever have a kindly greeting

from them you meet along the road.

FROM AN OLD GAELIC BLESSING & PRAYER

I

GENESIS

It begins with brainwaves, an idea: I want to see Ireland. Then, like a gentle breeze, enters emotion, a curious yearning, whispering: I *need* to see Ireland. Add imagination, and the lady is wearing a smile. A beautiful smile. A coquettish smile.

All right. All right. So the lady is a country, you were expecting a romance maybe? Well, all right again, her name is Rachel and she lives in Sligo. But that's its own separate story, and for the moment the subject is beginnings, so as I was saying, the Lady is sporting a smile. Dressed in soft green velvet, her shoulders support a shawl of lakes and rivers and mountains. And around her neck curls a single strand of wedding-white pearls, one each for Dublin, Sligo, Galway, Limerick, Killarney, Cork, and Waterford.

On her left wrist dangles a gold bracelet, heavy with the charms of song and dance, art, and the four Nobel Prizes for Literature, all jingling sweetly beneath the smaller Claddagh brooch nestled near her heart: two arms circling to join hands in friendship, then cradle a heart for love below the crown of loyalty, while in the center, twin emeralds sparkle to speak of the two Hs – History and Humor.

I suppose that is why she is not wearing a watch. For when the Carrowmore Tombs teach a text originating a thousand years before the Pyramids, and the pictures paint a painful but poignant panoply of tragedy and triumph in human nature's native colors, the lesson learned is live now and laugh as much as possible.

"Sounds good to me," I slide out through the grin curling from the corners of my mouth to light my face. And as I lift my eyes from the

1

Lady's figure spread out across the kitchen island to put a match to my pipe, synchronicity swells the grin full. For green tiles edge the counter's white face, and the tiny letters engraved on my pipe spell Peterson's of Dublin.

A coincidence? I consider, once again focusing on the Lady's smile and listening to her siren song. No, I don't think so, squirms the answer several seconds later, all I can see and hear swimming together to configure *secrets* in giant green letters. So many secrets, says the smile, and the song sings sweetly of so many shades of green, that somehow they must harbor a truth I need to know.

"Yeah....Either that, or you're losing what little's left of your mind," I crack sharply into the silence, seeking to shake free of the trance and noting how hot my kitchen has suddenly grown. As a luxurious defense against the Oregon winter, the thermostat is set at 70. And though calculated to create comfy-cozy, the spontaneous ideas swarming about now turn toasty to tropical as "You're going" teases off my tongue, then tiptoes several feet away to wait and see how it's been received.

"I am?" answers the left side of my brain, neurons spinning faster and faster in response to the mixture of anticipation and anxiety coursing through me.

"Uh-huh. For sure," responds the right side with growing confidence. "Hell, deep down you know it, I know it, we know it. So with the Father, the Son, and the Holy Ghost all in agreement, why not just face up to the fact that there are no real accidents in life, and start celebrating with a nice glass of wine."

"O-kay," I nod cautiously, security struggling for a foothold, a thin smile sneaking across my lips.

It widens as I pour the merlot, add chocolate to the burgeoning festivities, and then shuffle into my study in search of an article about Ireland I'd clipped out I don't remember when and carefully stored I don't know where. But the night is pregnant with surprise, and inside five minutes, I've located it, relit my pipe, and digested the fact that 20 million Americans trace their ancestral roots to the Emerald Isle. "Well, how about you, you got any Irish roots?" old Righty chirps cheerfully, still seeking to secure my commitment.

"Oh, sure," snickers Lefty. "I mean you're half Russian, one-quarter

Lithuanian, and one-quarter Hungarian. Does that ring a bell in St. Patrick's Cathedral?"

"Well, it has all the makings of an Irish stew," rips the reply. "And what about dreams, and adventure, and romance, don't they count?..."

In the renewing silence, the noun *dreams* turns slow-motion somersaults until a nerve is nudged and I reach for a favorite book of poems and slowly steer my eyes to savor Ireland's greatest bard:

> *Had I the heavens' embroidered cloths,*
> *Enwrought with golden and silver light,*
> *The blue and the dim and the dark cloths*
> *Of night and light and the half-light,*
> *I would spread my dreams under your feet:*
> *But I, being poor, have only my dreams;*
> *I have spread my dreams under your feet;*
> *Tread softly because you tread on my dreams.*

Oh, yes, murmurs through my mind as solace stirs to tranquilize doubt. Yes...Yes...Yes. 'Cause dreams are the children of hope, and they do indeed count. Big time, huh, Mr. William Butler Yeats. 'Cause they help hold you young and fully alive. They point patiently at purpose and invite passion. And they promise that if you really believe and *risk*, you will be truly *free*. No guarantees of course. But the precious package does include a limited warranty: There's magic even in trying.

"Okay...I'm in," escapes through a sigh when optimism rests to refuel. And as midnight arrives and I climb the stairs into bed, I smile through the darkness at the newborn dream of discovery, allowing *adventure* and *romance* to snuggle in around the edges and add to the collective cozy. "So many shades of green," I echo in whispers, nestling deeper into the pillow, "you must hold a truth I need to know."

Uh-huh, counsels my coy companion silently as I fall into sleep. And all you have to do to learn it is go slowly and tread softly.

II

DILEMMA'S DELIGHT

GO SLOWLY AND *TREAD SOFTLY* ARE THE FIRST WORDS TO ECHO INTO mind when I tumble out of sleep the next morning. Now, *slow* is not an adjective ordinarily applied to me, unless we're discussing my notorious lack of speed on the tennis court. So, true to form, after rushing through breakfast and the sports page, I follow the newborn dream out the door and purchase an airline ticket to Dublin.

What happened to Mr. Conservative? Oh, he's present and accounted for all right. It's January, and the departure date reads September 2, eight full months away. Time to plan and organize, to read and study. Time to ensure that Matt and Nick are doing well at college, and to share the summer when they are home. And, of course, plenty of time to cancel, I console myself with when *if you risk, you'll be truly free* also echoes into ear.

"Yeah, free to fall flat on your skinny little ass too!" I spit out sarcastically as I head my Jeep toward the bookstore. "I mean, risk is not some wimp you can screw around with. This dude you have to take seriously, you hear? As in plan, plan, plan," I lecture as I turn onto the freeway, doubt resurrecting itself from optimism's Valium to creep back into consciousness.

Now, planning a holiday may at first blush seem a simple task, an act of unadulterated joy as it were. However, in this instance, while the joy shines through like the rosy ruby of my birthstone, or make that gleams green as an emerald so as to maintain geographical correctness, one must nevertheless temper unbounded enthusiasm with two sobering realities.

First, while the Godperson simply laughs when man plans, in my case He-She becomes absolutely hysterical. And secondly, I am going alone.

Why? you ask. Well, I lost my wife to cancer thirteen years ago, and haven't remarried nor managed to attract a girlfriend. Why not? is one of life's sad mysteries, to be more fully explored in Sligo when we arrive there. For now, suffice it to say that I do have friends. Many, in fact, including even my two sons and daughter, as I'm a most likable fellow, warm-hearted, loving, and loyal as you are about to learn. Unfortunately though, for travel purposes, my kidlets are either gainfully employed or in hot pursuit of higher education, and my friends are all married and fully occupied with their families and businesses. Thus, if I am to satisfy my gnawing need to know Ireland and learn its truths, I must venture forth: me, myself, and I.

Naturally, in the face of journeying 6000 miles from home, this shadowy status of *solo* can be a bit scary. As if one conjures up becoming lost, there's no partner to scrutinize the map with, and the threat of loneliness does little to warm one's feet into a headlong sprint for the airport. However, like most facets of life, there are two sides to the proverbial coin. So, while shared experiences are not assured, they are still possible if one is open to them and willing to reach out. And in turn, the opportunity to see what you want to, when you want to, and for how long, all without argument or compromise, is a guaranteed gift from the tails side of travel's mintage. Problem is, this advantage leads directly to Mr. Scary's Sub-Sonata, a dandy little ditty founded on Fear's Theme of the Unfamiliar, music and lyrics by Doctors Freud and Jung. And though possessing the potential to graduate confusion into chaos, fortunately this malady can also be overcome in large part by the illusion of control created by careful planning.

I say *illusion* because as the equally learned Doctor Victor Frankl teaches, the only factor in life that you can truly control is you. Still, while this miniaturized rose may not retain Gertrude Stein's full fragrance, it nonetheless smells sweetly of calling the shots. And while I don't know about you, I absolutely, totally, and unreservedly love even this constricted concept of control. I mean, the nourishing notion of knowledge placing me safely in charge of what, when, and how long, warms me to the bottom of my anally retentive soul. Oh, yes, I know. Somehow I failed to include advanced anal retentiveness on my laundry list of quintessential qualities that make me likable, but you wouldn't want me to overcrowd my sentences, would you? And besides, I have confessed, and we're only two paragraphs removed. So, as I was saying, if the underlying uneasiness born from becoming a stranger in a strange land cannot be totally eliminated, over time it can be substantially muted by thoroughly acquainting yourself with the desired subject, thus allowing accumulated familiarity to gradually wear away the face of strangeness and replace it with a family of new friends waiting to share their treasures with you.

And how does one fashion this feat? Well, with books, and maps, and videos. A most timely subject too, as we've arrived at Powell's Travel Bookstore in beautiful downtown Portland. An entire establishment devoted exclusively to travel, its shelves are packed with happy helpers whose sole purpose in life is to pierce the clouds of confusion with shafts of golden sunshine. In fact, inside an hour, the glow is so welcoming that an application of sunscreen seems called for. As after I quickly discover DK's *Eyewitness Guide to Ireland*, along with National Geographic's map of Dublin, mystery marches toward reality and the doubt of where to begin is in full retreat. Then, when *Daytrips Ireland* jumps off the shelf to volunteer, the rainbow on its cover leads me to the fabled pot of gold.

Divided into fifty-five one-day adventures by car, rail, or bus, and complete with fifty-nine maps, each of which is numbered with salient sights that the text then illuminates, this absolute treasure-trove of the Emerald Isle's cities, towns, and villages, its art and architecture, its customs and culture, also addresses the practicality of how best to see the most inside a given time period. However, while this helper is straight from heaven, it presents a dilemma. A delightful dilemma to be sure, but an exquisitely aching interrogative nonetheless: There are so many wonders to visit, how does one choose?

A simple enough question on first sighting. But to Mr. Obsessive-Compulsive Me, one that became my constant companion, both tickling and torturing me for two wavering weeks as I explored and re-explored Patty Preston's *bible* on the sights, sounds, and smells of Eire, each marvel appearing more intriguing than the brother or sister before it. Until finally, on the brink of major madness, I was rescued by Peter Drucker. No, not a travel agent possessing the perfect itinerary. Instead, the Father of Modern Management and Prophet of The Five Principles, the first of which, Planning, mandates choice. And while I never fully appreciated Dr. Pete inside the hallowed halls of business school, I now engendered a genuine fondness for the fellow as I focused on my calendar and maps, his refined axioms coagulating into a common sense that commanded in neon-green blinking lights: BE REASONABLE AND CHOOSE NOW OR ELSE!

Having concluded that I could escape from life's responsibilities for three weeks, without being overwhelmed by guilt or threatening my financial status with bankruptcy proceedings, my first move was to subtract two days for air travel to and from. Then, ever so carefully I allocated the time-space of the remaining nineteen opportunities to allow visits north and west, and south and east – the charms on the Lady's bracelet beginning to become lifelike as I studied the stories of Dublin, Galway, and Cork, scrutinized the distinct cultures of mid-sized Limerick and Waterford, and then was so mesmerized by the landscapes and simplicity surrounding the small towns of Sligo and Killarney that I could feel myself trying to squeeze inside the large color photos I turned and re-turned each night before sleep. It was the villages, however, that threatened once again to interject insanity into the itinerary, the struggle continuing as I sought to add the likes of Ennis, Adare, and Knock without stealing too much time from the Burren and the Cliffs of Moher, geographic miracles complimented as *can't miss*.

"Hell, it's like trying to pick out one single pastry from a bakery crammed full of goodies!" filters my frustration into the early morning hours of late February, the bible's tantalizing tale of the Tipperary Trio of Cashel, Holycross, and Cahir rousing me from my bed and into yet another insomniac scheme of siphoning hours from x so as to include y.

"Yeah...for sure and then some," nods my head in full agreement, drowsy eyes surveying the map with amazement at how such a small island could hold so much history. Druids, Celts, Romans, Vikings, and the English hum into mind, the Hill of Tara then slipping into view, followed by neolithic Newgrange in the Boyne River Valley. On and on the reel runs with Kings, Queens, and castles, wars, politics, and the economy, until suddenly it's stopped by the sun's first slivers of orange sneaking over the hills that guard the bay out back.

Well, how about that, I muse, my mind slowly switching channels to now. A new day is coming, with fresh challenges and opportunities. In

Dublin and Killarney they're already well into the adventure, Irish style of course. So you guys just keep it going, 'cause I'm coming to join in, skips the next thought happily as I search the eastern sky for a glimpse of the River Liffey six thousand miles away, the *dream* shimmering on the sun's newborn rays. "It'll be awhile yet," I whisper into the sweetening silence, my smile a salute: "So meantime, top o' the mornin to ya. Top o' the mornin…"

III

TORSO OF TIME

THE GREAT NOVELIST LEO TOLSTOY ADVISES THAT THE GREATEST OF all warriors are these two: time and patience. And as February sidled into March, and March began wooing April and its winsome song of Spring and new beginnings, I retained the services of both champions as I slipped into the day-to-day details of Plan Ireland.

By this juncture, maps and books filled both my house and life, along with Irish rail and bus schedules and the steady stream of information pouring in from the Tourist Centres I had faxed in each of the cities and towns so carefully selected for visitation. In fact, during a clear-your-head cookie break, "Holy cockamolies!" suddenly combusts out of a pool of apprehensive amazement as I survey the mountain of materials that have miraculously managed to assemble. "Uh-huh, beware the Ides of March all right!" caution then instructs, "And while you're at it, watch what you pull from the pile too. 'Cause if it happens to topple in your direction, what's left can go to Ireland in an envelope!"

But, hey, "no problem," advises Tira, a most helpful hostess at Dublin's Busarus bus station. All I need is an Emerald Pass to allow me on any bus or train. That, and a happy hour on the phone listening to the lovely lilt of her voice as she lays out dates and times capable of transporting me from desire to desire. And "no problem," echoes Christine Jones, reservations manager at the Hotel Central, while expertly assisting me in securing accommodations, an echo that cheerfully reverberates from her equally friendly counterparts in six other hostelries chosen for their centered location and three-star status.

Now, it wouldn't be even remotely unreasonable for you to ask: Hob, old chap, have you never heard of a travel agent? You know, those pert little professionals whose expertise in such matters allows them to make a living advising amateurs such as you?

Well, of course I have, and they are most valuable creatures to be sure. Just not in this case, and advanced anal retentiveness has absolutely nothing to do with it either. I mean, you want to talk Paris, their eyes light up. London, they know intimately, and they're equally at home in Brussels or Florence. But mention Dublin, and the Vacancy sign flickers on. And as for Sligo and Killarney, well, suffice it to say that the adjective *blank* takes on new meaning.

No problem, however. Employing Tolstoy's Twins, all one has to do is match the Irish Tourist Board's Hotel Guide to City Center spots within walking distance of the rail and bus stations, make several telephone calls, and bingo: You're comfy-cozy and good to go! And, in addition, free of charge no less, you gain two highly appealing advantages. First, in speaking with Tira and Christine, you learn first hand how warm and friendly the Irish are, thus swelling capital the C in comfy-cozy. And secondly, one avoids the possibility of being talked into traveling by car, a most well-intentioned suggestion calculated to place you closer to the charm of the countryside, but one also dripping with the dual dangers of loneliness and getting lost.

Lost?…Uh-huh, as in the object is to reach Sligo and one ends up in Stuttgart, a nice enough place I'm told, but then again a frightening forum when one is alone and speaks English with an Irish accent so much better than German with any accent. And how could such a significant miscalculation occur? Easily, if you happen to be born with a natural sense of direction similar to mine. Which is to say, that it would be far more appropriate to label it rudderless, with an innate ability for misdirection. I mean, my Patty claimed that in the middle of the night, I could get lost going to the bathroom in my own house. "Hell," she would chuckle good-naturedly whenever I took my latest wrong turn, "you should wear a compass, not a watch. How's that sound for Christmas?"

Sad, to me. Very sad in fact. But also true. And hence my strong affection for and devout attachment to maps. Maps, maps, and more maps, each charm on the Lady's bracelet now dotted with destinations' green stars as I continued to study history, read biographies, and, when the hour straddled midnight, climb into bed to search for theatres and museums, pubs and restaurants. Seek, I did, and find soon followed: Cork dancing with Wicklow in my brain, the Nobel works of Yeats, Beckett, Joyce, and Heaney linking hands with Robert Emmett, Daniel O'Connell, and Eamon De Valera to spin tales of family, freedom, and a melancholy culture that spawned revolt against England and the Protestant Church, with St. Patrick, Brian Boru, Strongbow, the Great Famine, and the Easter Rising of 1916 all standing tall to tease mysteriously from history's shadows.

And more. Did you know that Ireland is 300 miles long and 170 miles wide, making it easy to cross from east to west in a few hours, and from the southern edge to the northern rim inside a day? Are you aware that no part of the island is more than 70 miles from the sea, and that no city lies more than 100 miles from a neighboring sister or brother? And do you realize that only 3.8 million souls reside within the Republic, almost the identical population of my Oregon? And the climate's the same too, rain, rain, rain, with the average temperature classified as mild.

In Dublin, at the junction of Grafton Street and College Green, there's a statue of Molly Malone, the celebrated "cockles and mussels" street trader from Irish folk song fame, while across the street, images of Edmund Burke and Oliver Goldsmith guard the entrance to Trinity College, founded in 1592 by the first Queen Elizabeth and home to the Old Library, which houses the original Book of Kells. You want theatre? There's the famed Abbey and Gate, the Gaiety, Peacock, and Andrew Lane. Mention music, and a chorus of pubs sing out their promise of nightly frolic, while architecture simply abounds, from the awe-inspiring Custom House of James Gandon to the elegant simplicity of Merrion Square and St. Stephen's Green.

And history? Why it's everywhere, leaping from Dublin Castle to Yeats' grave outside Sligo in Drumcliffe cemetery. In Galway's Eyre Square, there's the Browne Door, once the entryway to the mansion of one of the ancient fourteen tribes, while Limerick City features the medieval monuments of King John's Castle and St. Mary's Cathedral. Following suit, Killarney gifts a National Park not only holding natural beauty beyond belief, but Muckross Abbey from the 1440s as well, while Cork City traces its roots to the sixth century when St. Finbarr founded a monastery. And not to draw fame solely from its renowned crystal, Waterford offers Reginald's Tower, a thousand-year-old Viking treasure.

And still more. Much more. There are battlefields and castles, rivers and mountain ranges. The moon-faced Burren, and the Ring of Kerry. And Glendalough. And the Sally Gap. And the Dingle Peninsula. And… and…"You're only standing on first base, Hobman. So how's that grab ya, huh?" jabs the rising river of overwhelm, before fading into the smoke billowing from my pipe in the early morning hours of newborn May. "I mean, how in the holy hell can one little island hold so much?" I then chuckle, suddenly catching sight of the *Professor*, a character I created to serve as the hero's conscience in my last novel. Named Euripides Bartholomew Schwartz, the greatest of all Greek-Jewish philosophers, of which in reality there were none, I nevertheless invested him with a status equal to that of his collegial chums, Aristotle, Plato, and Socrates. Not as well known, of course, but equally well respected for his practical approach to sophisticated issues by those with Ph.D. credentials. And, in that I was sorely in need of a large dose of practicality, the sighting proved fortuitous indeed.

"Listen, Little-Boy-I-Want-to-Know-Everything," oozes his warm greeting, "Face it: You can't. Period! So why not just stick to basics, and rescue yourself from the Lost Land of Empty Statistics."

"Yeah…right," ventures my reply sheepishly. "Guess my enthusiasm's trying to do a little too much, huh?"

"A little?" he groans. "Hell's bells, you're trying to cram nineteen centuries into nineteen days! You can't know everything, or see it all. Who do you think you are, Albert the Einstein, or Newton the apple dropper?"

"No….Just curious me."

"Well, I'm going to lay off the old pussycat story, but I do have a news flash for you: You better stick to basics and rest your brain, Buster Brown, or the Synapses Union's going to file a formal grievance for abuse of overtime! Ya hear?…"

Somehow, I did. I listened. And in the renewing silence, soft and salutary, I heard. "It's not a test," seeps my morning motto after a good night's sleep. "You're just trying to avoid a blind date, that's all," I grinned out over my maps and books as I returned to my preparations. And magically, as if it too heard the call to basics, frustration faded and was replaced by a much friendlier companion, anticipation. An uncanny combination of desire, hope, raw excitement, and antsy anxiety, all shepherded by The

Dream, this infant, feeding relentlessly on restless energy, grows gigantic as June pushes July into August and my departure date looms large as the Atlantic and just beyond the tip of my nose.

"Wind up ye olde details," skips self-instruction as I busy myself paying bills in advance, providing copies of my itinerary to family and friends, and insuring that the kidlets' needs will be satisfied during my absence. Then, while returning several unused maps and books to Powell's, I receive a bon voyage gift. In a stand adjacent to the customer service counter, Nuala O'Faolain smiles coyly at me from the cover of her book and asks: *Are You Somebody?* Drawn instantly to the pretty face that speaks clearly of character, I learn from the back-cover summary that she writes about rising from a dysfunctional Dublin family to push constantly at the boundaries of Ireland's confining Catholic culture and become a highly regarded journalist. And spurred by intuition, impulse fathers a spontaneous purchase that will soon transform into *special* indeed.

Tick. Tock. Tick. The clock now leans into September, time's torso having gained as much weight as the single suitcase I have so carefully packed. It's Sunday, the same Sunday that seemed an eternity away eight months ago, but now stands smiling brightly at me, then begins rushing by, propelled by the electric emotion coursing through me so strongly that it threatens to fly me to Dublin without aid of a plane. A long hug from Matt. A short flight to San Francisco. And at 6:24 p.m., cozied into seat 12A of United's Flight 954 with Nuala, a diet Coke, and assorted nuts, we have lift-off!

And as the plane banks into the sunset, the great poet Keats whispers into my ear: "Beauty is truth, truth beauty. That is all ye know on earth, and all ye need to know."

Well, trickles the reply, my head nodding in affirmation. All those shades of green are waiting, time to find out!

IV

HELLO DUBLIN

And after a tasty dinner, a chapter with Nuala, and five hours' sleep, all tucked inside an eleven-hour flight, I stand outside Dublin Airport holding hands with the moment. My body clock says it's only 6:21 a.m., but my trusty Timex Digital reads: Good afternoon, Hob! Welcome to Ireland!

Yeah, and a wet one too, drips my observation, a light drizzle falling from the bruised sky as I walk toward the taxi pool pulling Big Blue, my suitcase, behind me. No problem, however, I muse as the homing thought, Hey, just like Portland, is suddenly submerged by the rush of Do you realize you're walking on *Irish soil?*, the actuality instantly spawning a smile that grows wide with triumph. In fact, I'm still wearing it when Brian the cabbie returns it, grants my request to sit up front with him, and heads us toward downtown Dublin.

Chuckling over the idea of being the first Irish person in my life, Brian, around forty, with a wife and two sons, freely joins in the conversation running from which suburb we're passing through to where I'm from and how did I know we need to take the O'Connell Bridge to reach the Hotel Central? Where, twenty-some sociable minutes later, he deposits me with a hearty handshake and a farewell "All the best."

From the sidewalk, for a long moment I admire the angular, orangy-red brick facade that speaks of the Victorian era, noting that the canopy over the entryway is faced with red and green stained glass. Then, entering the lobby to check in, I meet Christine Jones, the reservations manager, and discover that she's as lovely as the lyrical voice I listened to over the phone last April. If only you were thirty again, I chide myself playfully, settling into room 322 and slowly casting an approving eye over the warm wood-and-cloth furnishings, before hurrying to ready myself for a late-afternoon adventure. Ye olde unpacking can wait till bedtime, waves a green flag from the Master Plan, so as four o'clock approaches, I slip into my warm, waterproof jacket, pull on my backpack, and head downstairs and outside to see what I can while the light lasts.

This time I turn left when I reach the sidewalk, and head west on Exchequer Street till it turns into Wicklow one short block later, precisely as my memorized map said it would. Celebrating by lighting up my favorite Peterson as I walk, my eyes sweep in several directions to capture the narrow, brick-paved streets, lined with darker brick buildings housing shops of every description inside a quaint mixture of multi-colored new and older styled storefronts. Time slows to coddle curiosity, but still ticks to four-thirty when I reach Grafton Street and turn left again, now pointing north to where a five-minute stroll brings me face to face with the Bank of Ireland.

Serious is the adjective that floats forward to salute this landmark. As constructed of sober-gray cement, and sporting impressive dimensions, this icon of the economy is fronted by four towering columns supporting a canopy, on top of which appear two carved lions that appropriately inspire dual thoughts. One, the architects of ancient Greece would be proud indeed. And secondly, this Central Bank personifies perfectly the intended images of safe and secure. Which is precisely how I'm feeling, having successfully navigated the better part of one whole mile without a single misstep. Not cocky, mind you. Just pleasantly pleased that Map Reading 1 thru 1000 is immediately paying dividends, a smile finding my face as I continue northward on Westmoreland, Trinity College creeping into view on my right. Tomorrow, I mouth silently to the scholarly enclave as my walking shoes begin to earn their keep. Today is reserved for Temple Bar.

Described variously as Dublin's Greenwich Village, Left Bank, and Latin Quarter, I had map-marked this celebrated spot as just the place to squeeze into day one's abbreviated time-slot. A compact 2-block-wide by 10-block-long hodgepodge of narrow streets and alleys running between Westmoreland and Fishamble Streets just south of the Liffey, in today's vernacular, Temple Bar is "*the* place to hang out." Named after Sir William Temple, the Provost of Trinity College who lived in the area during the early seventeenth century, and redeveloped in the 1990s after its modern-day warehouses fell into decline, this revitalized island of activity is a magnet for the young and the restless, the avant-garde and the bohemian, and the artistic and the entrepreneurial. And as I reach Fleet Street and enter this cultural hot spot, an understated "Wow" whistles through my teeth, so taken am I by the off-beat charm that warms round me like an electric blanket.

For color is everywhere the eye turns. And people too, a veritable cross-section of size, shape, sex, and age, with tourists adding a multinational flavor. But the subject is color, and here every hue has a home. As housed inside a motley mixture of Georgian and Victorian architecture, restaurants, cafés, and bars, as well as shops, studios, and art galleries wear bright shades of red and yellow, blue, green, purple, and orange – a peppy parade of pigment that rivals even the most garish rainbow. And variety? As in almost too much to choose from? Try over 150 shops for clothes and crafts, books and gifts, jewelry, pottery, and toys. Then add music venues, the Irish Film Centre, and the Gallery of Photography to the mix, along with a spicy splash of hotels and dance clubs, and the full bounty of Temple Bar's buzz circulates into view.

"Holy molies, what a place!" spurts off my tongue, when, after a happy hour of roaming, I flop down onto a curb facing the small square that serves as the area's hub. A favorite meeting place, even as the dinner hour approaches, the plaza is well populated. On the near side, a street performer is strumming guitar, and as I listen to the folk melody float over the crowd, a striking blonde dressed in a sleek black pantsuit crosses diagonally and disappears up an alley. Oh, yes, what a place for sure! And not easy to leave either, my mind sighs as I pull myself up from my perch and head off to meet the River Liffey.

Eustace Street drops into sight inside three blocks, and just before I reach it I treat myself to a mocha from a cute café called The Joy of Coffee, spending my first Irish pound, nicknamed *punt*. Then, a right turn, and another short block lands me on Wellington Quay, where one blessing instantly follows another. At home, night after night I'd gazed at photos, but none had prepared me fully for the eyeful I now enjoyed. For even under leaden skies and the thinning light, *beautiful* echoes and re-echoes as my eyes search and survey. The Liffey, which cuts through the center of Dublin, immediately captures the core of my attention, steely gray yet softly peaceful against the ominous overhang, and crowned by a series of low-slung stone bridges. On both the north and south banks, buildings stretch east and west as far as the eye can follow. Most are constructed from various shades of brick, with stucco fronts of several hotels bearing bright colors, accented further by the facades of ground-floor shops and restaurants. And every so often, like a solitary candle on a cake, a church steeple rises over this multi-colored collage of old and new in sacred celebration of the beauty playing round its feet. North and south, east and west, and from ground to sky roam my ravenous eyes. And when they can hardly hold any more, "H-e-l-l-o, Dublin," finally escapes in whispers from my post on the Grattan Bridge. "I've come six thousand miles to meet ya, and if I had to leave right now, you're worth it!" tumbles my abject admiration, my head bobbing in agreement.

No need of course. The only travel required to continue perusing this picture-postcard is a short retreat to a nearby corner awning when rain suddenly starts to fall. And once positioned, I promptly renew my galloping gaze, sighting the turquoise dome of the Four Courts a half mile away as dusk begins to drop into Yeats' "light, and the half light," my mocha now tasting even sweeter with the realization of how comfortable I feel after only a few hours. It works. You study some, and make maps your best friend, and you can enjoy big time! I smile, suddenly recalling the horoscope I'd read on the plane. "Let go of preconceived notions and accept your pioneering spirit," it had advised. And as both conditions now appear highly appropriate for searching out new truths, I slowly raise my cup in silent salute.

Fifteen mesmerizing minutes later, the rain stops, and I start my feet back to Temple Bar in pursuit of dinner as the clock ticks toward six-thirty. As I had not eaten since cantaloupe and egg sandwiches were served an hour before landing, food centers my attention as I amble toward a famed pub, disarming me for the shock I was about to encounter. For just short of my destination, I stumble upon a fast-food eatery wearing the historical handle: The Alamo.

Stopping abruptly, my eyes locking onto the hot-red storefront's windows with their gold-lettered tribute to bar-b-q and Coca-Cola, for several sober seconds I focus intently on the glitzy incongruity, until finally, like a volcano, Oh…my…God, Texas has invaded Ireland! erupts to flood my suddenly feverish brain. I mean, you may think it's only a harmless little restaurant, spew the neurons, but take a brief glance at history, will ya? Those first farms and ranches in northern Mexico were also little. You know, simple settlements and all. Then, before you can say Sam Houston, bango, they grabbed the whole enchilada! dances the dialogue, a wry smile creeping out of the corners of my mouth to mock the gravity of the situation. Oh, I know their official position is that all they did was lower Mexico's border a tiny bit, but the truth is they kicked the holy hell out of Santa Ana's army and took it! Never mind that this tiny border alteration just happened to be larger than some countries, so I wonder if the Irish have any idea at all of the terrible danger they're in? And moreover, does our government know anything about this? I mean, what about the CIA and the FBI and…and…oh, hell, the problem's even more serious than first blush reveals: We've got a Texas cowboy in the White House, remember? Christ, he's probably in on it! And tricky Dick Cheney too! I mean, there must be oil somewhere on the Emerald Isle, don't you think? teases the tangent, pausing only long enough to allow me to shift my weight.

The only hope, optimism offers, is the Supreme Court. They could declare the whole bloody mess unconstitutional, and order us back to our own business. Then, Colin Powell can apologize for the inconvenience (Sorry, you know how rambunctious teenagers can be), and Congress can take a five-minute break from being confused to slip a few billion into the Irish treasury and make nicey-nicey. Only problem is, that after the political perversion in Florida, you can't count on the Court either. So, what we're left with, unfortunately, is pure trouble with a capital T, right here in downtown Dublin! the monologue meanders to a close, leaving me to add the postscript. "Yeah, right, Hobman," fuels the afterburner. "And you better find that pub quick, before Guinness is replaced by Corona, or maybe even Pennzoil!" I chuckle, finally turning away and shuffling on toward the olive-green facade that had caught my eye when I first entered Temple Bar.

At the corner of Anglesea and Fleet streets I find it, still sporting the large gold letters spelling out Oliver St. Gogarty, the name of the physician-writer who was both a friend and critic of Yeats. The friendly light glowing through its welcoming windows instantly issues a personal invitation, and upon my entry, the homey image grows real from hospitality's trio of a fireplace, live music, and the well-worn wooden bar where I seat myself and order a pint of Ireland's national drink. Then, after I've toasted both Eire and new beginnings, and supplemented my Guinness with a hearty stew, time floats pleasantly by amidst casual conversation and a local band's mixture of modern and traditional folk songs.

Nine o'clock finds me returned to room 322 at the Hotel Central, where, while unpacking, I savor both the day's successes and the comforts placed at my disposal. With my home away from home easily housing a king-size bed with oversized pillows, my eyes smile at the warmth flowing from the plush green bedspread that coordinates with the green-and-gold striped canopy and matching window treatments. In between the windows stand an oval table and two chairs, several feet to the left of which is a doorway into a spacious walk-in closet. And to the right, the *throne* room, half the size of the large living area, is truly a surprise, with its white-tiled floor leading to double sinks and up three wooden stairs to a bathtub with shower that could house four of me. Then, to crown these regal accoutrements, a skylight, on which the lightly falling rain taps a tender tune.

"Very, very, nice indeed, King Hob!" I enthuse, pleased with how well my choice had turned out, and for the moderate fare of 140 dollars. Celebrating with fresh coffee and a pipeful, I then reviewed tomorrow's prospects and telephoned the kidlets to advise that I was safe and sound, before reaching *sharing time* with Nuala.

On the plane, she had introduced herself as an opinion columnist for the *Irish Times*, the most respected newspaper in Ireland, confiding in me that despite some accomplishments as she reached her forties, "I'm no star," then asking wistfully: "Who decides what a somebody is? And how is a somebody made?..."

Tonight, she introduces me to her family, and I learn that Ireland in the 1940s was a living tomb for women, that they never went out, never had money, never stopped having children – and that absolutely no one accepts responsibility for the large Irish families that in generation after generation were ravaged by alcoholism. Her mother, without education or skills, and condemned to the role of homemaker, turned to drink and reading, "not to feed reflection, but to avoid it." While her Dad, a teacher, jumped into radio commentary and then journalism, and was away from home for long stretches of time, during which other women played prominent roles. Thus, the children were left to half raise themselves, with the oldest expected to help care for the younger siblings to boot.

"Boy, some rough beginning," I mutter as my eyelids grow heavy, and I climb into bed with a myriad of thoughts slowly turning over. How different my childhood had been in those same 1940s, I muse, with family stability and the added security of Grammy, Gramp, and Nanny Lou living right next door. But my life had been more traditional then too, I recall, with Dad the breadwinner and Mom cast in the role of homemaker. I wonder, did she feel unsatisfied? Miss having a career? And is that why she was so nervous when I was little? tumble the questions, funneling into a top that begins to spin.

I...don't...know, slips the sleepy answer, it needs more thought. What I do know is that it's been some kind of special day: The Bank of Ireland, Temple Bar, the Liffey and the Quays – not to forget for a moment, the Georgian buildings, which strangely speak to a warm spot deep inside me. "Oh, yes, the best Labor Day I've ever spent," I whisper into the darkness. "And thank you, Lord. Big time," half-steps my happiness, today's outrageously colorful storefronts and dusky bridges fading into tomorrow's promise of St. Patrick's Cathedral and Trinity College.

Yeah...for sure, travels the trail of gratitude into sleep. So, hello, dear Dublin, my new friend. And good night.

V

CHURCH, CASTLE, & COLLEGE

Tuesday dawns crystal clear, with the sun smiling out of a cloudless, cobalt-blue sky. And standing at my hotel room's third-story window sipping coffee at six-thirty, I smile back as my eyes steer west along Exchequer Street to where inside a block it joins Great Georges. Feeling excitement also awaken to prod me fully alert, for an unhurried minute I let my eyes wander over the snapshot of new sights awaiting me, before shuffling back over to the small table to pore over my maps and notes. Then, after a hot shower and a hearty Irish breakfast of stewed fruit, cereal, eggs with sausages, and more coffee, I join the Dubliners off to work and early morning shopping.

With history streaming into mind to fill my head as full as my stomach, I turn left when I reach Great Georges and begin a gentle climb, my eyes searching the myriad of shops housed in orange-brick Georgian buildings and earmarking in my memory bank the Market Arcade for a future visit. Two long blocks bring me to Stephen Street, where I turn west, following it through a district of office buildings into Golden Lane, noticeably narrower and more curved. Add a slight wiggle or two, and ten minutes later its arc meets Bride Street and I'm stopped in my tracks by my first view of St. Patrick's Cathedral.

A poetic philosopher once said that architecture is frozen music. If so, St. Patrick's is a symphony of lullabies featuring the sweet-soft sounds of the violin. For though Ireland's largest church by virtue of its 300-foot length and 140-foot bell tower, and while formed from impressive gray limestone, its classic lines speak simply to the absolute absence of pretension, whispering, "I'm special all right, please notice," while simultaneously smiling,

21

"Welcome!" Having frozen in place myself, several musical minutes sound before movement is able to reoccur. Maybe it's the two-block-square park inside which it sits that makes it seem so user-friendly, I muse when I finally resume walking and enter the grounds. Or, maybe it's the quiet strength flowing so humbly from its stately shape that over the centuries has caused it to be seen as the people's church, finishes my thought as I stop fifteen feet inside the gate to note a slightly raised stone slab surrounded by flowers.

"Wow, this is where it all began," escapes off my tongue as I gaze at the spot where in 450 St. Patrick baptized the locals from a then existing well, my mind racing on to recall how a wooden church was subsequently constructed nearby to honor him. And quite a story too, headline news today. For kidnapped from Britain to Ireland by pirates when but a boy, Patrick had later escaped to study Christianity in France before returning to convert the Celtic tribes. And in similar fashion, it was after the passage of centuries that in 1192 the church was reborn as a stone cathedral, with the bell tower restored even later, in 1370, by Archbishop Minot, thereby providing the steepled column with its name.

Holy molies! Ain't it something! bounces my brain in sync with the bells now chiming to announce the arrival of nine o'clock. And though an apt expression of the admiration coursing through me, when I then enter inside the Cathedral, my colloquial tribute proves to be an understatement of magnificent magnitude. Standing at the western end, one has an unobstructed view of the altar, a football field away, while overhead, a vaulted ceiling constructed of gold-tinted wood arches gracefully downward around windows whose stained glass kisses the sunlight to scatter jewels across the inlaid wooded floor. No less than totally awestruck by the warmth of the beauty before me, I slowly amble up the center aisle to within twenty feet of the altar and sit down to study the even larger and more intricate stained-glass windows above the dais. Though I'm not religious in a doctrinal sense, the overwhelming aura of peace permeating the air is so inviting that I am suddenly moved to pray, first giving thanks for being allowed to experience such beauty, then less selfishly, for peace in our troubled world.

Upon lifting my head moments later, my eyes fix on the raised wooden pulpit slightly left and ten feet to the front of the altar. It was here, history offers, that Jonathan Swift, the great political satirist and author of

Gulliver's Travels, preached when he was Dean of St. Patrick's from 1713 to 1744. And concentrating, I try to imagine him exhorting the congregation to wrestle with the irony of *do unto others* within the framework of bitter Anglo-Irish relations, my mind's split screen also returning to high school and my beloved English teacher, Eunice Schmidt, who had labored so lovingly to help us know Swift's genius. Grateful then, and even more so now, minutes later when I visit the Dean's grave behind the pulpit inside the north transept, I thank them both, bowing, then blowing a kiss.

Returning outside, I don't want to leave – I can't leave, so strong is the hold of history, so powerful the pull of peace. So, lighting up my pipe on a park bench facing Minot's Tower, I simply sit in the sunshine, luxuriating in its warmth while allowing my eyes to wander lazily over the subdued beauty of the Cathedral, then drop to the abundant flower beds bright with color.

"Do ya like it?" asks a surprise visitor, slicing a path through my relaxed trance to pull my gaze upward into the grin of a small man hunched over a refuse container on wheels. When I explain how truly special I find it, Joe, the head groundskeeper, shares with me that it amazes him too, "All over again, every day," and that the "comfort fix" is the chief benefit of his work. Then, after we trade talk about Ireland and England, where Joe lived for thirty years because employment opportunities were better, the discussion centers around how Ireland's finally enjoying an era of prosperity, thanks to the location of large installations by Intel, Microsoft, and Gateway, as well as entry into the European Union. This, in turn, leads to the sticky subject of world problems, with emphasis on the terrible violence in Africa and Palestine. "Hell," Joe ventures, shaking his head sadly, his voice remaining low-key. "People just can't get along. I mean, look at us Irish, we've got two groups from the same religion, and they're always at each other."

"Yeah, I hear ya," dribbles my reply, the fact that St. Patrick's is a Protestant Cathedral in an overwhelmingly Catholic community tripping into view. "Well, if we could just make the silly politicians sit down here for a year or two, maybe they could be friends like you and me," I smile, then thank him with a handshake after he takes my picture alongside my *favorite* Irish church. "I'll be back," I call after him as he strolls toward a hedge in need of trimming. "Right after I see some more of your beautiful country. You take care now, ya hear?..."

"You too," he returns, just as Minot's bells chime to signal an hour has passed. It seems like a whole day, I reflect, pulling on my backpack and slowly walking back to the gate, then turning to steal a final look. Frozen music, huh? follows the next thought as my eyes memorize. "Well no problem understanding why Handel chose your choir to debut his *Messiah*," I whisper before finally pushing myself through the gate. "No problem at all," I confirm with a nod of the head.

Still smiling when I reach the sidewalk of Patrick Street and turn north, my grin's afterburner kicks in when the joy of my rich discovery is topped with the consideration that though already a success, the day remains young and many historical treasures lie ahead. And as eagerness increases my pace, I notice that Dublin too is now fully awake, that cars and buses are humming to and fro, and that the path I'm pursuing is at present populated with people of all ages, sizes, and shapes going about their day's business. Mothers with children in strollers. Office workers carrying cups of coffee, and laughing and chattering away. Executives and professionals in pin-striped suits, lugging leather briefcases. And senior citizens out for a morning stroll, arms locked together. Ireland's capital city, alive and lively with its embrace of almost half the Republic's 3.8 million citizens, hustling and bustling about, albeit without the frenetic pace of New York, Chicago, or Los Angeles, and absent their aura of endless size that makes one feel like a solitary fish in the great Atlantic that separates them. It's more like my Portland, I muse as Patrick Street becomes Nicholas, then changes to Winetavern three blocks later. It's a large city, no question. But one that's walkable, and feels homey from its quaint mixture of old and new buildings, the vast majority of which are compatible and limited in height, so that one doesn't have to look up out of an artificial canyon to find the sky or the horizon. It's cosmopolitan all right, but comfortable. Like a pair of new shoes whose retrofit styling speaks of yesterday, while incorporating today's technology so as to eliminate the need for breaking them in. Boy, wouldn't the Celts and Vikings be amazed? pops the question as my feet pick up speed, my mind then wandering back over the centuries.

The Celts first arrived in Eire around 600 B.C., and over the next three hundred years mixed with the descendants of the Beaker, Food

Vessel, and Cinerary Urn peoples until they dominated. Then, from 250 B.C. until A.D. 800, during a long and relatively peaceful era, the tribes prospered and Ireland politicized into four geographic dominions: Ulster in the north, Munster in the south, Leinster in the east, and Connaught in the west. Each of these areas had a king, with individual chiefdoms carved out within the realm, and there was in addition a titular High King at Tara, an overall scheme of practical politics that was actually working quite well, history records. However, unlike time, history refuses to run in a perfectly straight line, insisting on an occasional bump in the road, some of them large with consequence. And it is precisely one of those bumps, colored a battle-bruised black-and-blue, which brings us, ten minutes and two sloping blocks later, to Wood Quay, the special spot on the River Liffey's south bank where in 842 the Vikings landed to found Dublin.

Though undeveloped, the area already had settlers. In fact the Greek geographer Ptolemy had pinpointed this location on a map 600 years earlier. But now, the ambitious Danes had decided the time had come to upgrade this scrawny settlement at the junction of the Rivers Poddle and Liffey into a city. A walled city no less. And along with it, no extra charge, create a story that would undoubtedly have headlined the "Evening News with Dan Rather"! bounces my brain as I sit down on a nearby bench for a smoke, then stare up at the modern Civic Office Complex that now stands where the fierce invaders once pitched camp. Yeah, they'd be amazed all right, my thought continues as I turn to gaze at the Liffey and try to imagine how raw and primitive Dublin, or Black Pool as it was called then, must have appeared. "What do you think? Huh, Professor?" I shrug to my famous but fictional guru.

"Well…I'll tell you," he answers slowly, choosing his words carefully. "Those Vikings would be pleasantly surprised all right. But they got an even bigger buzz when they found out they couldn't take over Ireland."

"Yeah?…"

"Uh-huh, you just bet. Oh, they had their day, but they couldn't dominate. And in 1014, when they were aligned with the army of the King of Leinster, old Brian Boru, the King of Munster, kicked their butt at the Battle of Clontarf!" he smiles, now warming to his subject. "After that, the Vikes just merged into the Celtic tribes. So at the end of the day, or millennium as it were, they started one hell of a city, introduced some valuable farming techniques, and best of all, added red hair – like on that curvy cutie that just walked by, or didn't you notice?"

"Yeah, I did. How could you miss that?"

"Well, good. 'Cause I was afraid you were only into old buildings, and the red-hair factor has a very important role to play. You see," he rolls on, "After the ass-whipping at Clontarf, the Leinster folk gradually lost their lands over the next century. So, finally, in 1166, old King McMurrough sailed over to England in search of help. No problem, of course, those Anglo-Norman lads were always hot to seize an opportunity."

"Ohhh, yeah, I remember. Strongbow, huh?"

"Exactly! And once Mr. Richard de Clare got a good look at King Mac's daughter – a lovely lass with long red hair and a body that wouldn't quit – and his cronies got equally turned on by the beauty and productivity of the Irish lands, they – "

"Decided to stay permanently," zips my interjection. "And there's been trouble ever since."

"Uh-huh. You got it, little buddy. Old King Henry II, who was financing the venture from back in England, declared himself overlord of Ireland, and the battle was on. And you know what? Old Strongbow's still here – I mean, lying in state, up the hill a bit. Wanna take a look?"

A cardinal idea, even though the subject sanctuary of repose is now under Protestant control. So, retracing my steps up Winetavern to where it intersects High Street, there, amidst the Old City that had sprung up from the Vikings, I meet Dublin's second great cathedral, Christ Church. Not as large as St. Patrick's, its cream-colored stone blocks, topped by a green-tinted slate steeple, make it appear more massive. A combination of Gothic and Romanesque architecture, its magnificent carved stonework and gracefully pointed arches, with delicately chiseled supporting columns, rise into the sky from the former site of a wooden church originally built by the Danes. In concert with Archbishop Laurence O'Toole, it was the recently married and now happily settled Strongbow who commissioned the stone reconstruction in 1172. And inside, the sixty-eight-foot, Gothic-arched ceiling of the Great Nave, partners with stained-glass windows and the attendant air of solemnity to spell out *impressive* in large letters.

But it is below ground that Christ Church Cathedral is truly unique, with its maze of stone caves, wall carvings, and arched walkways that some believe date back to the eleventh century and constitute Dublin's oldest surviving building. Here, amidst the dim lighting and musty smell, one can actually feel the weight of the shadowing centuries pressing in, and you almost expect to bump heads with Strongbow round the next curve.

When he fails to appear, however, I stop by his stone effigy near the main entrance before continuing my retreat back outside into the sunshine. Where, for several minutes, I stroll in the narrow gardens bordering the Cathedral's front and eastern sides, stopping intermittently to reflect on all the living that has breathed and died away round these storied walls, the Celts, the Vikings, and the Anglo-Normans. And it is history that remains in my brain's backyard, when I finally take leave and begin traveling west on High Street toward St. Audeon's Church, and the Middle Ages.

Three short, shop-filled blocks later, the object of my pursuit appears. But before approaching further to become more intimately acquainted, I stop for coffee – and a cookie. Hey, let's get serious now. One doesn't just go hippety-hopping off into the Middle Ages, you gotta be prepared. I mean, we're talking the *Dark* Ages here, history buffs, so you better bring along a little light, or you could get so lost that the combined resources of the FBI, the CIA, and Strongbow's Secret Police couldn't rescue you. And frankly, if one's looking for a spot of illumination, well, calorie for calorie, no better brightness exists than that from a freshly baked cookie! Especially, if it's large and iced! And as Lady Luck would have it, a generous measure of both attributes loomed in my immediate future. I mean, the cookie I spied in a nearby window looked like a pancake on steroids! And having been conceived during a romance between giant spices, this Godzilla-sized confection was smilingly smothered with a glazed icing that was doing its best imitation of Ben Bulben Mountain. Not only that, but if you looked closely, smack dab in its cream center was a message: *Hobman, I was made just for you!*

Now, serious soul that I am, and not one to ignore a direct command from the Sugar Gods, I immediately snapped into executive-decision mode, entered the enticing bakery, and claimed my prize. And for so dutifully honoring the Cookie Creator, I was instantly rewarded further with the sensuous sight of the attendant-angel Lisa, whose honeyed smile is the only thing in the entire world that's sweeter than the ecstasy melting on my tongue. I mean, mere adjectives and adverbs fall all over themselves in failing to adequately describe this luscious lady. Suffice it to say, that on the sacred scale of one to ten, she registers a solid twelve!

Most unfortunately, however, the Dark Ages are just that: Dark! And this heavenly cookie was *not* created for me, not in this lifetime anyway. Unh-unh. *No way* was the message I read this time. *You have a daughter who's older.* So, clutching my cookie with both hands, so as to preclude any possibility of kidnapping, I munched my way the remaining quarter-block, then settled onto a nearby bench in the well-maintained church-yard and began ogling a lovely lady from a different time and dimension.

A national monument, and currently under restoration, St. Audeon's is believed to be the only surviving medieval parish church in Dublin. Built of brick-sized, brownish stones, and fronted by a Corinthian portico and bell tower thought to be the oldest in all of Ireland, the well-worn exterior speaks of ages of use and service to working families, its tone humble but dignified, its pride still standing tall and ringing from three bells cast in 1423.

Ten minutes later, when they share with me their news that noon has arrived, I whisper, "So long" and head for the stone steps on the far side of the garden, which are six feet wide and wind steeply down to an arched entryway on Cook Street, some twenty feet below. And when I emerge, I slowly stretch forth my fingers to gently rub the rock walls that once surrounded Dublin, this section, built in 1215, still running for a half block in either direction. I don't know why, but ever since I can remember, old buildings and like antiquities have touched a tender spot deep inside me, pulling me back to times when life was more simple, the slower pace providing a strangely distant yet warm and cozy sense of comfort. And as my fingers lightly graze the stone face of long-ago yesterday, the yearning to have been there, to know it as only living experience can teach, softly aches inside my chest: a quiet but steady throbbing that slowly dissipates as I move on, the lingering sense of loss still accompanying me the entire distance of my climb back uphill to High Street, where I then continue westward.

A long block carries me past Tailor's Hall, Dublin's oldest surviving guildhall, to Cornmarket, an avenue so named because in the thirteenth century it was an important trade and street-market site. Two hundred yards further, and Bridge Street welcomes me to once again curve southward toward the Liffey, a faint smile curling out of the corners of my mouth as memory's map matches the plastic-coated edition in my backpack. A grade-A-on-your-homework grin, ten twisting blocks later it does a found-it-on-the-first-try encore when I stop in front of The Brazen Head, Dublin's oldest pub. Housed in a single-story structure composed of mixed shades of brown stone, with bright yellow, red, and pink flowers overflowing the hanging baskets on either side of the black signature sign studded with gold letters, this fabled institution dates back to 1198. Uh-huh, that's right. Eight hundred years old, says the simple but serious fact, adding a full measure of Can you believe? to my grin's repertoire as amazement slowly turns the number over in my mind. I mean, they've been serving ye olde booze here, from Strongbow all the way down to the Happy Hobman. Now let's see Starbucks match that! jabs my conclusion. And you know what else? I'm hungry, follows the next thought, Wonder Cookie having unionized the remaining hunger pangs and induced them to picket. So, what do you say we just join Mr. Strongbow for some refreshment? Who knows? Maybe he brought along the red-haired cutie? And maybe, even, she's got a sister? I crack, still shaking my head in wonderment at the incredible idea of an establishment staying in business roughly three times longer than the entire history of the U.S.A.

Inside, I toast the total enjoyment of the morning's discoveries with a pint of Guinness, reexamining in the dark beer's creamy head the Celts, Vikings, and Anglo-Normans I now know a little bit better, and imagining that St. Patrick and Brian Boru are winking their approval. Then, deciding that there's simply so much more yet to see to lose an entire hour eating, I purchase a roast-beef sandwich, slip it inside my backpack, and head back toward city center.

Journeying along the Liffey, my eyes smile back at the countless points of light enlivening its blue-gray waters, my feet happily bouncing from Merchant's Quay back across Wood to Essex, where, at its eastern end I turn right along the boundary of yesterday's visit to Temple Bar. This time however, on my pathway north, I search out a narrow, crooked street named Fishamble because the Vikings once used it as a fish market. Centuries later, it became a fashionable street and home to a music hall, now long gone. But on a plaque fastened to the current office building, it is still honored as the historic spot where the combined choirs of St. Patrick's and Christ Church cathedrals rendered the first performance of Handel's *Messiah* in April of 1713.

"Must've been one hell of a concert," I whisper, patting the plaque's bronze letters in gentle salute as the immortal melody swells my ears full. Then, adding my hum to the harmonious chorus, I restart my feet, and am shortly thereafter standing before Dublin's City Hall. A square, stone edifice of Corinthian styling, it plays host to the City Council. Which, for a buoyant moment, I am tempted to drop in on for a nice chat. You, know: Hi, there, fellow fans of Dublin, it's me, the Hobman, here. I just thought you'd like to know, that after the testworthy total of twenty-two hours of hands-on research, my carefully considered opinion is that your City not only tops terrific, but is rapidly approaching the scintillating stratosphere of sensational! I mean, it's just so special of you all to locate your famous buildings exactly where they appear on my map, that I'd be more than happy to put my endorsement in writing. And as for my fee, well, no problem at all. The recipe for Cookie Creation of the Century will do nicely, thanks. Especially if it could be delivered by Dublin's answer to Venus, so that I could have one more lovely look.

Most fortunately, however, the call of Dublin Castle is stronger than that to oratory, not to short-change the renewed grumblings from my stomach, and their immediate coalition serves well to propel me around the western wall of City Hall and the shorter part of a block to the rounded Record Tower, one of two remaining features from the original Castle built in 1214. For several seconds, I just stand still, stunned by the forty-foot height of the massive block walls. Then, shuffling slowly through the arched entryway into a central courtyard that could easily incorporate a football field, I find some elongated steps on the south side, slip off my backpack, and seat myself for my sandwich and study. After the third bite, my stomach loosens its hold on my concentration, freeing my eyes to perform the slow and steady survey necessary to fully capture the details of the sizable structure that surrounds me. For constructed on a stone base, no fewer than three stories of light-red brick form the facade, which is dotted with rows of white, wood-framed windows that run the entire circumference of the quadrangle until they merge into a blur. All three entrances are of stone, and styled Corinthian, with large pillars supporting triangular-shaped pediments edged in scroll. And across from me, above the roofline of the north face, rises an octagonally shaped belfry bearing eight carved columns that serve as a base for a turquoise-colored cupola. Boy, someone was certainly serious when they built this baby! bursts a brainwave, my memory then nibbling at pieces of history in sync with the continuing bites of roast beef.

Picking up from the Professor's Hanky-Panky Theory of Irish-Anglo Beginnings, I recall that while Strongbow and his legions of nobles had stayed put after assisting King McMurrough in reclaiming his lands, and had even constructed a fortress on this very site where I now sit, still, like the Vikings before them, their power had steadily declined over the next three hundred years. That is, it did until 1541, when King Henry VIII, having broken with the Catholic Church and abolished the monasteries, forcefully reasserted it. Thereafter, even in the face of English military might, Irish resistance remained fierce, as both the clans and the descendants of the Anglo-Normans had developed a decided preference for not taking orders from, or paying taxes to, those blokes in London. And when late in the seventeenth century, James II, a Catholic, ascended to the English throne, Irish hopes for independence bloomed like Spring's first red rose.

Unfortunately, red was simply a signal for bloodshed. For James II was soon deposed as King by his sister, a comely Protestant lass who promptly wooed the Dutchman, William of Orange, to oust Brother Jim and make her Queen of a lot more than their bedroom, thus altering history, while adding to its sex-inspired footnotes. Now, noticeably upset by his sudden demotion, without even benefit of a golden parachute, James II fled to Ireland, where the Catholic constituency rallied round him. And when William followed in hot pursuit, on July 1, 1690, a great battle ensued in which the English prevailed, crushing the Irish Dream, and establishing a British reign that would last for over two centuries, until the creation of the Irish Free State in 1919.

Jesus...H...Christ! shrugs my chagrin, the sandwich momentarily losing its tastiness as I reflect on how a would-be earlier Fourth of July had so miserably failed the cause of freedom. So that's how old St. Patrick's and Christ Church came to be Protestant, huh? gleans my melancholy musing. And that's also how the Irish flag was created: Green on one side for Ireland's Catholics, Orange on the other for its Protestants, with White in the middle for the hoped for peace between them. A peace, current events painfully remind, that still awaits fruition in the separated and divided dominion of Northern Ireland.

"Well," I mutter after several seconds' pause, glancing up and over the roofline. "At least the right flag's flying now. I mean, hell, it may have taken seven hundred years, but this old symbol of Empire isn't home to English Viceroys anymore. Unh-unh, now the Irish can use *their* castle, to celebrate their own Prime Minister," smiles my conclusion, the redness of the brick walls suddenly warming with charm, Ireland for the Irish reflavoring my roast beef. Then, having slipped inside and successfully steered through seven centuries of history, funneled finally into a happy ending, I just rest, savoring the sweet taste.

When I finally take leave, around 2:30, the satisfaction from having experienced yesteryear's struggles in an imaginary, yet strangely real sense lingers, incubating a vague feeling of having actually shared in the historical happenings. Call it learning come to life. Call it magic. But somehow, the simple acts of walking through Old Town, and running my fingers over remnants of the Middle Ages, have shortened the span of time between St. Patrick and now, allowing long-ago's life lessons to become more human, then personal, and finally, a part of me. And with intuition painting a relaxed but serious smile across my lips, as if a change is occurring, which I welcome, but do not yet fully understand, this *knowing*, even without proof, adds a bounce to my step as I travel up Dame Street past the Olympic Theatre.

Fifteen minutes later, I have returned to College Green and the same spot where I first spied the white-to-beige stone facade of Trinity College on yesterday's outing to Temple Bar. This time, however, I stop to study the stately lines of its architectural styling, my focus promptly fastening on the four enormous white Palladium columns rising to support a triangle-shaped pediment over the wooden-door entrance, the lapis-blue, gold-handed clock in the center, serving as a solitary sentinel. Behind this handsome face, the body is massive, rising three full stories and running along College and Nassau streets for a hundred and fifty feet in either direction to convey its message that this is a serious forum for higher learning. Just in case you managed to miss it, however, lifesize statues of two of Trinity's most distinguished graduates – political writer and orator Edmund Burke, and Oliver Goldsmith, poet and playwright – flank the walkway leading up to the arched entry, reminding one of the long tradition of high intellectual achievement, while simultaneously serving as greeters.

Suitably impressed, and now on the alert for *special*, I'm still not fully prepared for the boundless beauty of Parliament Square. Eye-openingly large, with equally super-sized buildings to the left and right, fifty yards straight ahead, the white-marbled Campanile soars a hundred noble feet into the azure sky over an ornately carved and arched stone base, easily capturing my attention, then eliciting a whispery "Wow!" of understated admiration. And after circling it several times to note that the first octagonally columned tower is tiered by a smaller-domed replica, with an intricately sculpted cross serving as a spire, I retreat to the wide stone steps on the Square's south side and plop myself down to further feast my eyes.

Recalling that Queen Elizabeth I had founded Trinity in 1592, as a college for the Protestant descendants of Strongbow and the Anglo-Norman nobility, as I stare across a hundred yards of cobblestone to where four carved columns reproduce a facade identical to that governing the main entrance, memory also reminds that the Palladium style of architecture takes its name from Pallas Athena, the Greek goddess of wisdom. And after turning my head to note yet a second matching face on the building behind me, I nod approval at just how appropriate the selection had been. It's a campus fit for gods, all right! bubbles my enthusiasm, a soft chuckle then escaping as I drop my gaze to the mere mortals streaming to and fro, the casual comparison triggering Lucy into mind.

I had met this vivacious sweetie several months ago, when she telephoned selling insurance, her Irish accent prompting me to share my plans for the upcoming trip, and her good nature then inspiring a visit to share a native's knowledge. In her late twenties, bright, sensitive, and a virtual treasure-trove of information, Lucy had not only helped me refine my itinerary, but had tutored me in Gaelic pronunciations as well. Uh-huh, my own *personal* connection to Trinity, I reflect, remembering also how Lucy had explained the serious sacrifice her parents had made to allow her to attend college, gratitude and pride gleaming in her large dark eyes. From a farm outside Cork City, all four kids to and through Trinity, concludes the replay, my desire to meet the Walshes growing as their achievement fully sinks in. But that's for later, of course, when I reach County Cork. So in the meantime, how about we go see some more of Lucy's college? I pose, hauling myself up and heading off through the Campanile's archway to Library Square and the Rubrics.

Built around 1700 of red brick, with ten-foot chimneys rising from a slate roof that slants gently upward from the fourth story and its row of dormer windows, the Rubrics is the oldest surviving building from Trinity's formative years. And for several minutes I just stand beneath one of several elm trees offering shade to its front, and allow my imagination to scan the generations of students who have come and gone. From the quill, to computers, traces a thought through the sand of centuries. But try as I do, the certainty of change is impossible to feel amidst the timeless quietude flowing forth from the surroundings, like a soft shawl settling serenely around my shoulders, my eyes wandering lazily onward to a small chapel tucked into the Square's left-hand corner. The only chapel in all of Ireland that is shared by all Christian denominations, it is both charming and the perfect symbol for the pervading peace, all inside the same glance.

"Uh-huh…Absolutely perfect," I whisper, flashing on the futility and waste occasioned by man's insatiable need to separate himself from his brother instead of uniting. Then, slowly swinging my eyes to the right of the Rubrics, I pick up the imposing outline of the Old Library. Forming the southern flank of its namesake plaza, the actual entrance is on the opposite side, in Fellows Square. Only a short stroll away, when I reach it, the large expanse of grass greening its center instantly rolls out the welcome mat. As peopled by numerous groups of varying ages who are enjoying coffee, tea, and each other underneath the warm sunshine, the call of camaraderie is contagious, and only the treasures which await inside keep me from accepting the inviting offer. A decision for which I am immediately rewarded, when after paying a small admission charge, I enter the Old Library, walk downstairs, and slip inside the Colonnades Gallery that houses the awe-inspiring Book of Kells. A hand-scripted and illuminated edition of the Four Gospels in Latin, it was created in the ninth century or earlier by monks at the monastery in the Irish Midlands town from which it takes its name. And lying inside a glass showcase in a dimly lit room, the ghostly glow from its ancient pages eerily transports you back in time as eyes narrow to scrutinize the brown and gold pages of medieval manuscript, embellished artistically with intricate interlacing spirals as well as human figures and animals. Each day a new page is turned for visitor viewing, and as the adjective *magnificent* holds hands with its sister *unbelievable*, I focus and refocus on Luke I, struggling to fully grasp the sheer depth of dedication it took to produce such a masterpiece. Not to forget talent and inspiration, either, I remind myself as I reclimb the stone stairway thirty mesmerizing minutes later.

And *masterpiece* is also the right word-helper to summarize the spectacular features of the second floor's Long Room. For recognized as the largest single-chamber library in all of Europe, this two-hundred-foot-long by forty-foot-high sanctum for scholars features the warm welcome of wood, from the golden shades of the floor to the rich browns of the arched and slatted ceiling. And housing over two hundred thousand of Trinity's oldest books in carved cases running from floor to ceiling, with marble busts of immortals such as Plato stationed to greet today's seekers at the entryway to each stack, this library is a living painting: picture perfect in design and construction, yet alive and breathing with ideas from history's greatest minds. A veritable museum by Michaelangelo, it not only displays ancient treasures such as Ireland's oldest harp, but serves equally as a priceless reservoir of inspiration for creating new works of wisdom that will further enlarge the sacred heritage.

For the second time this prized day, I don't want to leave, so special are the sights my eyes strain to capture in every detail, so earnest the empathy they evoke, so significant the meanings my mind struggles to frame, then freeze forever. Finally, however, after lingering to closely view the harp created from willows and attributed by legend to Brian Boru, the morning's hero for triumphing over the Vikings at Clontarf, I manage to pull myself away. Outside, the sun has begun its westward descent. And with my senses crowded to capacity with the sights, sounds, and smells of history's fitful but fascinating tale, I wander slowly away from the Old Library to New Square. Built in 1837, and containing yet another library and museum housed in classical buildings fronted by large lawns harboring elm trees, for a long moment of exhale, I just stand and stare, no effort made to search, or survey, or understand. Just relax the eyes and rest the brain, soothes a distant voice, the harmonious mix of architectural and natural beauty spread out before me supporting the sudden need for *no more*. One minute. Two. Then three. And finally feeling Mr. and Mrs. Overwhelm slowly begin to retreat, but still in need of calm and casual, I restart my feet and venture beyond the quad, where

I discover a rugby pitch. No one's playing, but several joggers are out and at it. And dropping down onto the edge of this green sea of tranquility, I simply sit and aimlessly watch.

Like a magical elixir, the brief interlude of R & R recharges my battery. And as I return across campus, the restoration process continues with short stops to view an artsy theatre building named after another famous graduate, Samuel Beckett, as well as some tennis courts centering a group of residence halls. The courts are empty, "So no chance to show Dublin your great backhand," I tease, a smile creasing my face as I stride on, then widening full when I reenter Parliament Square and a young Spanish couple asks for directions to the Old Library.

"If they only knew," gurgles a chuckle after I've walked them over and "De nada" has answered "Gracias." "Why the blind leading the blind, would be a perfect twenty-twenty by comparison!" I quip to the large white clouds that have drifted into the western sky in search of sunset. Shaped like creampuffs, they instantly spark a desire for a sweet treat, and propelled by the sudden rush of euphoria from having experienced so very much, without getting lost even once, I hurry my feet toward a bakery I had spied yesterday in Temple Bar.

Finding it easily, I soon emerge armed with a brownie, two cookies, and a custard tart. What? you say, shaking your head. After already one-upping the Cookie Monster, now you're pigging-out again?...Uh-huh. Exactly. In case you haven't already guessed, where sugar's concerned, the Sultan of Self-Control I'm not. Besides, my old lawyering skills kick-in to advise that what we have here is a religious issue. I mean, you know how the Muslims face Mecca five times a day? Well, let me assure you, that similar devotion to the Sugar Gods is no less important. No, sirrreee. They deserve to be loved and respected with precisely the same passion – I mean, *each* and *every* opportunity to demonstrate one's love and appreciation must be honored. Hell, after the wonders I've been treated to today, no way I'm going to be a slacker in the Thank You Department. Unh-unh. It may be a tough worship, all right, but duty is duty – and I, for one, have no intention whatsoever of disappointing the Supreme Creator of Calories! concludes my Magna Carta of Confections, Handel's *Messiah* then straining back into ear to accompany a prayerful bite of brownie.

Then, as I reverently munch my windowshopping way back to the

Hotel Central, a pipe in the Peterson shop catches my eye. A small, brown, billiard-shaped briar with a slight bend, it's the enamel band sporting the colors of Ireland that finds my heart like an arrow. Lighting it up as soon as I sign the VISA slip, it tastes delicious right from the first puff. Just like Ireland, I flash, focusing again on my first full day, a curious sense of satisfaction circulating through me. I don't know how, but all of a sudden I *feel* a little bit Irish, surprises my next thought, slowing my feet to a shuffle, the Professor then chiming in with, "Uh-huh. And the Pope's a little bit Jewish too!"

Now, just hold on a minute, surges my spontaneous defense, already well warmed up. I mean, hell, I've prayed with St. Patrick and Jonathan Swift, drunk with Strongbow, and ogled a red-headed Viking colleen or two. And if that's not enough, I've lunched at Dublin Castle, studied the Book of Kells with Samuel Beckett, and served as a tour guide at Trinity College. "Now that oughta make me a little bit Irish, don't ya think?" I whisper between draws on my flagship Peterson, smiling, but also listening seriously for an answer to the question of why it's so important?....

Ahead, the evening promises a long hot shower, followed by dinner at The Stag's Head, one of Dublin's favorite nightspots. As for the answer, well, we'll just have to see, I tell myself as my eyes pick up the hotel a block away. You've only just begun, and there's lots of time, and so much more to see before the secret can step out into the sunshine. Maybe tomorrow? Maybe next week? Who knows? I grin wistfully. We'll see. We'll just have to wait and see.

VI

POLITICS, POETRY, & PASTRY

N EVER, EVER, UNDERESTIMATE THE VALUE OF A LONG, HOT SHOWER. Emphasis on long. As after yesterday's exhilarating exploration of the Old City, topped by music till midnight at The Stag's Head, Wednesday's alarm clock is met with a sleepy smile and a body blanketed by ache. A happy ache. A satisfied ache. But an ache nonetheless, and one sorely in need of a warm, soothing massage. And as the steady stream from the showerhead slowly kneads my muscles awake, and me along with them, last evening's fun and frolic return for an encore.

First up for replay is the tasty meal of Caesar salad and roasted chicken breast with raspberry sauce, stirring to life hints of hunger and a quickly passing thought of breakfast. Music promptly enters next: a vibrant, passionate parade that echoes ebulliently into ear to warm my heart, in like fashion to the water working its magic. No people holds music in higher regard than the Irish. In fact, Ireland is the only country to have a musical instrument, the harp, as its national emblem. And in upholding this anciently rooted tradition, the quintet that performed last night certainly did it justice. Composed of three males and two ladies, and featuring the flute, two fiddles, and both the piano and two-button accordions, for just under two hours they treated their audience to a mixed menu of melodies, from Gaelic love songs, some of which dated to medieval times, to more modern folk tunes. Playing happy, playing sad, upbeat and down, they even musicalized the political with "Remember," a haunting ballad honoring the Easter Rising. Sung by Ilia, a tall, slim blonde around thirty, the lyrics' tribute to freedom quickened the pulse and stirred the blood. But it is the melancholy harmonies from long ago yesterday that truly tear at the heartstrings. As mournful, yet still hopeful, their tear-stained tones capture more eloquently than words Ireland's agonizing struggle over the centuries to be Irish – the living and loving and laughing amidst the pain and sorrow of loss, and the desperate desire for freedom.

Is that what's drawn you here? explodes a testy query from the subterranean field of surprises, the music fading but still playing in the background. Huh? Is that it, the curious mixture of happy and sad? The melancholy underlying the smile of: Hey, everything's okay now, but how long will it last?...For several steamy seconds, I turn the intruders round and round, as if a closer inspection will produce an answer. Then, when only silence visits, I satisfy myself with: Well, you certainly love an underdog all right, memory's screen suddenly surfacing to feature reruns of my lifelong struggle to be me. The daydreaming child in grammar school arrives first, climbing the backyard avocado tree to stare at the sky, then ponder why the world is so large and he feels so small? Adolescence adds a second layer of shyness, for not fitting in to the high school scene of clubs and cliques. And then after college and law school, alienation steers a sharp curve even further away from the stifling society of Beverly Hills, 902$$, to Deputy Public Defender in the black ghetto of Compton, where the prejudice and poverty that plague the American ideal could be explored up front and personally. There, somehow, little boy lost fit. There, amidst unanswered questions and vaguely veiled class warfare, he strangely belonged. And there, in the courtroom, fighting for the downtrodden against the reigning power of the establishment, the heat of battle had bizarrely brought him a tangible yet fragile sense of *home*. Not an address. Not the safe identity of city, state, and country, or the secure comfort of neighbors, friends, school, and church. But instead, a loosely outlined promise of *meaning*: a hazy *wholeness* that flirts, then floats like a mysterious cloud on the edge of the horizon. Still far away, but closer and warmer than ever before.

"Yeah, sorta like Ireland's fight against the English, huh?" rolls my response into the cascading water, my return from distant places birthing a wry smile at the suddenly emerged simile. "'Cause somebody's always gotta be the boss, and tell the other fella what to do," I finish, turning off the shower and reaching for a towel. But let's not dwell on that sad story, we'll see what happens, follows fresh thought, the wail of weeping violins finally fading out. Let's just go get some breakfast, then start our day.

An easy choice, right? Wrestle with demons, or enjoy coffee and croissants with the *Irish Times*? Well, no problem here putting off the difficult. 'Cause it won't get lost, it'll just catch up and find you later, that's all. Only who knows? Maybe by then, you'll have found some allies? wisecracks hope through a smile, my feet then christening the new beginning by carrying me to a visit with Ms. Molly Malone. A happy hop, short skip, and jaunty jump to our prearranged rendezvous – upon arrival, "Good golly, Miss Molly!" echoes into ear courtesy of Little Richard, the upbeat then rock 'n' rolling my reappearing smile all the way from my lips to my eyes. Now, before you get too excited, let me explain that she isn't real, though I most certainly wish she were. 'Cause this lady's such a babe, she could've posed for *Playboy* if Hugh Hefner had been a Viking. I mean, we're talking a full centerfold layout here, with Playmate of the Year honors in the bag! Instead, however, cast in bronze, and rightfully awarded a commanding location at the foot of Grafton Street, this fish monger from once upon a time serves as the perfect reminder of just how pretty the Irish ladies are.

Now, actually, I've been meaning to comment on this lovely phenomenon before, but delayed in order to prevent jumping to the proverbial hasty conclusion. But now, having enjoyed over forty-eight hours in which to collect blonde, brunette, and redheaded evidence in support of my original observation, the truth of it, the whole sensuous sooth of it, is that I fully understand why Strongbow couldn't leave. In fact, inside the short space of a single, solitary hour, one could fall in love here five hundred times. I know. 'Cause I have. I mean, no problem at all. None! All you gotta do is open up your eyes, and zap, instantly your heart's a goner! You like soft skin, so clear, and clean, and marble-white it gleams? How about if sometimes it's flushed ruddy-red, to highlight sky-blue eyes? Or do you prefer violet, or green, or the deep darkness of midnight with a thousand stars shining? Care for high cheekbones and a finely formed mouth? Or is a rounder head more to your choosing, with flatter features and pouty lips? And don't worry about discrimination in favor of faces either, 'cause equal treasures are to be found in the accompanying physiques. You like tall and slim, do you? Or maybe shorter and slightly fuller? No problem. How about lithesome legs, and flat tummies fronting tightly-tucked tushes that tease till your eyes dance? And if, by chance, you're a fan of the bulging bustline, well, you've simply arrived in paradise, that's all. I mean, the entire experience is like being in a candy store that carries all your favorites, each of which is carefully made by a loving Lord while in the best of humor, and using only the finest ingredients!

The only problem, and most unfortunately it's an excruciatingly large one, is that the vast, overwhelming majority of these adorable angels are young. I mean, *young*, as in under the age of thirty. Mere children, to sixty-year-old eyes, the experience necessary to fully appreciate their glory easily trumped by just enough wisdom to see also that some dreams are simply fantasy. Well, no charge. And hell, you never really wanted to be twenty-something again anyway, floats the gentle reminder, accompanied by a repeating reel of school, the Public Defender years, and the joy of Patty flowering over the piercing pain of her loss. No, one bleeding ulcer is enough, thank you. And besides, gratitude grins, I had my turn, and I wouldn't trade for a minute. Not for anything, memory affirms, as my old but life-loving eyes return to their survey of Ms. Molly and her comely curves.

Well, you match up with the current hotties, A-okay, pretty lady, follows my next observation, but they sure do outdress you. For to celebrate their genetic gifts from God, in large part, Dublin's women are smartly dressed in a wide variety of stylish sportswear or dressy pantsuits, with designer shoes and accessories to match. In fact, while their male counterparts are neatly to modishly attired, and almost no one is overweight, it is the ladies, with their fresh faces, fine figures, and careful attention to couture and coiffure, who sparkle at the head of the people parade.

No doubt about it. Boy, what must Nuala think? I entertain, next, her description of growing out of puberty and into adolescence in a Catholic boarding school, calling into focus the contrast posed by the young women my eyes follow in several directions as they hustle and bustle about their business. No, these young ladies are not the "prudish girls of University College Dublin in the nineteen-fifties." Unh-unh, no way. Instead, their self-confidence shows clearly in the purposefulness shining on their fresh faces, in the pricey cut of their clothes, and the business-like pace of their stride. They not only had arrived, but gave every appearance of knowing exactly where they were going. And as I turned away from Ms. Molly and headed east on Nassau Street, her song,

"In Dublin's fair city, the girls are so pretty," hummed happily inside my head, history creeping in to fight for space.

After the Battle of the Boyne resulted in a decisive triumph for William of Orange and England, I recall, as I traipse along toward Kildare Street, Ireland came firmly under the rule of Great Britain and its Protestant Church. And with the dawning of the Georgian Age ten years later in 1700, the English nobles enjoyed an unprecedented era of prosperity by reaping the rewards of the Irish soil, while suppressing the Irish peasantry. And a heavy foot it was too, as under the Plantation System, native Irish farms were uprooted, and their lands given to Protestant settlers. In fact, so harsh was British rule that Catholics were not even permitted to buy land, and instead could only become tenant farmers.

In the last quarter of the eighteenth century, however, the influences of the American and French revolutions seeped into Eire, and stirred the beginnings of a movement for Irish independence. Finding a fertile field, this fresh energy soon fostered the local formation of an Irish Parliament in 1782, followed by an armed insurrection of the United Irishmen under Wolfe Tone ten years later. Unfortunately, both of these routes to self-rule failed, leading Great Britain in 1800 to legally incorporate Ireland into the Empire via the Act of Union. Once ignited, however, the flame of freedom could not be fully extinguished. And though Ireland's nineteenth century was stained with tragedy, still the flame burned, and fresh hope salved the wounds of oppression. In 1820, for a prime example, Daniel O'Connell, known as "The Liberator," organized peaceful rallies of up to a million people and succeeded in getting the Emancipation Act passed, providing a limited number of Catholics the right to vote.

Tragically, however, just as freedom was gaining force, in 1845 the Great Famine struck, visiting upon Ireland its darkest hour and delaying further progress. Instigated by blight that produced a total failure of the potato crop, the Irish populace was devastated during the next three years by a million starvation deaths and the emigration of three million more of their countrymen who were without visible means of support. A wound so severe, that there are those who argue that the Irish soul will never fully heal whole.

"Well, no problem understanding that," I drawl slowly when I reach Kildare Street, turn right, and stop in front of the Irish Genealogical Office, the flashing photo of an emaciated Patty in the hospital cutting off the flow of history. "I mean, with half the population gone in an eye-blink, no wonder Nuala says it left an *inferiority* complex. Hell, after all they've already been through with the English, and now they can't even feed themselves!" I mutter through the smoke from my pipe, then focus on the details of the house dedicated to Irish heritage.

Constructed of beige-colored sandstone, and styled Venetian, this two-story structure, featuring a columned entry, as well as intricate carvings of animals around the window ledges, is not only home to Ireland's chief herald, but also the only museum in the entire world that focuses exclusively on tracing ancestral roots. Sure, I think, with an exodus that makes Moses' look like a jolly jaunt in the desert, finding home's a full-time job all right. Christ, there's three times more Irish descendants in America alone than in the entire Republic. I mean, how in the hell do you treat this hole in the national psyche, huh? ends my commiseration with this sad and sorry episode, my mood then brightening as I move on to the literary Eden housed in the National Library next door.

A massive stone edifice with a rotunda-shaped entrance, the Library features the domed, first-floor Reading Room where James Joyce sited the literary debate in *Ulysses* – and not only is a first edition on display, but also present within its scholarly walls are like originals by Jonathan Swift, William Butler Yeats, George Bernard Shaw, and Oliver Goldsmith. Now, how's that for a distinguished club of poets, playwrights, and novelists? I ask myself. Wanna join?…

"Ohhh, sure," rings the rejoinder, the Professor suddenly intervening. "Never mind you're a little light in the genius department, just argue you've got the heart for it. Besides, they don't have a Jewish member, so you could add a little flavor. You know, like a chocolate chip in one of those cookies you're always eating. I mean – "

Okay. All right, I concede, closing him out with a smile. It was just a thought, let's not get anally retentive about it. And with my mood now in full retreat from the dark doldrums of the Irish holocaust, I exit the literary hall of heroes and walk across the street to where it meets Molesworth. A few yards further, and I'm standing in front of Buswell's Hotel and Bar, housed in a Georgian brick building. Near the entrance, a plaque advises that their pub was a special favorite of the fabled James Joyce, and for a fanciful minute my imagination's eye captures him coming and going – slim and scholarly looking, dressed in black, wearing dark glasses

43

and carrying an umbrella...sometimes locked in scintillating conversation with cronies, more often alone, with thoughts twisting and turning to run feverishly through him, like the literary *stream of consciousness* he invented...a chronicler of life so obsessed with detail, he once claimed that if Dublin disappeared, it could be faithfully reconstructed from the pages of *Ulysses*...a pilgrim in such diligent pursuit of perfection, he devoted seventeen years to writing *Finnegans Wake*, words flowing, then ebbing into silence...eyesight failing...moods rollercoastering up, down, and sideways, happy in love, sobered by poverty, haunted by demons dancing inside passion...the struggle continuous, the search unending... always, always, seeking *home*.

Tick. Tock. Tick. Seconds sliding into a mesmerizing minute. The past growing more and more real. In fact, so real is the reverie that for an instant I'm tempted to enter the pub for a confab with ghosts. Did you find it?...Huh?...At least for you?...'Cause I want to know, cries the voice of *need*, my foot taking a step. Instead, however, the toot, toot, toot of traffic pierces the thin veil, ferrying me back to the world without answers, the sea of history then swaying me to resume my own odyssey, carrying me northward another half block to Leinster House.

Originally built as a Georgian-styled home for the Duke of Leinster in 1745, today the elegant edifice serves proudly as the official seat of Ireland's government: Dail Eireann, the House of Representatives, and Seanad, the Senate. And as my eyes wander over the stately stone structure, featuring a 140-foot facade, with two three-story Corinthian columns on either side of the entrance, what jumps out to quicken my heartbeat is the flag of the Irish Republic flying freely overhead.

"God...bless!" I drawl slowly, as history's troubled tale flows back into mind. And spell that with a capital T, too. For after the Great Famine was finally defeated, so also were the armed uprisings of Young Ireland and the Fenians, which occurred soon after some semblance of normalcy was restored. Then, as if to add torture to the catalogue of calamity, in the 1870s, thousands of Irish tenant farmers were evicted by their British landlords when plummeting agricultural prices denied them the ability to meet their rents. This time, however, instead of seeking emigration, the dispossessed rallied behind the leadership of Charles Stuart Parnell and the Home Rule Party, the dream of independence still alive, the flame of freedom still burning in spite of the century's trail of tragedy.

And campaigning arduously against further evictions by ostracizing targeted landlords, and in particular the powerful Captain Boycott, whose name then slipped into the vernacular, this economic tactic proved so successful that Prime Minister Gladstone was forced to sponsor the first Home Rule Bill in 1886. Unfortunately, however, while feeling fully the pressing force of change, the British Parliament defeated the proposed legislation, buffeted as it was by the even greater pressures leading up to World War I. And when the Great War then exploded into a bloody reality of unforeseeable length, yet one more time, the festering situation in Ireland slipped into limbo.

Until, that is, the Easter Rising of 1916, I recall, relighting my pipe, then glancing back up at the Irish flag. Perhaps the most celebrated event in modern Irish history, in what was supposed to be a national uprising, on Easter Monday, 2500 armed insurgents seized the General Post Office and several other government buildings in Dublin and held on for five days. Five short-lived days of glory, as the tale tells, but with large, long-lasting consequences. As when the revolt failed to inspire action on a national scale, the insurrection in Dublin was soon crushed by superior military force, with the British Government then court-martialing all fourteen leaders of the rebellion and executing them by firing squad at Kilmainham Gaol. This latter act, however, proved to be a portentous political blunder. For rather than satisfying its objective of silencing the Irish populace by intimidation, it served instead to further inflame public opinion, and to make martyrs of men such as Joseph Plunkett, James Connolly, and the poet Patrick Pearse, who had read the Proclamation of the Republic from the Post Office steps.

"Ohh, yeah...Mr. Pearse was a writer too," I murmur into the gentle breeze that sharply contrasts the winds of war that were blowing back then. For raising the burnt banner from the ashes, Yeats, Ireland's greatest poet, had written, "Now and in time to be, Wherever green is worn, Are changed, changed utterly: A terrible beauty is born." And born it was, I note, the story spinning onward. As in 1919, an unofficial Irish Parliament was convened, and shortly thereafter, led by Michael Collins, the War for Independence was commenced against the occupying British forces. Blood, blood, and more blood was shed, but this time: Victory! In 1921, under the Anglo-Irish Treaty, the Irish Free State was finally born, now, the only *terrible* modifying *beauty*, the sad separation of the

Emerald Isle, six northern counties having elected to become Northern Ireland and remain a part of the United Kingdom. Still, shining like a soaring sun, celebration centered this day of deliverance: After seven hundred years of strife and struggle, Ireland at last belonged to the Irish! And after a brief civil war between the Pro- and Anti-Treaty forces, the Irish Constitution was signed in Room 112 of the nearby Shelbourne Hotel.

High on my list of special spots to see, ever since I first spied its regal brick and white-trimmed facade in one of my guide books during my patented late-night study sessions, the Shelbourne is now less than a block away, reports my memory map as I leave Leinster House and push past the National Museum to the end of Kildare Street. A sharp right, a short half-block, and the famous hostelry jumps out of the photograph to become real. Five full stories of red brick real. And after I cross the street to better view the stately structure, my eyes slowly travel from the stone-columned entryway adorned by sculpted Nubian princesses to the dormer windows just below the roofline, all the while, its storied history meandering through my brain's backyard. For dating back to 1824, the Shelbourne has not only held hands with the people and events that form modern Irish history but also played host to world leaders, literary giants, and stars of stage and screen.

"Yeats stayed here," I whisper, slowly turning around to face St. Stephen's Green, another favorite stomping ground of the great bard. Originally one of three ancient commons in the Old City, this twenty-two-acre park was first enclosed in 1664, then laid out in its present form in 1880. And generously landscaped with trees and shrubs of various types, this leafy oasis also contains a lake, a gazeboed bandstand for summer concerts, and numerous pieces of statuary, including a bust of James Joyce and a memorial to Yeats by the renowned sculptor Henry Moore. Ohhh...yeah, I'll give you sculpture all right, murmurs my mind as I enter The Green, as the locals call it, and sit down on a bench overlooking the lake. Looks to me like the whole park was sculpted by God. I mean, it's so beautiful, it's perfect! purrs my brain as my eyes fasten upon two white swans swimming slow circles. And a perfect place for lunch too, follows my next thought as I pull from my backpack some cheese and an apple left over from breakfast.

The apple is sweet. The cheese tart and tangy. And with my soul singing a song of satisfaction from the freedoms formalized in the shadowing Shelbourne, and my hunger now sated by a simple but delicious meal in the heavenly setting spread out before me, add contentment to the day's growing list of perfections. Uh-huh, as in I don't ever want to move again, I confirm, before lazily speculating on whether Yeats may have sat on the very same bench I now occupied, my imagination drifting to watch him stroll along the lake, his senses filling with such beauty that even he would be hard pressed to adequately capture it with pen and paper. Yeah, it'd be a challenge all right, I muse, especially if one considers that soon after the Constitution was born, old W.B. was busy serving as a Senator in Ireland's first free Parliament. "Uh-huh, politics and poetry make for a busy bee indeed," I shrug out, pulling my mind back to the present and my body to its feet. "And speaking of busy, Hobman, a whole afternoon of fresh sights, sounds, and smells is still waiting for you, so how about getting it in gear?..."

No argument. I simply promise myself a return visit on the way home from the afternoon's travels, and my feet obey. First up, after I re-cross the street to the Shelbourne, is the dark brick house adjoining its eastern boundary. Here, Oliver St. John Gogarty lived. Poet, surgeon, and senator, Gogarty was an intimate of Joyce, Keats, and the revolutionary leader Michael Collins, and entertained them in regular Friday evening salons at his home, along with other famous literati of the day such as George Moore, AE (George Russell), and Lennox Robinson. One of the great lyric poets of the day, according to no less an authority than Yeats, Gogarty was equally accomplished as a physician. And noted for his generosity to the poor, he was said to have the kindest heart in Dublin, along with the sharpest tongue. Like Yeats, a member of Ireland's first Senate, after he was kidnapped and escaped during the Civil War, in 1924 he released a pair of swans into the Liffey in celebration of his survival, and it is believed that the silvery sweethearts that swim the Liffey today are all descendants from this pair. A living legacy, smiles the thought as I salute the good doctor with a nod of the head, then push on due east. And how appropriate for a poet, eh?...

A half block later, on Merrion Row, I stop to visit the Huguenot Cemetery, a small seventeenth- and eighteenth-century graveyard now locked behind wrought-iron gates and serving to remind just how much Dublin has grown since it was in use. Noting some green shrubs that have been painstakingly topiaried into a striking Celtic Cross in the center of the courtyard, I move on, reaching Merrion Street shortly, where I turn left and proceed through two long blocks of highly impressive buildings which house the various departments of the Irish Government.

How proud the freedom fighters who sacrificed so much would be, marches into mind as I slow my pace to allow my eyes to survey the massive marble and brick structures, noting that despite their great size they appear graceful. And when I reach Leinster House for the second time, I stop to admire the view from its western side, its classic lines of architecture calling into mind that some say James Hoban, the Irish-born architect, used it as his model when he designed the White House. Proud indeed! I grin as I continue on my way. All Ireland can be proud!

My next objective is the home of Oscar Wilde, the great playwright, poet, and novelist. And ten minutes' further stroll down Merrion Street to where it meets Merrion Square North brings me face to face with the elegant Georgian residence where he lived from age one to twenty-three. Originally constructed in 1762, the first floor is faced with flat panels of white stone, over which rise four floors of red brick. And armed with a fresh cup of coffee secured from a nearby neighborhood café, I stand back to study its stately lines, a wistful smile curling out of the corners of my mouth to meet Wilde's sad-happy history as it filters into view through the smoke from my pipe.

Oscar, who would later moralize that "the only sin is stupidity," was born into privilege, his father being a prominent eye surgeon, his mother a poet famous for her salons. Educated at Trinity College, and at Oxford to which he won a scholarship, at age twenty-four Wilde settled in London where six years later he married Constance Lloyd, a woman with a considerable fortune, and with whom he had two sons. Boyishly handsome and charming, Wilde's first great theatrical achievement arrived in 1892 when *Lady Windemere's Fan* resulted in his becoming the most fashionable and talked about playwright in London, leading Wilde to quip that "there is only one thing in the world worse than being talked about, and that is not being talked about." Nonetheless, increasingly famous as *A Woman of No Importance* and *An Ideal Husband* followed to rave reviews, as well as for his fastidious dress, including the wearing of an ever-present green carnation, Oscar continued to climb over controversy to score ever higher marks in British theatre and dominate the Victorian scene with his wit and personality.

All of Wilde's plays combine the drama of social intrigue with witty high comedy. In each, he brings together an intolerant young idealist and a person who has committed a social sin in the past. They meet in a society where appearances are everything, and the effect is always to educate the idealists to their own weaknesses and to show the need for tolerance and forgiveness. In *The Importance of Being Earnest*, Wilde's masterpiece, and what is generally accepted to be the best light comedy in English, social hypocrisy and the Puritan idea of earnestness and sincerity are likewise lampooned, laughing at our human foibles once again the vehicle for overcoming them.

Tragically, while at the peak of his career, with three hit plays running simultaneously, Wilde was accused and convicted of having homosexual relations and sentenced to two years in prison at hard labor. The tolerance and forgiveness of human aberration for which his genius had labored so ardently were cruelly denied to Oscar – who, ruined in health, finances, and creative energy, died in France at only forty-six, three years after his release. And standing there, staring solemnly at his home, the sad irony suffered by one who taught us so well to laugh and learn from ourselves, dying as a total outcast, strikes me full, his poignant wit echoing into ear as an exclamation point. "We are all in the gutter," he murmurs hopefully, "but some of us are looking at the stars!"

"Well, thanks for looking at the stars, Oscar. And God bless," I whisper out, forcing a smile before finally turning away and slowly crossing the street to enter a park. Named Merrion Square, it was laid out around 1762, and famously centers four blocks of Dublin's finest Georgian architecture – its twelve acres of tree-lined walkways and lavish flower beds framed by rows of reddish-orange to brown-bricked townhouses along its south, east, and northern borders, while its western perimeter showcases Leinster House, the National Gallery, and the Museum of Natural History. And as I stroll southward, I am quickly captured by its overwhelming beauty and oasis-of-peace ambience. While only half the size of St. Stephen's Green, its multitudinous variety of flowers and shrubs are absolutely equal in splendor, and in similar fashion, its statuary includes the Danny Osbourne likeness of Oscar wearing an ironic half smile beneath his high forehead and melancholy eyes, as well as the legendary Rutland Drinking Fountain erected in 1791 for use by Dublin's poor.

Wow! is the word that escapes off my tongue several times before I reach the northern boundary a dreamy half hour later, only to be spontaneously combusted into "Holy cockamolies! Wouldja look at that!" when I emerge onto Merrion Square North and spy its charming collection of Georgian castles. A homespun colloquialism, inspired by outright amazement at the unique blend of understated elegance and the rich rainbow of color rippling from the brightly painted doors, as I slowly saunter along the sidewalk to scrutinize the myriad of details, from the original wrought-iron balconies to the ornate doorknockers and intricate fanlights, my amazement soon marries admiration. I mean, where I come from, doors are doors – you know, they open and close, help greet and say goodbye, or if screened, permit the entry of a welcome breeze on a hot humid evening. But here, they are virtual works of art, as though Michaelangelo or Leonardo might have been the design consultants, and celebrated with their customary passion for perfection!

To begin with, each door is framed by an arch constructed of plaster and painted moon-bright white. Then, on each side of the door stand single or double columns with molded feet and ringed heads, on top of which sits a flat or tiered pediment that is in turn crowned by fanlights, some shaped so intricately as to make the most creative spider proud. The size of the archways varies in proportion to the doors they are accentuating, which run from the standard eight feet by three feet to those currying favor with the National Basketball Association at ten by six. And seated on their hinges, like kings and queens on their thrones, are the stars of the show, the doors. Bejeweled with gleaming brass knobs, knockers, and mail slots, and all enrobed in bright color, they collectively present a smile that one will never forget.

And did I say rainbow of pigment a paragraph or two ago? Well, let me confess that amongst my many talents, I possess a genuine gift for understatement. I mean, we've got red, orangish-red, and orange all by itself. We've got avocado green, forest green, and several shades in between. And do you like blue, the color of cool and calm? 'Cause we've got cerulean, cobalt, and ultramarine. Now how about yellow? Any fans for warm and cheerful? 'Cause we've got lemon yellow, gold-like-the-sun yellow, and pale yellow for those of the more subdued persuasion. And that's not all either. No, we've got violet, we've got purple, we've even got pink – all together, a sensuous and scintillating smorgasbord of the color wheel. I mean –

"Sorta like'm, do ya?..." interjects the Professor, suddenly terminating my train of enthusiastic observation.

"Like'm?...Hell, I love'm! It's like walking into an art gallery run by Baskin-Robbins, and you get to sample all thirty-one flavors. It's awesome, don't you think?"

"Uh-huh," he returns slowly with a smile. "And so are you, in a warped sort of way. I mean, who else could drag ice cream into a socio-historical discussion about doors?"

"Hey, listen, Dr. Wisenheimer," jets back my dazzling defense. "First of all, the only problem that ice cream presents here is that I haven't had any lately. And as for history, sir, I've already filled the folks in on the Georgian Age and its incredible architecture, and I was just about to share with them the famous people who lived on this lovely street, when I was so rudely interrupted by the Satanic forces of the Sugar Police!" concludes my counter-attack, squelching the flavorless indictment.

And illustrious personages they were too, the occupants of these gaily decorated dwellings, meanders my next thought as the good Doctor retreats to the far recesses of my mind and my feet resume their journey. For at Number 50 resided none other than Daniel O'Connell, the great Catholic Emancipation leader, while a quarter of a block farther east brings us to Number 82, where a plaque informs that William Butler Yeats lived here from 1922 to 1928 while serving as Senator. Nor did he suffer for literary company either, as right next door lived his close friend and fellow poet and playwright, George Russell, commonly known as AE. Distinguished company, all right. And for a long moment, I stop and strain to imagine their long-ago comings and goings. Then, eager to continue the afternoon's adventures, I press on, slowing at the corner for one last eyeful of color and charm before turning right onto Fitzwilliam Street and heading due south.

After having visited Buswell's Bar with James Joyce, walked St. Stephen's Green with Yeats, and shared Merrion Square with Wilde, as I stride briskly along toward my next planned encounter, the birthplace of George Bernard Shaw, excitement sidles side by side with the solid sense of satisfaction pervading me from the multi-treasures already enjoyed. "Thank you, dear God, for letting me see such beauty and share the lives of such masters," escapes my joyful gratitude as indelible imprints of Leinster House, birdbath-centered flower beds, and the Parade of Doors slowly fade enough to allow my eyes to roam anew.

Fitzwilliam Street is wide, more like a boulevard, and lined with unbroken rows of four-storied Georgian buildings housing flats over shops and offices of every imaginable type, from software companies to solicitors. And with the great playwright's home some three miles distant, there is time to take it all in, my eyes spinning like a lazy top. Within minutes, I arrive at Fitzwilliam Square, like Merrion a beautifully landscaped park, only unique in that it is private, its use restricted to the residents of the surrounding apartment houses. Hey, look, tennis courts! Care for a hit, old man, teases a thought when I spot two inviting and unoccupied oases amidst a sea of greenery, my feet pattering onward. Several blocks later, however, I slow to a stop for a surprise visit to the one-time home of Jack Yeats, W.B.'s brother, and a painter of considerable renown in his own right. Then, as I pick up the pace once again, the minutes glide by most pleasantly amidst occasional shared greetings with fellow Dubliners and my continued casual study of passing neighborhoods.

When I reach Adelaide Road, nearby church bells chime out two o'clock, gently awakening me from my relaxed reverie and calling attention to the fact that an unexpected addition to my itinerary was now close at hand. Earlier that morning at breakfast, while reviewing the route to Shaw's home, I had noticed a yellow Star of David on the map, not far from where Fitzwilliam intersects Adelaide and directly on course toward my meeting with George Bernard.

Now, why, you might ask, is the accidental discovery of a temple important to our literary quest? Was Shaw Jewish?...Well, no, dear reader. But as previously disclosed, I am. And while that falls somewhat short of an artsy eye-opener, it does explain why the yellow star's sudden appearance served to strike a chord of curiosity within me, one that quietly swelled to naggingly champion a capital C. For even though Ireland's overwhelmingly Catholic culture has comfortably accommodated a small but fully integrated Jewish community ever since the Spanish Inquisition, with Robert Briscoe even serving as the Lord Mayor of Dublin during the late 1950s – still, try as I do, my ear just can't hear Hebrew being pronounced with an Irish lilt. So, slip an idiosyncrasy into an offbeat mind, and the idea forms to drop by, say hello, and give a little listen.

The only problem is, I can't find it. When I reach the map-designated spot, I find myself staring incredulously at an office building. No problem, I tell myself, maps aren't infallible. Maybe the star was placed on the wrong side of the street, or was meant to appear a short distance farther west. A logical explanation. Reasonable. And one I pursue assiduously for the next fifteen minutes, tracing and retracing my footsteps on both sides of the street for the better part of two blocks. All to no avail. In fact, the only thing I found was frustration, a feeling further fueled by the Professor poking at me with: "Are we lost, little boy?..."

"No," snaps my return. "The temple is! Somehow, it fell off the damn map!"

"Ohhh, a tad testy, are we?" he follows, smirking.

"Uh-huh, you got it, all right. And you would be too, if you'd added an extra mile for nothing. You ever hear of the Lost Tribes of Israel? Well, what we've got here, Bible Believers, is the Lost Temple. You happen to know where it is, Mr. Smarty-Pants?..."

"Nooo," he oozes back at me. "It wasn't here when I last visited around twelve hundred. But may I suggest that since the subject of record is Mr. Shaw, you cease your imitation of Moses wandering in the desert and move on forward. After all, for one with your absolute genius for getting lost, you've actually been doing quite well."

It was true. For over two days now I had been exploring storied Dublin, and not once had I failed to find my desired destination. Over fifty hours without a major miscue, I calculated, my mood returning to its previous good humor as the failed prospect of an Irish-accented Sh'ma was soothingly drowned out by past successes and the immediate opportunity to meet another fellow scribe. So, with the charges against the offending map gratefully reduced from a high-grade felony to a minor misdemeanor, I quickly negotiated a trade with my backpack for a fresh pipe. Then, chuckling at my capacity for obsessive-compulsiveness, I resumed my journey westward, Shaw's life story beginning to trickle into view.

Born in 1856, the third child and only son of George, a partner in a milling business, and Elizabeth, a classical singer, George Bernard would later say that he was "the fruit of an unsuitable marriage between two quite amiable people," explaining further that "he and his two sisters had to find their own way in a household where there was neither love nor hate." When he was still a small boy, I recall upon reaching Harcourt Street, a servant in charge of G.B.'s outings frequently took him to visit her friends who lived in squalid tenements in the slums, an early learning experience from which he developed a lifelong hatred of poverty, writing later that "I saw it and smelt it and loathed it."

A poor student, Shaw did not attend college. Instead, in his teens he worked for land agents, doing well and being promoted to chief cashier, while devoting his leisure hours to the theatre. Then, in 1876, at age twenty he followed his mother over to London where she had settled after separating from her husband. Finding employment as a music critic, Shaw soon became successful, and in 1884 helped found the Fabian Society, an organization of socialists working for political and economic change through reform.

Interesting, huh? Only son, poor student, politically left of center, I muse, stopping the march of G.B.'s history parade when I reach Synge Street, then turn left a half block and finally find myself standing in front of the house where he was born. An unimposing box-like structure, composed of reddish-brown brick and containing two stories, for over a minute I simply stand and stare at its clean square lines, noting that its sole distinguishing feature is its aqua-blue front door of similar style to those on Merrion Square. Then, narrowing my focus onto the bronze plaque to the right of the entryway; I am struck full with surprise. "Well, I'll be damned, we share the same birthday!" I sputter out, now feeling an even truer kinship with this great playwright and essayist whom I had so long admired. But ever faithful to his life's work of popping my balloon before it can overinflate, the Professor promptly produces a pin.

"Ohhh, sure, Hobman," he drones with soft sarcasm. "But July 26th is *all* you have in common."

"Oh, yeah?" I refute with lightning speed, my lawyering instincts snapping to attention. "Well what about the poverty issue? I was a Public Defender and represented the poor, you know?"

"Uh-huh. I remember. But let's not forget either, that G.B. is ranked amongst the most important literary figures of the twentieth century, a Nobel Prize winner. Whereas, dear friend, the only award you're in danger of collecting is Man of the Year from Haagen-Dazs – although, considering your unbridled capacity for inhaling sugar, they might just make that Consumer of the Century, even with ninety-nine years still left to run!" he tacks on, breaking into a wide grin.

"Ohhhkay…I hear you," I chuckle back at him, dropping down onto the sidewalk to simply sit and share with Shaw. His early plays, I recall, were not immediately popular because of their radical subject matter. In *Widower's Houses*, he attacked slum landlords, then followed with *Mrs. Warren's Profession* and *Arms and the Man*, which argued against the causes of prostitution and war. By 1904 however, public hostility had begun to thaw, and G.B. soon became hugely successful with *Candida*, *The Devil's Disciple*, and *Caesar and Cleopatra*.

Yeah, that's right, I nod slowly, confirming his use of the theatre to teach as well as to entertain, the reel then running on to *Man and Superman*. For it was here that Shaw introduced his theory that *life force* was the energy that dominated people biologically, and that if harnessed by human will, it can lead to a higher, more creative existence. And following that tasty tidbit of moral philosophy, G.B. enlivened the scene further with *Saint Joan*, a drama about the individual in conflict with historical necessity. Although this play is widely considered to be his masterpiece, some critics prefer *Pygmalion*, an ironic Cinderella story about how a professor of phonetics demonstrates the absurdity of class distinction by transforming an ignorant Cockney lass into a counterfeit aristocrat by changing her speech.

"My favorite too, G.B.," I whisper, slowly pulling myself up off the pavement and smiling my emphasis to one of the second-story windows. Almost expecting the white lace curtains to part, and G.B. to nod his bearded head back at me, my gaze is suddenly interrupted by a large raindrop striking my nose, *My Fair Lady's* "The rain in Spain falls mainly in the plain," echoing into ear.

"Right, G.B. And on my head too!" I chuckle, drawing my umbrella from my backpack as the rain picks up. "And you know what, Mr. Birthdaymate, sir? I want to thank you for all your special words, and tell you that maybe, just maybe, if I live to be ninety-four like you, I might get lucky and add a few that would be A-okay, in your book. Meanwhile, so long, dear friend," I whisper, taking one last long look before I turn away, his exquisite prayer following my footsteps: "You see things; and you say, 'Why?' I dream things that never were; and I say, 'Why not?…'"

Cradling a cup of coffee against the dampness, one hour later I have managed to thread my way back to the opposite side of my late-morning visit to St. Stephen's Green, where I easily locate the massive stone buildings that form the campus of University College Dublin, founded in 1740 as the Catholic University of Ireland. The rain that had accompanied me during my return journey has thinned to a misty drizzle, then a few minutes later ceases entirely, kindly allowing me to stroll around the College's perimeters underneath a hazy sun meshing with patches of blue sky.

As my eyes sweep over the classical lines and elaborate plasterwork of Newman House, named after John Henry Newman, first rector of the university and a celebrated cardinal, memory also reminds that this is where my bedtime companion Nuala had attended in the late 1950s, her recollection of Dublin as "dark and dramatic, the streets drifting with smoke and rain," causing me to reach for my pipe. "Not many people got to college thirty-odd years ago," she observed frankly, "and the students moved like guerrillas around the centre of the city, hardly visible. They walked everywhere. They borrowed each other's coats. They lent each other books and ate egg-and-onion sandwiches and chips with mince sauce...And everything I was learning was new to me. Caring about issues was new. Politics was new. Nationalism was new...and knowing men and boys as companions was new."

Yeah, quite an awakening, all right, I ponder, halting to try to fully appreciate the degree of difficulty facing a shy young woman from a dysfunctional family, trying to expand both her educational and personal boundaries of experience. Able to relate somewhat due to my own adolescent shyness, and the accompanying confusion and self-doubt during my freshman year at U.S.C., still, I felt unable to truly fathom the complexities of Nuala's environment, or her sizable courage. "You're a better man than I am, Gunga Din," I smile out softly, turning away from UCD, as she called the College, and shuffling across the street to The Green. "I told you I'd be back," murmurs my greeting as I enter its leafy environs and once again inhale its peaceful beauty. My watch reads five-forty, and as I stroll along in the gathering dusk, I am joined by Dubliners returning home from work, or reading books and newspapers on a bench, or sharing a picnic on a blanket, like the two lovers I just passed, sipping wine and holding hands in front of a flower bed overflowing with red and yellow blooms. It's like a Monet painting, floats a thought, my head affirming with a gentle nod, my pace slowing even further to let it all seep in.

Fifteen free-hearted minutes later, I pass through Fusilier's Arch, a handsome stone pass-through dedicated to Ireland's war dead, and emerge onto Grafton Street. The spine of Dublin's most popular and stylish shopping district, Grafton, which is closed to cars, is almost always crowded full with pedestrianized shoppers and talented street theatre artists known as "buskers." Running south from St. Stephen's for several blocks till it junctions Nassau Street and Ms. Molly Malone, whom we encountered earlier today, Grafton's cobblestones are lined on both sides with multi-storied Georgian buildings housing a rich roster of shops, restaurants, cafés, and department stores. In fact, so total is this tribute to the Passion of Purchase that it justly lays claim to the title, The Holy Grail of Shopping! – as from Dublin's most elegant and exclusive department store, Brown Thomas, to an almost unlimited supply of smaller shops selling a vast variety of clothes, cookware, and candy, art works, jewelry, and music, it can truly be said that there's something for everyone's taste and budget.

Relaxed, but still stimulated by the peripatetic scene my eyes sweep in amused amazement, the surging river of shops and shoppers quickly drowns the fading fragment of thought suggesting a one-block detour to visit Mansion House. It's Slow Down Time! announces the left side of my brain with authority. You've walked over ten miles today and seen one whole hell of a lot. So sorry, Mr. Lord Mayor, but old Hobman can't come for late-afternoon tea with you, 'cause it's time instead to simply slow down and shop. A humanitarian proposal, it is heartily seconded by the cry of "Great idea!" flowing from my tired, aching feet, closely followed by their faithful selves slowing to a shuffle as I snake my way through the crush of chattering citizenry to participate in the party.

Stopping every so often to view a snappy leather jacket, Laura Ashley's linens, and Butler's homemade chocolates, at the Dublin Bookshop I break from my penurious pattern of window-purchases to buy a small collection of essays by John Keane, a highly popular Irish humorist. Then, with the pursestrings pried fully open, Mr. Big Spender indulges himself with an Edding Gel Roller Ball Pen and a couple of extra notebooks for journal keeping from The Card Gallery next door. Finally, at Number Forty-Four, I arrive face to face with Bewley's, Dublin's legendary café and restaurant that also houses an appealing shop selling its own brands of coffee, cookies, and cakes inside its red-bricked premises. Standing on the site of Samuel Whyte's former school, whose illustrious roll included Robert Emmet, leader of the 1803 Rebellion, and the Duke of Wellington, this institution has been a favorite of the locals for a hundred and fifty years. And upon entering, I am immediately captivated by its charming Victorian ambience, and its magnificent array of pastries.

Seating myself on the balcony overlooking the first-floor shop, for several minutes I just rest and people-watch, instantly bemused by the mixture of guesstimated ages, occupations, and conversations. Soon, however, hunger stirs, provoking a portentous poem to jump into mind: Maybe a Napoleon/Maybe a Raspberry Tart/How about a Cookie/Just to start?/The Brownies look good/So does the Apple Pie/Hell, you deserve it/Here's sugar in your eye!

And after it has run its devilish course, I place an order for one of each underneath the growling glare of the Professor. After all, I reason, wasn't it Oscar Wilde himself who taught us that "the only way to get rid of temptation is to yield to it!" Hell's bells, concludes my rationale, the day has been filled with such truly special rewards that they must be celebrated! And grinning gratefully, as streaming sugar marries memories of Joyce, Yeats, and Shaw, I pull from my backpack yesterday's baseball news which Matty had faxed me. You know, I tell myself in reverent tones, happiness humming inside my head: Sometimes, life is wonderful indeed!

VII
NORTH OF THE LIFFEY

THURSDAY MORNING ARRIVES SLOWLY, THE ALARM CLOCK HAVING TO pry me away from my dream of living opposite Merrion Square amongst Yeats, AE, and O'Connell. But as my gears gradually slip from just beyond stupor's sluggish to simply sleepy-slow, I manage to stir awake.

Now you're probably thinking: Never mind slow. It's a miracle the Hobman's alive! After all, not everyone safely survives a Pastry Pig-Out at Bewley's featuring a self-induced sugar coma! And you're right. But fortunately, the whole sweet truth of the matter is that I have. True, I did order the entire heart of the pastry menu. But kneeling also at the altar of the Deity of Discipline, I ate only bites of each, carefully storing the precious remainder of my goodies in my backpack for today's lunch. So, with the Sucrose Issue successfully resolved, and your mind now resting at ease, Good morning! Ready to meet north Dublin?...

Well, good. Me too. And after securing a soothing shower and a bite of breakfast, we're off, briskly retracing Tuesday's steps to Trinity College. Only this time, no stops. Instead, the charted course leads up Westmoreland to Ashton Quay, and then across the Liffey on the O'Connell Bridge. Named for the Great Liberator, who also served as Dublin's first Catholic mayor in 1841, the stone span logically leads onto O'Connell Street, the northside's major thoroughfare. And there to greet one, not more than fifty yards from the bridge's lip, is Daniel himself, standing tall and proud atop John Foley's magnificent bronze monument. Rising like a celebratory cake off a cream-colored stone foundation, around which are seated four life-sized carved angels, overhead the circular-shaped second layer is crowded full with sculpted images of Irish freedom-seekers from various walks of life, several of whom raise their arms hopefully toward the multi-tiered pedestal occupied by their caped hero.

The intricacy of Foley's detail is absolutely amazing, meanders a thought as I return the Great Liberator's serious but friendly gaze, my next brainwave bringing Lincoln and the similarity of their emancipation missions into mind. "Yeah, good job for sure, Danny, my man," I whisper, smiling as I lower my eyes and make ready to leave. "And by the way," I toss up to him, my feet beginning to move: "It may have taken Mr. Foley nineteen years to capture all of your glory here, but it sure was worth it, don't you think?..."

Uh-huh. You just better believe it! ripples the imaginary answer as I proceed further north for two blocks, then turn east on Abbey Street Lower and continue on toward the morning's first highlight, the Abbey Theatre. Reaching it inside five minutes, at the juncture with Marlborough Street, with a warming sense of satisfaction I pull out my pipe to celebrate. For founded almost a century ago by W.B. Yeats and Lady Augusta Gregory as Ireland's National Theatre, the Abbey has become synonymous with many of Ireland's greatest writers, a must-see long ago marked on my map. Now suddenly present, and standing still as a statue with sweet-flavored smoke billowing from my flagship Peterson, my mind's memory wheel slowly spins forth its storied history, from debuting classics such as *The Playboy of the Western World* by John M. Synge and *Juno and the Paycock* by Sean O'Casey to encouraging works by today's rising stars such as Sebastian Barry, Marina Carr, and Michael Harding. And though housed today in a modern-style brick-and-glass building, as my eyes pass over its simple, clean-cut lines, imagination's eye hearkens back to long-ago yesterday, and for a wistful moment I see the horse-drawn carriages pulling up and Yeats and Lady Gregory, and Dr. Gogarty and AE and Sean O'Casey himself climbing down, all dressed in their finest clothes, laughing and chattering away amidst their excitement.

The beep of a passing bus pulls me from my reverie. And after nodding my appreciation to the literary scene and its proud history, I smile so long, then stroll further east toward the Custom House and startling surprise. For even though studying color photographs has more than casually familiarized me with the beauty of this building, when several minutes later I round Beresford Place and gain first sighting, I am stopped in my tracks by the sheer splendor of its size and artful construction. Absolutely breathtaking, is the phrase that springs into mind as my eyes struggle to fully capture it. And though true, it is nonetheless an understatement of considerable magnitude. All right for a beginning, but standing alone by itself, not fully adequate either. In fact, speaking of beginnings, one cannot start to properly appreciate this architectural wonder without gaining some distance from it, so great are its dimensions and grandeur. So hastily retreating back across the Liffey by way of the Butt Bridge, I settle onto George's Quay, slip off my backpack, light up a fresh pipe, and have myself the proverbial good gander, "Wow!" wheeling out to complement *breathtaking*'s previous failure to achieve full justice.

For openers, Custom House, constructed to pay homage to trade, runs in width the entire distance of its namesake Quay, some 650 feet approximately. Large?...Is sugar sweet? Or water wet? Does immense light the lamp of understanding?...Yet amazingly, as enormous as it is, the impression of graceful it softly brushstrokes onto the canvas of your eyes is simultaneously equal, lending new meaning to the word majestic. Designed by the English architect James Gandon two hundred years ago, the main facade is composed of pavilions at each end with a Doric portico in its center, and over the second story sits a matching stone cupola topped by a turquoise-tiled dome on which stands a sixteen-foot statue of Commerce. Then, at street level, the arms of Ireland crown each of the two pavilions, and a series of fourteen allegorical heads by Dublin sculptor Edward Smyth form the keystones of the arches and entrances, one each for Ireland's thirteen major rivers and the Atlantic Ocean. Used today for government offices, with its huge Georgian windows offering unparalleled views of the River Liffey, should one look up the adjective *awesome* in the dictionary, one is likely to find a picture of Custom House, no words needed. In fact, I can't find any that seem adequate for my journal either, so resting my pen, I simply stand and stare in complete admiration. Until finally, several minutes later, the subconscious need to push on pokes its way into stalled reality, and after murmuring, "I'll never forget you," I move on, winding my way back to O'Connell Street.

Actually, *street* is a misnomer. For O'Connell is almost twice as wide as any street I have encountered. So wide, in fact, that in addition to its broad sidewalks, it includes a twenty-foot pedestrian mall centered in its midsection and running its entire length. Street?...No. Boulevard, yes. And Avenue, better yet, I muse as I stroll north, my rested eyes now filling with the mix of architectural styles that house the hotels, restaurants, and shops of every description which line both sides of this busy thoroughfare. Immediately struck as I am by the *avenue's* diversity of old and new, large and small, glitzy and drab, when I reach O'Connell's halfway point, once again history's badge bounds from the shadowy pages of yesteryear to stand and stir the boiling broth of bittersweet curiosity. For shining proudly in the late-morning sunshine is the General Post Office of sorrowful Easter Rising fame. Built of brown brick and stone in 1818 according to the designs of noted architect Francis Johnston, this last great public building of the Georgian era, with its Doric-columned portico, is the single most important symbol of the Irish struggle for freedom. For it is on these steps where I now stand, memory reminds, that Patrick Pearse proclaimed the Irish Republic on Easter Monday in 1916. It is here that bombs fell and the freedom fighters bled and died and Yeats' *terrible beauty* was born. To my right, on the outer facade, bullet holes are still easily seen. And when I move closer to run my fingertips lightly over them, I also find nearby, etched into the stone, the fateful words from freedom's voice. "Ohhh, but what a good fight you put up," I whisper to Pearse, Plunkett, and Connolly after I've walked across the street to better view the grandeur of the building. "I saw inside the statue of the mythical warrior Cuchulainn, and you did him proud for sure, each and every one!" sings my sympathy softly as I strain across the years to try to appreciate the pain of their sacrifice, my eyes then tearing at the sight of the Irish flag waving freely in the wind. And suddenly, unexplainably, I can see them, all the martyred fourteen and their lost comrades, standing arm in arm around the flagpole and smiling back at me. Smiling wider and wider and warmer and warmer: A smile so great, that it swallows the sadness in their eyes.

Several seconds later, when emotion has wound down and my smile is my own again, I silently salute them with: God bless!, then slowly move northward once again. A half block, and I reach Earl Street where I turn right for a full one to meet my old friend Marlborough Street. Then, fifty yards north, and I stand in front of St. Mary's Pro-Cathedral. The street is shady from the multitude of trees, and not yet fully recovered from my emotional encounter at the GPO, I drop down onto the grass across from the landmark and rest amidst the surrounding flowers. With the locale empty and quiet, after a minute or two, my trusty pipe acting as companion, I feel myself fully returned to me. How can I be sure?...Well, a strong craving for sugar is calling, and after pulling from my backpack a piece of Bewley's Brownie, I slide it inside my mouth to the accompaniment of my tongue's loud applause. Then, fully refreshed, I employ my eyes in a study of St. Mary's, Dublin's sole Catholic cathedral – though only an "acting" one as *Pro* designates, because it has not been anointed official by the Pope.

Interesting is the adjective that slips into mind as a summary of first impression. Constructed of light-colored stone, and occupying the better part of half a block, St. Mary's Pro combines two unique architectural styles for Dublin: a Greek Revival facade with a six-columned portico modeled after the temple of Theseus in Athens, and waiting inside, a Renaissance-style interior reflecting the design of the church of St. Philippe-le-Roule in Paris. And though at first blush St. Mary's is most certainly impressive, it still pales by comparison to the elegant beauty of St. Patrick's, or the towering triumph of Christ Church. In large part this results from St. Mary's backstreet location, which at the time of its dedication in 1825, before Catholic emancipation was fully effectuated, was the best the City's Anglo-Irish leaders would allow. So, while St. Patrick's is seated in a lush park, and Christ Church stands alone surrounded by a carpet of lawn and blanketing flower beds, St. Mary's is cramped by neighboring properties on an ordinary, albeit leafy street. In fact, seated as far away from the entrance as geography permits, what with the fenced grounds of Tyrone House and the Irish Department of Education at my back, I am still only able to glimpse a small fraction of the turquoise dome rising behind the statues of St. Patrick and St. Laurence O'Toole that flank St. Mary atop the pediment over the portico.

Now, chances are, I muse, that Mr. O'Toole, the twelfth-century Archbishop of Dublin, and the City's patron saint, wouldn't be too pleased about this. And old Patrick, who was known to display a mighty temper when injustice entered the fray, would be downright pissed off! I mean, in a country that is arguably more Catholic than Rome, and the Protestants manage to twist the Trinity into the Father, the Son, and the Holy Left Out! Jesus cockamolies Christ, what the hell is going on here? concludes my fury-flavored indictment, snapshots of the long British occupation flashing forward, then quickly fading away. "Ohhh, I know…I know," trickles a whispery stream of resignation. "More trouble's been caused by religion than anything else man's dreamed up. Hey, what was it I read in John Keane's little book: 'That Ireland consists mainly of Catholics and Protestants, some of whom are even Christians!' Well, right on the money, John," I chuckle, pulling myself to my feet and beginning to amble back toward O'Connell Street. "Right square on the money."

With Keane's keen observation having resuscitated my good humor, upon returning to the junction of Earl Street and O'Connell, it is further nourished by the Anna Livia Fountain, a multi-spouted monument erected during Dublin's millennium celebration in 1988. Designed to represent the River Liffey, Anna Livia in Gaelic, and popularized as such by James Joyce in his works, a nearby statue of the master smiles approvingly at the sculpted mermaid that highlights the memorial, despite the fact that most Dubliners bemusedly refer to her as the Floozie in the Jacuzzi. "Now listen, sweetie, I don't know about this floozie business," I wink to the lithesome lass as I pass by. "But if you're free for dinner, how about ringing me up, okay?…"

Yeah, yeah. I know. Talking to buildings and statues is one thing, but asking a naked lady made of marble to dinner is a full step beyond serious. It just goes to show what can happen to a person who's ingested too much sugar. Or, on the other hand, maybe not enough, provides a second thought as I meander up O'Connell in search of Parnell Square. Browsing here and there as I progress further northward, when I approach a half mile my eyes are suddenly lifted to the skies by the upward thrust of my objective's namesake monument. For shaped like an obelisk, and composed of blanched yellow stone, the four-sided shaft shoots some fifty feet into the air to celebrate liberty's torch, while at the base stands a life-size bronze likeness of the great Charles Stewart Parnell, the nineteenth-century Champion of Home Rule. Remembered fondly as the Uncrowned King of Ireland for his unrivaled courage on behalf of Irish independence, from his pedestal Charles Stewart now oversees the small circular park which also bears his name. Dating back to 1748, and second only to St. Stephen's Green in age, this tiny urban oasis warmly welcomes visitors with large urns of colorful flowers dotting the circumference of its cobblestoned center, while further enhancing the surrounding neighborhood.

And a distinguished locale it is too. For just twenty-five yards or so farther north of Mr. Parnell sits the legendary Gate Theatre, the launching pad for such famous actors as Orson Welles and James Mason, and home each summer to a Beckett Festival. Residing in a building originally constructed in 1784 as part of the adjacent Rotunda Hospital, it was converted to its present artistic use in 1930, and is renowned for its staging of contemporary international drama. Next door, however, the companioning hospital, which dates back to 1751, continues to serve its medical function and to enjoy its fame as the first hospital in Ireland to specialize in maternity care. Built in the Palladium style of Leinster House, it also contains a unique chapel featuring striking stained-glass windows and a Rococo plasterwork ceiling by Bartholomew Cramillion. And after a ten-minute tour, highlighted by sharing the chapel's beauty plus some chit-chat with a charming couple from Norway, my explorer's batteries are fully recharged and eager to fuel my northern journey one block further to the Dublin Writer's Museum.

How about that, an entire museum devoted to wordsmiths! squeals my excitement as I peruse the eighteenth-century, three-story, red-brick townhouse which now serves as home to voluminous literary exhibits. I mean, we're talking comprehensive with a capital C, word worshipers. For not only is the gallery's focus trained on Shaw, Yeats, Beckett, and Heaney, Ireland's four Nobel Prize winners, but numerous other famous writers are showcased as well, from my old friends Swift, Wilde, and Joyce, to O'Casey, Behan, and Binchy. Talk about died and gone to heaven, for the better part of two golden hours rapture rolls forth from a cathedral whose religion coddles the creative cravings of my soul. As spread out before me is the history of Irish literature over the past three hundred years, with displays of rare editions, manuscript notes, and assorted memorabilia. On the first floor, I meet Henry Grattan, born in 1746, who both wrote and worked for Irish Independence. And for company, nearby are original manuscripts by Oliver Goldsmith and the dramatist Richard Sheridan. Then upstairs, I am introduced to the work of Thomas Moore, who was known as the National Poet of Ireland in the early nineteenth century, and his distinguished company includes Patrick Pearse, Joseph Plunkett, and Thomas MacDonagh, three poets whose passion for freedom placed them at the heart of the Easter Rising. Nodding my appreciation to each for a poem appearing in longhand, when I reach the third-floor gallery of portraits and busts, I find them waiting, their lively eyes sharing the moment with me, before a nearby oil of Mary Lavin captures me completely. "I'm busy for dinner," I whisper flirtatiously to her upon parting after several fantasy-filled minutes. "But how about lunch? We could talk over nouns and pronouns, mix in a verb or two, and you know, sorta get acquainted."

Regrettably, Father Time prevents her acceptance. The notion of lunch, however, lingers and is greeted most enthusiastically by the hollow creatures bouncing around in my tummy. So, after purchasing a snack from the first-floor coffee shop, my appetite and I adjourn to the Garden of Remembrance, located directly across a narrow street from the Museum's entrance. Noting its rectangular shape, and the crowd of flowers and trees, I quickly find a seat on a bench overlooking the large cruciform pool which occupies center stage. Dedicated to all who gave their lives in the cause of Irish freedom, the garden was created in 1966 on the fiftieth anniversary of the Rising. And as I take note of the mosaics on the floor of the pool which depict broken weapons as a sign of peace, I am seized by the thought of how perfectly appropriate this special spot is to give thanks for their supreme sacrifice and honor their rich legacy. For sure, and then some! sounds gratefully into mind. And after murmuring a prayer for peace, my simple celebration of cheese, croissant, and apple could not have tasted better, topped as it was by the last bites of my Bewley's brownie.

At one o'clock, the bells of the neighboring Abbey Presbyterian Church wake me from my sunbathed siesta and its dreamy review of history's heroes and the morning's magnificent architectural monuments. Standing up, then stretching, as I pull on my backpack, the Gothic style of the Abbey suddenly reminds me of my house and draws a smile. The Abbey was built in 1864 with a large donation from a local wine merchant named Alexander Findlater, causing locals to call it Findlater's Church. As my eyes climb the steepled tower adjacent to the Museum, then pass over the triangular-shaped body to dwell on the bell tower rising above a pointed arch, I also see the smaller, distant cousin that cradles the front door to my home. Do you miss it? asks an intruding interrogative. Huh? Do ya?...

Nooo...not really, shuffles my answer after several seconds. But the question doesn't disappear. Instead, it shadows me as I return south along

O'Connell Street, pressing me for further attention even as I wrestle with a difficult choice: Detour east of O'Connell to visit the James Joyce Museum? Or remain inside the cocoon of *Relax Time* initially spun inside the Garden, and experience more of the living, breathing environment weaving threads in all directions along my adopted avenue. The afternoon has turned blue and warm. Absolutely lovely. And with reason arguing that I've already met Mr. Joyce three times, intuition closes out the quandary with: He'd tell you, never mind the dusty manuscripts. Just open your eyes and ears, Writer-Man, and have a look and listen!

Yeah?...Ya think? I smile. Well, all right, no problem, finishes the thought as I head inside Café Maud and purchase a raspberry ribbon ice-cream cone, then drop down onto a bench in the Mall near the foot of the statue of Father Matthew, the founder of the Abstinence Movement. Uh-huh...That's right. But before you get lost in the moment's iridescent irony, let me remind you that I did fully honor the spirit of Father Matthew's mission by summoning forth my full powers of discipline in order to resist the shopkeeper's Satanic offer of a double-decker. I mean, hell, three scoops was not entirely off the menu, ends my defense, a large bite following to celebrate my victory, the sweet cream also flavoring my feeling of being unusually *comfortable*. And that's precisely when Mr. Interrogative regains his voice, jumping out of the shadows and seizing upon my innocent use of the word connoting *homelike* to ask: Why?...

I don't know...I'm just comfortable, that's all, drowses my reply with understated brilliance, my eyes searching the buildings and trees and the faces of passers-by for a real answer, the knowledge that I am a stranger from a foreign country, with a different religion, absent even a drop of Irish heritage, and knowing absolutely not a single soul trailing into mind to occupy the spotlight. *Interrogation lamp* is actually more accurate, as Mr. Nag instantly follows up with: Okay...Then why are you *so* comfortable? Huh, old boy, who's shy and never feels at home easily?...

Well...for openers, the answer slowly begins to form, the buildings aren't too tall. There are no skyscrapers to blot out the sun and erase the horizon, confirms observation, my eyes easily able to pick out Bronze Daniel some three blocks away. Then, too, the mixture of old and new is extremely well balanced. I mean, look, over there's the Gresham Hotel built in 1817, and a little further up is Clery's Department Store from 1822, and the GPO from 1818, with all the small shops and their modern fronts and merchandise tucked cozily in between. I mean, you can have high tea at 3 p.m. in the Gresham with Queen Victoria, then find U2 and Snoop Dog across the street in the neon-signed music store. It's like they've got both feet firmly planted in the present, but their heels still touch yesteryear, saying: We know where we are, and hopefully where we're going. But we didn't forget where we came from either, and don't want to. Our roots lie in the land, and that's why even in urban Dublin, we do parks and gardens big time, filling them full of flowers and trees, from Parnell Square and the Garden of Remembrance to Merrion Square and St. Stephen's Green.

"Yeahhh," ambles agreement off my tongue, understanding trickling in as I sit in the buttery sunshine, my eyes shifting to study the steady stream of people going about the business of living. For if architecture and horticulture have created a comfortable stage, what about the actors? pursues the insistent interrogator, still perched on my shoulder. Well, to begin with, they're just people like you and me, replies first thought, my gaze gathering in young, old, and the middle-aged from the serpentining parade of doctors, lawyers and stockbrokers, housewives, shopkeepers, salesclerks and repairpersons. And first impression also says they're busy, bustling about with their hopes and dreams, worries and fears, all mixing to fuel their daily chores and long-range plans. They work hard. They play hard. They laugh and cry, grow frustrated and find oases of peace. They fall in love, form families, wrestle with bills, and sing and dance and curse and pray. And what was it I read, that you can measure the character of a city and its citizenry by its energy?…Well, Dublin's certainly got plenty of that, deduces my next brainwave, synapses now shifting into higher gear, the hustle and bustle of business interplaying with nightlife's theatres, concert halls, and cafés to form a flood of energetic endeavor across the map of my mind.

And yet, a quiet voice interjects when I interrupt the flow to shift my weight, this energy is different from that flowing through the streets of New York, Chicago or Los Angeles, London, Hong Kong or Berlin. It's slower, and friendlier. It's vibrant, to be sure, but somehow less hurried, less stressed. It's alive, and enthusiastic, and even passionate, but not frantic or crazed. A big city?…Yes, no question. But not driven by the fires of bigger is better, and there isn't a second to waste. Instead, there are roots that run a thousand years deep, and more than casually connected, breathe balance into daily life along the Liffey, whispering faithfully: "It's nice to be important, but it's more important to be nice!"

For several serious seconds, the ancient axiom's simple philosophy sings to me like a psalm harmonized by St. Mary's celebrated Palestrina Choir. Then, smiling with satisfaction, I bid Father Matthew farewell, promising to curtail the promiscuous consumption of sugar before turning away and heading for Moore Street and its open-air market. A right turn one block later at Henry Street, followed by another after a short walk westward, and presto, I'm instantly injected into a scene in which the mythical Molly Malone would be fully at home. For centering two blocks of Georgian buildings housing shops below overhead flats, Moore Street's cobblestones, closed to vehicular traffic, host a bevy of vendors selling fresh fish, fruit and vegetables, and flowers along with T-shirts, leather goods, and costume jewelry from their four-wheeled carts. Crowded with an interesting assortment of people, add the pandemonium of chatter to the folk tunes strumming out of the first-floor music store and the pungent smells punctuating the air, and Moore Street Market easily validates its reputation as one of Dublin's most aromatic and noisiest attractions. It's an experience that also produces an ear-to-ear grin as one waltzes back inside a bygone era to sample the various wares while sharing conversation with sharp-witted vendors and fellow shoppers. In the Earl Butcher Shop, Sam enthusiastically explains to me the advantageous quality of his skinless boneless chicken breasts over those of his next-door competitor, while outside I purchase an apple from a young lady who could've worked alongside Eve in Eden, what with her hip-hugging jeans, halter top, and bare midriff. You see, Father Matthew, I can make nutritious choices, smiles a thought as I thread my way back through the crowd of rich Dublin dialects to Henry Street and say so long to the cheery scene. In fact, counting that bakery I passed up, make that two counts of being good, chuckles the tail end of my plea for recognition by the Purity Patrol, my feet padding on forward.

At 40-42 O'Connell Street, I meet Eason & Son Ltd., a book shop that has been operating at this very same location for over a hundred years. *Shop* is their name of choice, but the reality is a very large store with a huge selection of books and stationery items, all offered inside a warmly colored modern layout encased in yesteryear's Georgian brick facade. Happy second century, and many more! whisks my wish as I take leave, now picking up the pace as the Liffey comes into view. The famed Four Courts is the final destination on today's tour, about a mile or so to the west. So, upon reaching the river, I turn right onto Bachelor's Walk, the first of four quays leading to the headquarters of the Irish Justice System since 1796. Even as four o'clock approaches, the afternoon remains pleasantly warm, with the azure sky now unfolding a curtain of clouds over the western horizon. And as I stroll along the Liffey, I feel fully the contentment created by the day's discoveries, my smile widening further at the sight of several couples holding hands and sneaking kisses on the benches facing the river. Hey, you guys, I tease: This walkway's for bachelors, don't ya know?…On the other hand, however, hope, once again springing eternal, suggests: Maybe one of you sweetie-pies might just happen to have a widowed mother? Or a divorced aunt, or friend? You know, someone age appropriate, like late forties or early fifties. I mean, you do have some older women here in Dublin, don't ya?…

They must, I answer myself as I pass the Arlington Hotel, a three-storied classic painted mustard yellow and flying several flags on each side of the green, white, and orange of Eire. Ormond Quay appears soon thereafter, diverting my train of thought to a speculation on why the name is so popular as to cause the succeeding dock to be celebrated as Ormond Quay II. "Ormond must have been one of those rare older beauties you've been searching for," I quip softly as I stride steadily onward, scanning the Liffey for boats, eyeing people on the bridges. Then, as Inns Quay finally appears, so does our majestic objective. And though tripping off my tongue to repeat itself, having rested since being used this morning to describe Custom House, *majestic* is nonetheless the appropriate adjective to apply. As once again James Gandon has worked his magic, this time producing a distinctive, bone-colored stone building of Georgian style, running some 450 feet in length, and featuring a gracious six-columned Corinthian portico whose pediment is topped by carved figures of Justice, Mercy, Wisdom, and Moses. This central section is in turn flanked by two wings containing the original four courts of Common Pleas, Chancery, Exchequer, and Kings Bench. And just to ensure that this queen beauty stands out in the Dublin skyline, Gandon crowned her with a massive sixty-four foot, copper-covered, lantern-style dome supported by matching Corinthian columns.

"As if someone could possibly miss it, huh?" I smile as once again

I have to retreat across the Liffey in order to gain enough distance to fully appreciate the work of art swelling my eyes' capacity full. And emulating my morning experience at Custom House, likewise, words cannot capture the true depth of my admiration. "I don't want to practice law anymore, Mr. Gandon," whispers my weak attempt. "But your genius building sure makes it tempting." Then, fixing my stare so as to freeze each and every detail, for several minutes I am lost inside its mesmerizing magnificence.

A horn beep from a passing barge brings me back to Merchant's Quay, and slowly I shift my eyes to follow its journey west. Dusk is dropping hints, and out on the horizon, the sun is settling into a pink puddle. Thoughts of dinner flicker into mind, followed by the need to pack, as tomorrow I will leave for Sligo. I'll be back though, I say silently to Dublin as I begin the stroll home to Hotel Central, crossing Wood Quay reminding me that this is where She was born a thousand years ago. And when I then slow to a stop where the Vikings first stepped ashore, suddenly, unexpectedly, Dublin spins a celestial circle about me, stars winking to catch my eye. North of the Liffey, on the welcoming width of O'Connell Street, the General Post Office sparkles as the sure-most symbol of Irish freedom, with the Great Liberator standing guard, and the Garden of Remembrance promising peace to countless others whose selfless sacrifice made possible the liberty that could birth a James Joyce and fuel the bustling but unhurried life-energy of the Moore Street Market. Then, to the south, twinkle Trinity College, Dublin Castle, and the Cathedrals of St. Patrick and Christ Church, St. Stephen's Green, Merrion Square, and Grafton Street all shimmering in support. If the southside, harboring the Old City and today's Temple Bar, is the heart of Dublin, enters a thought, sparks flying, then the northside, carrying liberty's torch and a literary flame, is its soul. And if at the world's table of power and politics, Dublin might not exert great influence, follows the fuel of ripening understanding, the world would do well to look, listen, and learn. For yesteryear's roots, which are retained and celebrated, rather than abandoned, order priorities and temper the pace of life to where nature is never far away, nice is not nerdy, and comfortable is an investment of capital worthy of being cherished. "Better to be nice, indeed!" I whisper prayerfully north and south. Then, smiling wistfully, I light up my pipe and stroll into the falling night.

VIII

TRAIN RIDE TO SLIGO

THE TINY TRAVEL CLOCK CHEERFULLY CHIRPS ME AWAKE. WIDE AWAKE, and instantly able to feel the nervous anticipation of seeing Sligo hollowing a home for butterflies in my stomach, Drumcliffe, Yeats, and Ben Bulben marching spryly into mind as I slide out of bed and stroll into the bathroom to shave. "Uh-huh, and as Grampy used to say, we're up before breakfast to see'em too," I mutter to my reflection as I turn on the hot water, then retreat to the sitting area to snap on the coffee maker.

Add cream and two sugar cubes, and my movements ramp up to full speed ahead. Inside an hour, I'm showered, dressed, fully packed, and downstairs at the desk checking out, having whispered good-bye to Room 322 and left a Thank You note and five pounds for the house-keeper. Len, the attendant, shares in my excited chatter, tipping me off to the Half Moon Pub in Sligo as well as other special eateries in Galway and beyond, before escorting me to the waiting cab and waving alongside his "All the best" as the driver pulls from the curb.

Ten minutes later, I'm lighting up my pipe outside Connolly Station and studying the gray bank of clouds that have lowered the sky's ceiling and produced a finely falling mist, a slight twinge of sadness at leaving Dublin and my comfy home at the Hotel Central rubbing up against the eager anticipation of the day's adventure ahead. But no problem, no real time to miss what has somehow become so familiar in such a short time, as I have to find my train. Also no problem, as the bright lights on

72

the Arrival-Departure Board quickly advise that Train 75 will be leaving from Track 3. And at eight-thirty sharp, the train's first lurches find me comfortably settled on a cushiony seat inside a smoking car, my journal and camera spread out before me on the table, with friendly conversation already under way.

Three hours and 150 northwest miles will pass between Dublin and Sligo, and Mary, a sweet-faced, middle-aged housewife provides a most amiable beginning. For though she is traveling only an hour's distance up the track to Mullingar to visit an ailing uncle, her good-natured curiosity spearheads a steady but relaxed dialogue. I explain about Oregon and Portland, my family, and the switching of careers from lawyering to writing after Patty's passing, and she shares her thoughts and feelings about working-class Irish families, keynoting her hope that education and the technology age will raise the prospects for her children, before warmly encouraging me to look up my newest literary companion, Mr. John Keane, for a possible chat when I reach Killarney. Then, when Alice joins us after our first stop at Maynooth, the purring pot of conversation adds seasoning to grow even more flavorful.

A pretty lady in her mid-seventies, with delicate features and sparkling blue eyes that belie her age, Alice softly radiates refinement, from the tasteful blue suit and matching overcoat to the educated quality of her speech. She, too, was traveling only a short distance to Longford to visit relatives, but it's long enough to share her treasured memories of living in Chicago when her now deceased husband was stationed there by his insurance company. Lake Michigan, the Loop's skyscrapers, concerts, theatre, and close friendships tumble off her tongue as if it were only yesterday, the genuine enjoyment of that life experience sunlighting her smile, while outside the window miles of green fields flow by, growing greener in the light rain, their lush folds dotted with haystacks, stone walls, and clusters of cows and sheep.

All too soon, Mullingar Station looms, and Mary makes ready to depart. I had confided in her that my literary hopes were tied to a novel being considered in New York. And now, after pulling on her coat, she hugs me while adding "I hope I'll see you again at a book signing. Remember, we Irish *love* love stories." Then, when Longford appears shortly thereafter, Alice charges me to "Take the best of care, and enjoy

Ireland," punctuating her warm wishes with a firm handshake before disappearing from view.

Still smiling as I return to my seat and begin an entry in my journal, the pen has barely begun to move when I am surprised by the sound of someone calling my name. Glancing up, then right, my eyes fix on a small man two rows forward. A hint of a grin is fighting for birth on his lips as he motions for me to join him. And when I reach his table, he quickly adds, "Sorry, but I couldn't help but overhear your conversation with the ladies, and you seem like such a regular fella, I want to know ya. Name's Jerry McDonald, but my friends call me Jerry Mac," he ends, extending his hand.

The grip is firm, and his infant grin now widens to match mine as I slip behind the table and peer across at him. Sky blue, the eyes are lively beneath a full head of closely cropped gray hair, and his nose, mouth, and cheeks are finely drawn, as if carefully measured to fit his narrow face. Dressed in stonewashed jeans, with a crisp white shirt accentuating his black blazer, the snug fit highlights the leanness of his slight frame. Not exactly basketball material myself at five-foot-six and a hundred forty pounds, I guessed that I was an inch taller and outweighed him by a similar margin, judging further that the weight of his years was also slightly less than my sixty.

Opening our dialogue by presenting a riddle, his voice tone was low-key and lightly accented. The details about a farmer filling bags of potatoes escape me, as did the answer, my focus having centered on the current of playfulness curling out of the corners of his mouth to light his face.

No problem, however, that the answer proves elusive, a second chance is immediately provided. And when I flunk that test as easily as the first, Jerry Mac just chuckles while revealing the answers and then creating my excuse. The problem is, it seems, that I need a drink. Deemed an urgent necessity after a half second's careful consideration, the second half includes his eager offer to furnish same. And after refusing my request to pay on the grounds that "You're *my* guest," he promptly heads for the bar car.

During his less-than-two-minute absence, I mulled over the issue of whether I'd fallen in with a good-natured but slightly mischievous Irish elf. And when he returns, bearing both beer and Jameson's Irish Whiskey "to add a bit of punch," the verdict is sealed. It's only ten o'clock in the morning, flashes my thought, and you're having an Irish Boilermaker for breakfast – not to mention, on an empty stomach! Hell's bells, counsels caution: Did you say a *little* mischief's afoot? You trying to win the Understatement-of-the-Year Award, are ya? Well, not to worry. For while Mr. Mischief is indeed tiptoeing about, it's his co-conspirator, Mr. Good-Nature that strides purposefully to center stage, and after a quick sip or two of Guinness, announces: Let's share! Which, aided by the freedom-fostering properties of our nourishment, we do. Like me, Jerry Mac had lost his wife to cancer. And as he describes his daughters, Jenny and Liz, a sliver of sadness softens the mixture of pride and gratitude sounding inside his voice, before echoing into mine as I reciprocate with details of Amy, Matt, and Nick. "Well, I've got ten acres or so," he picks up. "And I gave each of my ladies one of 'em to build their own houses on. Pretty sneaky trick to keep 'em close, eh?"

"Yeahhh. For sure," I nod, watching the corners of his eyes crinkle with glee, affordable housing having been high on my list of reasons for moving the boys to Portland. "But how'd you manage to grab onto ten acres?"

"Oh, I raise sheep, like my folks and theirs before 'm. Land's been in the family a long way back, you see."

"Right. I hear ya," trickles my reply, trailed by a brief outline of my family's shopping center business in California.

"Then you left lawyering and property, to be a writer?" he queries, curiosity creeping into his tone.

"Uh-huh. Guilty as charged," enters my plea. "I just wanted a more simple life, with time for the boys. But then too, some strange creature inside me said I really need to do it. Sounds crazy, huh?..."

"No, not to me," he shakes out, smiling as he adds another shot of Jameson's to our beer. "Shows character, if you ask this old farmer. Besides, writing's important," he tosses out, lifting his mug.

And after we toast my decision, and ask the literary gods for their blessing with a second, the conversation ages past comfortable, switching gears to spontaneous. Flow, flow, and more flow, as any and everything mixes with fleeing miles and minutes to churn chitchat into comradeship. Now how about this? I consider, relishing my good fortune as music and art, poetry, politics, and pretty ladies parade past. Just five days ago

I was in my kitchen in Portland, and now I'm cooking up conversation with an Irish shepherd on a train to Sligo. What a strange and wonderful world, eh? I smile, as Jerry Mac slants off onto religion, and the beloved John Keane arises for the second time.

"Know what he said?" Jerry Mac sidles out slyly, raising his eyebrows for effect. "He viewed that Ireland is composed of Catholics and Protestants, some of whom are even Christians. And if you ask me," he chuckles, "he hit the old nail squarely on the head. I mean, hell, the whole damn world's fought more wars over who's got the right church, than anything else – when all we gotta do is reach out a little and be friends like you and me, right?" he concludes, having echoed the same sentiments I espoused during yesterday's visit to St. Mary's.

"You got that right. Big time!" I chime, the rollercoaster then running on and over the Great Famine that led to the enormous wave of Irish emigration to America, to JFK, the Clintons, and soccer before finally settling on the delights of traditional Irish music awaiting me when I reach Doolin. Then, seemingly in an eye-blink, the call on the train's speaker is Carrick on Shannon. Rising, Jerry Mac hugs me, and when our eyes meet, says: "Remember. On your next visit, you can stay with me." Then, as my thank-you toned "Take care" echoes back into ear, he's gone.

For several seconds, I just stand and stare at the empty doorway, my head still bobbing. Then, before happy and sad can mix further inside me, for the second time I hear my name called out and spin round to meet the smiling face of Tommy McPartland. A strapping fellow seated three rows beyond Jerry Mac's pew, Tommy advises that now it's their turn to talk, pointing to the half-dozen folks seated near him, several of whom nod their greetings.

Time is short, as my audience will depart at one of three stops during the next fifteen minutes. But after Tommy, who had retired from the merchant marines last year at fifty with a bad back, proudly announces that he had visited Savannah once for three days, we make the most of it. When I confess that I had never visited Georgia, Tommy replies that he hasn't been to many of the spots in Ireland on my itinerary either. And after I explain how mysteriously drawn to Erin I am, and how truly beautiful and friendly I was finding it to be, a fusillade of questions flows my way. What was New York really like? And how about San Francisco,

Dallas, and Boston? Say, did we Americans ever feel lost in such a large country? And, of course: Where exactly, is Oregon?

They all know California, so I guide them north, like from Dublin to Belfast. And when I share with them how much Oregon is like Ireland, with its rivers and lakes and farms, and almost as green with forests and mountains, they nod and softly chuckle their appreciation, each of them then shaking my hand or patting me on the shoulder as the tiny towns of Boyle, Ballymote, and Collooney arrive and they depart.

Then, suddenly after all the wondrous commotion, I am alone. Totally. The sole passenger in the now empty car, I slowly wander back to my original seat and slump down beside my backpack, voices echoing all around me in the silence. Mary. Alice. Jerry Mac and Tommy. All gone now, but not before making a minor miracle. For inside three hours, they'd walked into my life and warmed a stranger with laughter, stories, and shared pieces of their lives. The car is empty all right, but I'm oh so full. For each and every one who welcomed me with an open heart had left footprints on mine. "Footprints of feelings that will last forever," I whisper to the flowers outside the window as the train rumbles on. And when the phrase, stranger in a foreign land, filters into mind as I carefully tuck the small empty flask of Jameson's into my briefbag for safekeeping, "Not anymore," murmurs through my smile as the gift continues to settle, the outskirts of Sligo now sliding happily into view.

IX

SWEET AFTERNOON
IN SLIGO TOWN

YOU KNOW HOW SOME PLACES YOU HAVE TO GET USED TO, TO FEEL comfortable in? The kind that have to grow on you, like some people who are a bit standoffish, and it takes several experiences over time before the ice melts and a rapport is reached?…

Well, not Sligo. No, this lively little market town of seventeen thousand souls wedged between Ulster and the Atlantic is neither shy nor intimidating. Instead, ideally situated in a valley between the two mountains of Ben Bulben and Knocknarea at the mouth of the River Garavogue, with Sligo Bay on its western shores and Lough Gil to the east, Sligo smiles immediately upon making your acquaintance, and welcomes you with open arms. In fact, wide open, bounces a happy thought as I return the warm greeting and firm handshake of my grinning cabbie, Jimmy Murphy, and settle into the front seat alongside him for conversation on the ride to the hotel.

Our route takes us along the western edge of town, then south, my eyes roving in all directions as Jimmy and I chatter away. The buildings winding into view, both commercial and residential, are scaled down from those in Dublin, and Jimmy quickly confirms that two stories is the historical height limit, and that most of what I see has been in place since the early 1900s. Constructed of stone, brick, and plaster, the houses and shops are in large majority simply styled and well maintained. And collectively, they paint a picture of *homey*, with their unpretentious design and the exuding aura of rustic stability.

"Oh, yeah. Right," Jimmy verifies. "Change doesn't happen quickly here, or come very often. What you see is what you get – the simple life, with a comfortable pace, and almost everybody knowing everyone. It's not exactly exciting, but it sure is friendly. And you can count on tomorrow, if you know what I mean?…" he ends, steering into the driveway of the Sligo Park Hotel.

I do. And then again, I don't. I mean, I've read and heard about life in a small town. But growing up in Los Angeles, the closest I ever came to experiencing it was my three years away at law school in Berkeley, and even then I was bordered by big-city Oakland next door and San Francisco across the bay. The idea of a more simple life, with a slower pace that offers time for family and friends, had always remained with me, even transformed into a dream. But after law school, work and the struggle to get ahead soon combined to reinforce my urban roots, fogging over the dream with a flurry of life activities. It didn't die. I could still see it during quiet moments before sleep, or during break times at work when I would stare out the office window and imagination would carry me far far away. But as the years passed, and some success arrived, it served only to attach additional strings and push the dream even further away. So, after learning that my room is not yet ready, it is with a quiet but growing sense of excitement that I set off to explore Sligo, not only a small town, but one whose rural roots run fifteen hundred years deep. "Uh-huh, that's right. Sligo was founded around 450 by Bishop Bronus, a disciple of St. Patrick," I chirp merrily to myself as I head north into town on a road named for our old poet-friend Patrick Pearse.

"Yeahhh…Good job, Bronus old boy!" bounds my good humor, nourished by the knowledge that my watch reads only twelve-fifteen and a whole afternoon of adventure lies ahead. Even the chilly breeze off Sligo Bay, and the threatening gray clouds overhead, fail to dampen the feeling of relaxed enthusiasm welling inside me. No, homey has been sighted, and a lifetime of curiosity canters forth to easily fuel the search engine, not that a full supply is necessary. For less than two minutes into my journey, first impression is solidly reinforced by the red, yellow, and beige sides of several row houses and the eye-catching charm of a totally quaint cottage I stop to admire. Small, at about twelve hundred square feet, with rich red flowers and thick green foliage blanketing both sides of the entryway to offset the dark brown shakes forming the vaulted roof, it exudes country charm, the elements of pure and wholesome wrapping their arms around comfy-cozy to perfect its personality. I wonder if Jimmy the Cabbie is going to live in such a cutie after he gets married next month, I muse as my eyes climb to the smoke whispering from the single chimney into the heavy sky. He told me that he and Julia were looking, and from that picture he showed me, they'd match perfectly, handsome couple that they are. No problem with room for the children to play either, not with the stone-fenced yard, and flowers and trees everywhere, rises my river of speculation. And they can afford it too, what with Jimmy owning his own cab and in business for himself. Plus, here, you can get a nice little house for what wouldn't buy a bathroom back in Portland, I shrug, smiling at my vicarious enjoyment of a life I can somehow feel, even though I'm touching it only in passing. Oh, they'll never have a ton of money, or a hot nightlife in Temple Bar, adds the opposite side of the coin. But they've got love, and they're surrounded by family and friends in a life that's under control. Hey, maybe their options are somewhat limited, but so is the old stress level, and that's not a bad trade-off if you ask me. Hell, it's a damn good life! I conclude, resuming my journey toward town, contented with my deduction that there are good prospects afoot for their happiness.

Fifteen minutes later, I stand at the corner of Thomas and Castle streets in the heart of downtown Sligo, where homey, already firmly formed in my psyche, is now polished to perfection. As to my left, running along the narrow passageway for three blocks and an equal number of name changes, is a central shopping district that would make a stroller along Sinclair Lewis' Main Street feel right at home. For composed of colorfully crafted storefronts situated below two stories of flats, all housed in one-hundred-year-plus-old buildings that are mostly plainly styled and painted subdued hues of white, beige, and grey, the aura floating forth is one of ageless casual comfort. Like a favorite sweater, whose warmth has sheltered so long you can't remember when not, I muse as I walk the narrow sidewalks from Castle to Grattan to John Street. It's Friday, and time to shop for the weekend, I gather from the crowds filling the narrow corridor so full that one could easily be pushed off the walkway into the street. And how two-way traffic manages to negotiate this thin thoroughfare without accident is a salient question indeed. It does however. And as I windowshop a drug store, an electrical repair shop, and a small market whose fruits and veggies lip the sidewalk, I am accompanied by the warm feeling that I have walked these streets many times before, and will do so again and again.

I also feel hungry, Big Time! As with only Jerry Mac's beer breakfast for sustenance since I awakened nearly eight hours ago, the need for nourishment has now notified me by special messenger. And special is precisely what pops into mind too. For eight months ago, when my initial plans for Eire were forming, one of the very first photos that emblazoned itself on the hard drive of my mind was the color picture of The Gourmet Parlour Bakery featuring its specialty, a three-by-three inch square of shortbread, topped by a quarter-inch layer of creamy milk chocolate. And though I do fear an angry outburst from the Professor, not to forget the gloomy glare of Father Matthew, the knowledge that this long dreamed-of treat is less than half a block away still spills a wide grin across my face while adding a pitter to the patter of my quickening feet. To poignantly paraphrase Shakespeare however: Alas, poor starving Hobman, pastries should be made of sterner stuff! For when I reach the holy spot of confectionery creation, my tongue tingling with desire, I am met by a storeroom whose abject vacancy is so glaring that its rays transform the empty image into the dumbfounded expression now clothing my face. A portrait so sad that fortunately it does not escape the eagle eye of a lovely lady passing by, who stops to render assistance. In her seventies, with snow-white hair accenting the blue of her eyes and matching suit, along with her white gloves and pearl necklace, she is the very embodiment of the Irish Godmother I had always envisioned. And when she immediately grasps the urgent complexities of my problem, and promptly solves it by advising that the beloved bakery has moved to Bridge Street, I instantly elevate her status to that of Grand Dame Fortuna meets the Irish Tooth Fairy.

"You see, no problem," I whisper after thankfully shaking her hand. "Not if you'll have a little patience, that is." For Bridge Street lies across the River Garavogue in north Sligo, not a great distance away, but also not slated for a visit until a couple of hours later. So, taking the edge off my hunger by lighting up my pipe, I then proceed up John Street to where it corners Temple, home to two historic cathedrals. Greeting me first is the Cathedral of the Immaculate Conception, a Romanesque styled stone structure of good size that dates back to 1874 and features sixty-nine stained glass windows. It is the smaller but older cathedral next door, however, that is of particular interest to me. For it is here, inside this Gothic building designed by the German architect Richard Castle in 1730, and bearing the bisexual title St. Mary the Virgin and John the Baptist, that William Butler Yeats' parents, Susan and John, were married in 1863. W.B.'s legend is what originally called my attention to Sligo. For though he was born in Dublin two years later, it was Sligo, his mother's birthplace, and where he spent so much of his childhood, that in his heart of hearts W.B. always called home. In fact, in his writings, Yeats exalted Sligo and the magnificence of its surrounding countryside, as *The Land of Heart's Desire*. Not only high tribute, but a perfect poetic image as well, I acknowledge from my vantage point on the sidewalk, smoke drifting from my pipe as I survey the brown-stoned setting where it all began, imagination soon focusing on the horse-drawn carriages delivering the wedding party. And when my mind's eye finally tires from straining to see the smiling faces of the homespun but radiant young bride and her dashing groom from big-city Dublin, a recent graduate of Trinity College, the eyes in my head follow suit, unlocking from the large wooden front door to make a final sweep of the two square towers flanking each side of the Cathedral's courtyard. A smile creeps out of the corners of my mouth when I notice that the grass is in need of mowing, my friend Joe from St. Patrick's flashing into view. "Well, when you've cushioned almost three centuries of life, and celebrated the beginning of W.B.'s sad-happy tale," escapes a thought, "what's a little haircut between us friends, huh?...So you take care, now. I gotta go walk the poet's town."

And walk, I do. North and south. East and west. Up hills, down curvy lanes, and across the flat spaces. For the better part of two hours, know it, feel it, touch it, are my watchwords, feet padding the pavement, eyes seeking and searching, while memory maps the sights, sounds, and smells of a small town whose simple charms, like a soft shawl, slip weightlessly about my shoulders, the wind whispering to spell *special* in lower case letters, the imprint on mind and heart nonetheless indelible.

At the top of Temple Street, I spy the Hawk's Well Theatre, housed in a modern styled building surrounded by trees. Named after one of Yeats' one-act plays, this year-round hub of theatrical activity carries on the long legacy of Sligo's great literary traditions, and tonight features a troupe of traditional Irish dancers from Cork City. A left turn a half block later heads me downhill on the Lungy, a steep and narrow street leading to the Sligo Presbyterian Church, which dates back to 1828. Then, following the aptly named Church Street I reach Harmony Hill, high ground that offers a spectacular view of the town below. I can make out Castle Street, half a mile distant, and wave "Hi!" before traipsing on eastward to High Street, which dates to medieval times, and which also holds the uniquely styled Dominican Church, commonly called the Friary. For though of modern design, and erected as recently as 1973, it sits on the grounds of a 1545 Renaissance Gothic edifice and incorporates the apse of the original church in its rear section. "Now, how's that for blending the old and the new into a happy hybrid?" I chuckle, heading back uphill to Teeling Street to view the post office and court house. Though its updated stone facade brings Sligo's legal center clear recognition as a symbol of sober authority, still, both buildings' small scale and unpretentious design are consistent with the City's central theme of simplicity, and after a quick hello and good-bye, I move on, trailed by the thought: Who would want to commit a crime, or breach a contract in such a nice place? Not long afterward, at the bottom of Teeling, where it intersects Abbey Street, I have my answer. For fewer than fifty yards to my right lie the ruins of Sligo Abbey, the City's only surviving medieval building. Built in 1252, the Abbey was once the proud burial ground for Sligo's kings and princes. But now, only the nave, choir, arched tower, and three-sided cloister survive, along with one of the few medieval altars in all of Ireland. "And if that isn't a crime, then maybe the Pope's Jewish after all," I charge, patting the ancient walls gently after entering inside.

"Oh, really?..." intervenes the Professor, suddenly reappearing after being AWOL for two days. "Would that be a misdemeanor or a felony?..."

"A felony, first class!" shoots back my reply. "And you can make all the fun you want, but old buildings like these are truly treasures, and should never be allowed to decay."

"Why?" he presses. They're just a bunch of old stones."

"Oh, no they're not. They're roots, a foundation. They're part of yesteryear, where we come from."

"Well, that may be, my friend," he concedes, his tone that of a spider luring the fly into his web. "But do you r-e-a-l-l-y know why you love them so much?"

"Yeah, I...think I do," trickles my answer slowly. "I've been wrestling with why? for years, and seeing Sligo has helped me finally pin it down. It's because they represent a more simple time, a slower, more certain way of life. And what's wrong with that?…"

"Nothing," he smiles. "Nothing at all. The computer-speed pace of change today – faster, faster, faster – is very dislocating, so I don't blame you one bit for wanting to slow down and find something to hold onto, something you can call home. Just as long as you realize, of course, that nothing's perfect."

"Perfect?…You want perfect, then die and go to heaven," I chuckle back, patting the revered walls again before moving on up the street, the realization that had traveled years to tumble out still sinking in.

Five minutes later, having strolled the Mall to the Kennedy Parade, then followed its two-block-long walkway alongside the River Gara-vogue, I cross over the smooth flowing waters onto Bridge Street. Once arrived, I inquire as to the exact whereabouts of The Gourmet Parlour from two amiable gentlemen in their mid-thirties, who graciously inter-rupt their conversation to point a half block straight ahead, then add through warm smiles: "The best! Enjoy!" And after hustling on up the street, indeed I do! As once again, the long-ago studied photo jumps off the page and into life, this time dragging along my taste buds for the treat of treats! Delicious?…Hell's bells, when applied to a Chocolate Bar, *understatement* implodes on its own axis. I mean, words simply fail. Yeats himself would be at a loss. In fact, as the soft and crumbly shortbread mixes with the creamy milk chocolate, and the surprise addition of a sumptuous layer of caramel, *culinary genius* is the feeble thought wafting off one's overwhelmed tongue. And the only possible way to even come close to accurately articulating the enveloping sensation is to say that it finishes second only to sex! I mean –

"Oh, for God's sake," groans the Professor. "Have you no shame! I mean, I'm shocked. And as for Father Matthew, well, he's having a full-fledged conniption fit!"

"Why?…" chirps my cheerful defense. "I only bought two. And Christ, if that isn't restraint, then it doesn't exist."

"You call beer for breakfast, followed by enough sugar to found a plantation, restraint?…"

"Uh-huh. The problem is, you're not looking at the situation from the proper perspective. Now, first of all, God's two greatest inventions are sex and sugar, in either order depending upon the quality. You following me?…"

"Yeah…kinda."

"Okay. Now God created these two ecstasies to show us how much He-She loves us, by letting us come as close as possible to the Lord's Loving Light while still living on Earth. And all God asks in return is that we show our love by appreciating these gifts. Most unfortunately, circumstances prevent me from demonstrating the depth of my affection for sex, so the least I can do is show the proper amount of enthusiasm for the greatest pastry in history. See?…" I end, taking another bite and smiling triumphantly.

"What I see, dear boy, is an utter incorrigible. Please know that I'll be praying for you, while you escort us to Yeats' house. That is, if you can walk that far in your hallucinogenic state."

No problem. As fortified with a half million calories or so, I bid a grateful farewell to the green-and-white trimmed Temple of Miracles, then amble happily north on Bridge Street. A left on Stephen Street a half block later, and both my sugar-sweet mood and I arrive at the Sligo County Museum and Art Gallery. Though equally fueled by a growing excitement to see W.B.'s family home, now only half a block away, with a nod to the resuscitated Father Matthew, I restrain my urge to bypass the Museum in favor of satisfying my primary desire earlier. For which I am rewarded with a viewing of Yeats' 1923 Nobel Prize, as well as the surprise of several magnificently lifelike watercolors of Sligo's surrounding landscape by brother Jack. In fact, my newfound appreciation for his mastery of making nature live and breathe on canvas walks alongside me the entire distance to O'Connell Street, which this time honors W.B., instead of the Great Liberator, with a bronze bust. Then, halfway across the Douglas Hyde Bridge, named for Ireland's first President, I catch my first glimpse of the red-brick, Victorian-styled house that was home to the Yeats clan. Charming, with its slanted roof lines and gabled windows, its three-storied size surprises me. Somehow, I had expected something smaller. But instead, I find a house whose frame is large like its master's was. For W.B. was a big man, over six feet tall with a massive physique, memory reminds as I enter inside and begin shuffling slowly through the living room. Always well dressed after success arrived in his early thirties, the picture of him that hurries into mind shows masses of gray-black hair slanting over his forehead, brown eyes, and a soft, full mouth which hints of a readiness to cry. Complex is the dominant adjective to describe him and his seventy-four-year journey through life, bounds my next brainwave, a flashback to his parents' Cathedral wedding then propelling memory's wheel into full spin mode.

Did the bride Susan, who had been raised in highly comfortable circumstances, have even an inkling that there would be money problems? That separated from her close-knit family in far-away, big-city Dublin, there would be struggle because dazzling husband John desired to paint rather than practice law? And that in addition, she would shoulder almost all the responsibility for the care of W.B. and two sisters, Lolly and Lily? Onto center stage strut the testy trio of problem posers, where they promptly curtsy, then cock an ear. And the answer?…Most probably not, according to Yeats' biographers. But with equal certainty, it does explain why there were frequent and increasingly longer family retreats to Sligo, where as her children's childhood years slipped by in her parents' home, Susan slowly but surely began her retreat into a dreamworld of her own choosing. In the meantime young W.B. devoured books he thought would please Mom and roamed the countryside he loved upon first meeting, and whose great natural beauty would inspire many of his most beloved poems. When his father suddenly removed the family to London for two years during W.B.'s ninth year, his formal education was begun at the Godolphin School. Uncharacteristically for the intellectually oriented youth, Yeats didn't particularly like it, and failed noticeably to distinguish himself, as was also the case at the high school in Dublin upon the family's return. And as a result, W.B. did not attend college, I recall with renewed curiosity while strolling from the living room into the smaller and less formally furnished parlor. Instead, at the direction of Dad, W.B. studied painting at the Metropolitan School of Art, where he met AE, the mystic poet who became a lifelong friend. And it is at this uncertain time, aged twenty, that his first poems were published in the *Dublin University Review*.

Two years later, the habitually restless Papa John again removed the family to London, this time igniting a momentous period of twenty years during which W.B. would shuttle continuously between London and Dublin, working feverishly in both cities, and calling each home. For it is during this peripatetic period, confusing as it was with its mixture of work, fragile love affairs, and still more work created from ever-escalating effort, that Yeats' literary output flowered, and both great recognition and fame followed. In fact, by his late forties, his work had been compiled into eight volumes, and his poems were studied in schools and learned by heart. And it is precisely during this period that *complexity* not only came to rule W.B.'s heart and mind with respect to his writing, but also influenced his personal life in equal degree. Complex?...I consider, seating myself on a small chair near a window on the drawing room's west wall. Jesus, that's like understatement being an understatement! For between his early twenties and the remaining fifty years of his life's tortuous path, Yeats was both sustained and tormented by his love life and the occult.

To begin with, whispers the whirling wheel, when W.B. was only twenty-three, the legendary beauty and passionate advocate for Irish freedom, Maud Gonne, visited the Yeats home in London. Almost instantly, he fell in love with her, and the strange twists and turns of their relationship are best summed up by W.B. himself, when he wrote, "From this time the troubling of my life began." For Maud traveled in higher social and political circles, and was consistently linked to other men, leaving the already insecure W.B. to further wrestle with quandaries about his sexuality. Always drawn to women, he remained a virgin until the age of thirty, when he had an adulterous liaison with Olivia Shakespeare, the beautiful, unhappily married author of six novels. However, instead of this romance liberating him, W.B. responded by not making love to another woman for seven long years. And even though in his forties, he gradually overcame his reticence and was able to flirt, date, and have an occasional affair, Yeats was never able to fully vitiate his profound fear of the sexual connection. Believing, as he wrote, that "his reverence for Maud had made him puritanical and slow to develop," his biographers consider this the reverse of the truth: "that his fear of sex had locked him into the safe pursuit of an unattainable woman."

Uh-huh. And that explains why old W.B. didn't marry until age fifty-one, I muse, shifting my weight inside the chair, Yeats' heavy involvement with the occult then catching the corner of my mind's eye. Oh yeah, floats my next thought, let's not forget to add this spicy tidbit to the stew. For belief in spirits ran strong throughout the Yeats family, and W.B. carried this search to new heights, beginning with his initiation into the Hermetic Order of the Golden Dawn in his twenties. A middle-class, unisex, secret society of mystics devoted to the practice of medieval and Renaissance rituals of magic, the Golden Dawn adopted as its basic text the Hebrew mystical interpretation of the Old Testament known as the Kabbalah. Moreover, because its teachings inspire an open mind, commitment to the Golden Dawn did not bar other roads to the supernatural, leaving Yeats free to explore direct communication with spirits, numerology, and astrology over a thirty-year period. In fact, his heavy involvement with the latter two schools of paranormal activity strongly influenced W.B.'s decision to finally marry, twisting the tale in a new yet old direction, the wheel continuing to weave its tangled web.

For now aged fifty-one, and widely accomplished, but with no home, no family, and tired of the bachelor's life, when his introduction to Miss Bertha George Hyde-Lee by mutual friends coincides with his astrological chart's advice that October 1917 is an auspicious time, after a short but intense courtship W.B. proposes and is accepted. Attractive, with piercing, intelligent eyes, curly, reddish-brown hair, and markedly high color, Georgie, as she was called, was at twenty-five less than half Yeats' age. The daughter of a retired British Army officer who inherited modest wealth from an uncle, Georgie was well educated, widely traveled, and at ease in both French and Italian. And, most importantly, she enjoyed an intense spiritual life of her own, being psychic herself, and a member of the Golden Dawn. To be sure, this shared commitment to the supernatural soon bonded the bride and groom into a close-knit and arduous partnership in *automatic writing*, whereby with Georgie as the medium, W.B. sought knowledge from the spirit world, the answers flowing through Georgie's pen as she sat in trance.

This *Script*, as Yeats called it, covers 3,600 pages over some 450 sittings, and from it he created his greatest poetry. As convinced that *images* come from a universal storehouse called the Anna Mundi, the world soul, W.B. believed that the chance to draw on this pool of accumulated imagination and wisdom offered a way out of the solitariness of the self, of crucial importance, since in his view reality is hidden and image is all that we see. Then, building upon this arcane base, W.B. proceeded to create through a tortuous process of composition. Often having written his first thoughts out in prose, he put almost every poem through innumerable revisions, constantly trying different words, tenses, and rhyme schemes in an obsessive effort to capture not only cosmic truth, but to also achieve a desperately desired but equally elusive sense of inner peace. Try. And try. And try again, consoles the whispering wheel as it slows to a close. As for all his remaining life, W.B. would continue the incessant struggle to locate himself between his mother's withdrawn dreaminess and his father's assertive rationality.

"It must have been totally exhausting," I murmur after leaving the house and walking a few yards away to lean on a railing and look out over the river. Tired myself, from the fullness of the day's activities, as well as the added weight from W.B.'s melancholy life-journey, I inhale deeply then release a slow sigh in an effort to free myself from the haunting similarities we share, the fruitless, guilt-fueled effort to please parents, problems with the ladies, and the pursuit of the paranormal. Success arrives, when the high points of W.B.'s life pour into mind, the Nobel Prize, his son and daughter, his role in the attainment of Irish Independence. And after flowing forth through my smile to merge with the Garavogue as it tumbles over the rocks below the bridge, the wheel's bittersweet web is finally replaced by the postcard scene running east along both banks, the various shades of red, yellow, and white clothing the buildings behind the walkways, winking their warmth back at me. A real-life watercolor, brother Jack would stamp his seal of approval on for sure, I muse, falling under its restful spell for several minutes, my trusty Peterson for company.

"You know what?" I quip when I finally return from my drowsy daydream. "It's time for dinner, and some music. How's that sound?…" You mean *real* food? teases my response. Hell, that could damage your reputation with the Sugar Gods. But say, isn't that the Half Moon Pub that Len from Hotel Central mentioned? follows a query when my eyes suddenly discover the quaint-looking stone structure across the street, my mind racing back to his hastily tossed tip as I climbed into my Dublin cab some twelve hours ago. Seems like another lifetime, but yeah it is, sounds the answer as I stroll toward the front door, the rich and rewarding events of the day making a cameo appearance as I enter inside.

As if Lady Luck had not already met her quota, when I reach the brass rail of the wooden bar, she serves up her second serious surprise, this time in the form of lovely Louise, the hostess at the Yeats Home Memorial, with whom I had enjoyed a brief conversation. Seated with friends at a nearby table, after calling out to me, she invites me to join them, introducing Molly and her boyfriend Ian, and ordering me a Guinness before

I'm fully seated in my chair. Her warmth and sparkling blue eyes are irresistible, and once again I have to remind myself that my daughter is older. There's no crime in talking however, Mr. Public Defender counsels, nor is it even a misdemeanor to dance. And so, over the next couple of hours, I enjoy both in abundance, with a tasty lobster to boot.

Louise is actually English. She moved from Manchester just over a year ago with her Mom and Dad, who operate a beauty salon and practice architecture. Their attraction: the slower pace and more simple life, and especially the clean air and the lakes and beaches. "Sligo has it all," she tells me as we share a slow one on the dance floor. On the other hand, Ian, a native, thirty-three-year-old doctor, had studied in Dublin, but decided to return to Sligo because he likes "knowing everyone" and having time to pursue his two passions, fishing and Molly. "Oh, reverse it, of course," he chuckles when I poke fun at the order of his interests, Molly, who manages a dress shop, then chiming in with, "Aye, you hear the man, do ya?" the love between them shining shyly in both sets of eyes. They're all surprised by how much I know about Yeats, and Ireland in general, but generously add to my storehouse nonetheless as the minutes tick through music, art, and politics, hairstyles, soccer, and local tales to reach the hour that warns it's getting late. Time to part, but not however before a polite fight over the check, during which they acquiesce and I'm allowed the honor of buying dinner. And even then, only after a round of hugs, and for me, a kiss on the cheek from each colleen, do we finally say so long.

Back outside on O'Connell Street, my watch says it's ten-fifteen as I start for home. The wind has picked up, and it's chilly, but as I tread along the now familiar streets, the comfy-cozy layout of Sligo keeps me warm. When I reach Castle Street and look left to where it becomes Abbey, then right to where it switches to Grattan and John, I christen it the Street of Four Names, chuckling at the thought that it bests the Trinity by one. What a truly nice town! follows the next brainwave. Not too big, not too small. Easy to get around. Why you can walk to most places, or bike, and there's plenty of shopping too – all the basics you need, and most of the extras you could want. But best of all, life's not too complicated here, sings the silent sentence, then stops when its tail end asks for further consideration.

All right, listen…I didn't say UNcomplicated, the key word here is *less*, argues analysis after a moment's hesitation. Hell, I know life's full of complexities, and that living in a small town isn't a free pass from reality! rushes reason as I reach Pearse Road and begin the two-mile climb to the hotel. And I also know that human nature didn't suddenly detour in the direction of heaven's angels, just because the population's under twenty thousand. No. No way…. But still and all, counters collective evidence, the life they've got here is more simple, more slow, and that adds up to a whole lot less stress and more time for family and friends and plain old-fashioned fun. Christ, you wanna talk about life's daily hassles, like commuter parking lots on the freeway, or wall-to-wall people rushing around like bugs in a bowl? Doesn't exist in Sligo. Oh, they've got traffic, sure, but no jams. And there's a little hustle and bustle down on Castle Street, all right, but that only creates an air of casual excitement, not a New York City nervous breakdown. No…here there's a feeling of peace, of contentment. It's a soft, quiet feeling, but you can hear it. And you can see it too, in people's smiles, in their eyes, and even between the lines in their faces, I muse, grinning back at the crowd jumping out of the shadows for a repeat encounter, chuckling when I again listen to their laughter, nodding my appreciation for their friendliness. Oh, sure, they've got their dreams and their disappointments, just like everyone else, soothes the silent soliloquy. Only their expectation level is more reasonable, 'cause there's time to think, and plan, to reexamine and ask: What do I *really* want?…And, oh yeah, I know, some critics would argue that small-town life is so simple, it's boring, and people are trapped inside its humdrum walls. But the truth I see is that folks in Sligo *choose* a less complicated life. They're not inmates in a Prison of No Choice. Instead, they elect to pay attention to basic values, root their priorities accordingly, and live close to nature. Why, Hell's bells, Yeats lived here, and loved it, and he turned complex into both a science and an art form! Old W.B. climbed the worldly ladder of success, all right. Big Time! But when ye old push came to shove, Sligo was his oasis of peace, his Paradise of the Ground Floor, and he couldn't get back here often enough! ends the flash flood from a wellspring deep inside me, Louise's "Sligo has it all," echoing to further lift the cloud of doubt, even as those overhead thicken with rain.

Holding off until I reach the hotel's front steps, by the time I scurry inside, a good old-fashioned downpour is under way. Thanking the Water

Gods for their forbearance, I then note how warm and welcoming the Sligo Park lobby's traditional woods and log fireplace are, in comfortable contrast to the more modern facade with its large glass windows and skylighted entryway. A nice blend, just like Sligo itself, I hum silently to myself as I stroll down the hallway to Room 210. It also proves quite nice. Generously sized, it follows the general ambience to the proverbial T, with the bed and nightstands of modern design, and the padded headboard and quilted bedspread warmly clothed in traditional colors of red and green. Two full windows center the eastern wall, and with the aid of some hazy light from the hotel's first floor, I can make out the dim outlines of a lovely garden through the rain which has now tapered to a light drizzle.

Intending to review tomorrow's plans, then cozy in bed to share a chapter with Nuala, I find myself too relaxed, and too tired. Lord, what a wonderful day! shuffles a thought slowly as I slip between the sheets, the people and places parading forth to say good-night. Mary back home in Dublin. Alice with her family in Maynooth. And Jerry Mac in his farmhouse, all tucked in too. Or is that spunky friend of mine still out with his cronies, hoisting one for the road at his favorite pub? teases a thought. "Well, be careful walking home, buddy," I whisper into the darkness, nestling further inside my pillow. "And thank you too, Tommy, my man," trickle my weary words as I fall into sleep, the lovely lady on Castle Street, the helpful fellows near the bridge, and Louise, Molly, and Ian all smiling Welcome!

X

MAGICAL DAY

SATURDAY BEGINS IN THE SPELLBINDING LAND OF SLEEP. TWO EXTRA hours' worth, nourished by stardust sprinkling sweet dreams of Sligo: a quaint cottage, a curvy colleen to warm my heart and bed, fervent friends to share the day with, and yesterday's question, Could you live here? answered with the smiling echo of *I do...I do...I do....* A beneficent bonus, brought to me by the luxurious ten-thirty starting time for the tour of Sligo's surrounding countryside, after a long hot shower and a full Irish breakfast of cereal, fruit, and sunnyside-up eggs with bangers, I'm feeling seriously sunny myself, despite the light rain falling outside. "Go away," I chirp cheerfully from my comfy chair next to a lobby window, trading the *Irish Times* for Matt's latest baseball fax. And when it does, shortly thereafter, my mood climbs the Scale of Satisfaction all the way to a perfect ten.

Stepping outside to enjoy a smoke, a smile curling out of the corners of my mouth, I watch the sun win a game of hide-and-seek with the flock of clouds overhead, patches of blue emerging in the widening gaps. A grateful grin, it enlarges to full when Sligo Tours' Mini Bus pulls into the parking lot five minutes early, and Ray, our guide and driver, beams me aboard with a high-spirited, "Morn'n! Glad to have ya!" In his early thirties, and of medium size, with sandy-colored hair, a fair complexion, and bright blue eyes that twinkle with the active sense of humor flowing from his gentle nature, Ray will soon prove to be the day's second bonus, this one a gift from the Travel Gods and spelled with capital letters. As soon after the bus turns right out of the parking lot and heads east, my eight companions and I find ourselves listening to a leader who is part historian, part geographer, and part sociologist-psychologist, all bubbling forth from a fountain of storytelling spiced with humor.

Almost immediately, in less than a mile, Sligo is left behind and we enter into a landscape of green fields gently rolling toward the mountains on both sides of our little bus. And with equal speed, Ray is teaching that the hills to our left, where Ben Bulben lies out of sight, are the Dartry Mountains, while those to the east are the Ox range, the oldest mountains in all of Europe. Calling our attention to Mount Knocknarea, their tallest member, and specifically to a small ridge rising above the summit, he then informs us that this cairn is believed to be the burial tomb of Connaught's legendary Queen Maeve. And having been instantly transported back two thousand years in time, we are then treated to a colorful account of one of Ireland's most famous mythological stories, the Cooley Cattle Raid. It seems that Queen Maeve ordered a raid on Ulster in order to capture a prized brown bull, and was initially successful despite the heroic defensive efforts of Cuchulainn, Ireland's most renowned warrior of ancient times. After licking their wounds however, Ulster warriors, joined by secret reserves and now led by King Conchobar, came to the rescue and drove the invaders from the north, leading Queen Maeve to plot revenge against Cuchulainn, causing his death several years later by supernatural means. It also appears that the notorious Maeve was a bit eccentric, dressing only in a loin cloth, and covering her body with black paint to match her waist-length black hair. "A sexy sight, she must have been, this grudge-holding lass," Ray sums up, several minutes full of lush landscape having rolled by. "It earned her the title, the Black Queen of Ireland. But to those really in the know," he chuckles, "the Black Bitch says it all!"

Geography. History. Mythology. And all wrapped neatly inside a blanket of green countryside that stretches as far as the eye can see. Then, just as it appears that the valley holds a monopoly on magnificent scenery, the bus stops at the top of Cairns Hill, and so does my heart at the breathtaking view of Lough Gill, the lake that so captivated Yeats. No problem understanding why, bursts a brainwave as I leave the bus for a closer view. For seven miles long by two miles wide, and surrounded by gently sloping hills that are heavily forested, the *Lake of Brightness* easily lives up to its Gaelic name. As everywhere the eyes roam, pinpoints of sunshine spring off its blue-bright surface to startle me with their silvery song: Stop! I'm special!…Look at me! As if one possibly could not, murmurs my next thought, my heart now slowing to a peaceful rhythm in sync with nature's pulse, my eyes finally able to locate the smallest of the lake's islands as W.B.'s fabled words pour into ear:

> *I will arise and go now, and go to Innisfree,*
> *And a small cabin build there, of clay and wattles made:*
> *Nine bean rows will I have there, a hive for the honey bee,*
> *And live alone in the bee-loud glade.*
>
> *And I shall have some peace there, for peace comes dropping slow,*
> *Dropping from the veils of morning to where the cricket sings;*
> *There midnight's all a glimmer, and noon a purple glow,*
> *And evening full of the linnet's wings.*
>
> *I will arise and go now, for always night and day*
> *I hear the lake water lapping with low sounds by the shore;*
> *While I stand on the roadway, or on the pavements grey,*
> *I hear it in the deep heart's core.*

"Amen," whispers my tongue when the poem has passed and it's time to reboard the bus, Ray's assurance that we will revisit later that afternoon from the northern shore the only consolation for having to leave a picture that only God could paint. But, as if that treat were not enough, and synchronicity needs to be honored in the meantime, inside seven minutes the bus stops again, this time at Tobernault. Meaning a secret place of worship, and situated in a glen just off the narrow roadway, this pristine spot is revered for its Holy Well, a natural spring made famous by St. Patrick, who baptized pagans into Christianity with its waters sixteen hundred years ago. Stone steps lead down to the surface in an alcove three or four feet below ground level, while overhead, similar pathways wind upward to several stations carved out of the hillside's dense foliage, with a sculpted statue of Jesus on the Cross at the summit, and twin altars for prayer below, all combining into a Cathedral of Sky and Water, with the tallest trees serving as guardian angels. Ireland is unique, I recall, for being the only land into which Christianity was introduced without bloodshed, courtesy of the sincerely simple yet deeply devout and highly persuasive ways of St. Patrick. And as I stand in his footsteps a second time, I am struck fully by the firm feeling that he would approve of his Outdoor Cathedral even more than his elegant namesake in Dublin, such is the holiness, the closeness to God one feels in absorbing the ideal beauty of nature. In fact, as we prepare to reboard the bus, Olive and Nile, two fellow pilgrims from Belfast, are expressing the identical sentiment, making the vote unanimous that this special spot is not only the perfect place to pray, but is in itself a sublime prayer for peace.

Back on board five minutes later, Ray chats us up with the fact that the narrow pathway we're following toward Lissadell House is aptly named Frog Road, because "amorous frogs in hot pursuit of immortality" leave the forest to cross it on their way to spawn near Lough Gill. Then, slipping on his archaeologist's hat, he goes global in scope with his fascinating recital about how the large mounds we see popping up every so often in the flat fields to the east are the Carrowmore Cairns, burial tombs built in 5500 B.C., or 3500 years before "those copycats at Stonehenge." And to round out the fruitful feast on wheels, he then trades archaeology for the arts, the sound system soon filling the air with the educated tones of professors reading Yeats' poetry, interspersed with melancholy tunes from traditional Irish music, as our tiny bus rolls along through a half hour of forested miles and limestone ridges to reach the sandy shores of Sligo Bay and the approach to Lissadell House.

I say, approach, because one doesn't just drive up and park alongside. No, indeed. Instead, the winding gravel driveway leading from the roadway passes through a wondrously wooded and planted Wildlife Preserve which is part of the twenty-two-acre estate, and the journey from the street to the front door takes almost four minutes. Then, finally, upon arriving, one is further impressed by a massive gray stone home constructed in the Grecian Revival style that could easily be mistaken for a palace. Originally built around 1830 to house the politically prominent Gore-Booth family from England, from 1900 on, Lissadell House was also home to Yeats, who enjoyed a long and close friendship with two descendant sisters, Eva and Constance, and over the years frequently visited for extended stays. In fact, the "great windows opening to the south" off the drawing room appear in several of W.B.'s poems. And as I stare out upon their fantabulous view of both Sligo Bay and Ben Bulben, it's sure easy to understand why, I muse, my eyes filling to overflow.

A minute or two later, in the adjacent two-story art gallery lined by Doric columns, two photos of the sisters atop the grand piano catch my eye. Eva, a distinguished poet in her own right, looks sweet but serious inside her oval frame in black and white, her dark eyes softened by the ivory cameo resting at her throat. A foot away however, and in color, the mischief that characterized Constance seems to twinkle from the blue orbs over the high cheekbones and finely formed mouth. I can feel your fire, forms a thought, memory recalling that this Englishwoman was such a passionate activist for Irish Independence that she took part in the Easter Rising, and was spared the firing squad solely due to her sex and the Victorian mores which excused her feminine involvement. Actually preferring to join her less fortunate compatriots, this strikingly beautiful firebrand subsequently became the first woman ever elected to the British Parliament, only to choose instead to take a seat in the first free Irish Parliament, and thereafter serve as the first Minister for Labor in the newly formed Irish Free State. Wow! How about that? A real lady, with solid brass balls to boot! I enthuse, smiling as I plant a kiss with the tip of my finger, then inch toward the front door. And see?...You don't have to be Irish, to be Irish!...

The twenty-minute drive from Lissadell House to Drumcliffe church-yard once again features a landscape that gives new definition to the color green, with panoramic views of Sligo Bay and Ben Bulben added for special effect, the famous mountain's loaf-like profile rising abruptly out of the plain to form an eerie silhouette against the cloud-patched sky as we draw closer and closer. When we arrive, it's lunchtime, and my companions scurry toward the Visitors Center where snacks are available. The Hobman, however, has no appetite. Not for food, anyway. As already piqued by Lissadell House, and its role in Yeats' life, and now standing only fifty yards from his gravesite in the shadow of his beloved flat-topped mount, the anticipation of *meeting* him at long last moves me straight ahead to St. Columba's Church, a small, white-speckled, gray stone structure, fronted by a much taller square bell tower topped by Gothic spirals at each corner. To the left of the entryway is a small cemetery, and to its front, stands a simple stone slab marking the final resting place of Ireland's greatest bard.

The inscription, "Cast a cold eye/On life, on death/ Horseman, pass by," immediately draws my attention. Penned by Yeats himself, his only other request was that he lie at the foot of Ben Bulben, which my eyes in turn quickly scan through the trees to the right before returning to center stage. For almost a minute, I simply stand and stare across the ten-foot gravel rectangle lying between me and the marker, noting the bundle of dead flowers that some visitor had laid at its base. Then, as a shy smile plays in the corners of my mouth, my heart finally speaks. "Hi, there, W.B.," I whisper slowly, unsurely. "I'm Hobman, and I've come a long long way to meet you. I'm not really sure why…. But somehow, between your poetry and your plays, your politics and the melancholy nature of your life, you lie near the heart of Ireland, and somehow that heart calls out to me. It's funny," the words stumble out, trying to step through time. "'Cause we're not really cut from the same cloth at all, what with me being born a year after you died, you being tall and a Christian, me, small and Jewish, and you a Nobel Prize winner, while I've struggled to publish just twenty-two poems. In fact, some of your poems, I can't even understand, while you'd probably think I'm downright nuts for writing that Sex and Sugar are God's two greatest inventions….But still, strange as it is, we also have a lot in common," I tell him, my mind's eye searching his finely formed image for some sign of awareness, and finding only that he appears guarded.

"All right…that's okay," seeps my next thought as I shift my weight. "'Cause I know, I understand the problem with your parents. Hell, I haven't ever been able to please mine either. Still can't," I add through a pinched smile. "'Cause it's hard, isn't it, when you're born different, and your first remembered thought is of not fitting in? Of how excruciatingly difficult it is, when the world appears so huge, and you feel so small trying to find your spot?…Ohhh, yeah, W.B., then add Mom and Dad's expectations, and a potful of pressure fueled by guilt, and you've got Neurosis City faster than you can say Sligo! Uh-huh, that's right. It's true. And let me tell ya, that shaky old childhood can carry over to problems with the ladies too. I mean, that acute vulnerability, that serious sense of self-doubt we share, sure can make one shy and slow to develop, right?… Hey, listen, I understand about Maud too, you were just too young and inexperienced to weave between the lines of social strata. Hell, in college, I lost my first love the exact same way, and later, Angel Patty to cancer to boot. So I know how much the pain hurts, and how the loss never leaves, and how they can drive you to seek and search for something more than this plane of reality provides. Ohhh, yeah, I've experimented with the paranormal, all right. Not as *big time* as you got involved with, but I've tried to reach Patty every which way, and I've even studied the Kabbalah. Hell, I'm Jewish for Christ's sake, so that was an easy step," I chuckle, humor bubbling up to lighten sorrow's load. "And you wanna know what I learned?…Well, for openers, I think this plane of reality we call Earth is a school, and we come here to learn one major lesson: to know and love self, so that we can better know and love God. Not really a problem, till ego, other people, and worldly pursuits get in your way, trying to define you. So it usually takes several lifetimes to get it right, and you don't graduate until you do. Now how's that square up with ya?…"

No answer, of course. But the chill wind blowing from Ben Bulben stops, and the sun suddenly feels warmer. "Okay," I nod to him. "I'll take that for a yes. And listen, Mr. Poetman, before I go, I want to say thanks for all you added to Ireland. It's really and truly a special place, and so is your Sligo. From what I can see, they're like a poem, they follow the heart's truth. Maybe it wasn't always that way, since Eire had to win its freedom first, had to overcome the pain of loss. Not forget it, mind you, 'cause you can't. But overcome it, and learn to live and laugh in spite of the hurt. To be itself: content, and cautiously optimistic, with hopes and dreams. You said, 'I have spread my dreams under your feet… Tread softly.' Well, W.B., Ireland does. It truly does. And maybe…just maybe…that's why I had to meet you…not only to see this truth, but to actually *feel* it!" explodes the gathering nucleus of newborn knowledge, the fallout pouring amazement across my face, my head nodding slowly in support. "'Cause you're exactly like your Ireland. You struggled and struggled, and when you were tired and bloody and beat up, you struggled some more. And in the end, you triumphed, you won the prize, while Ireland *is* a prize! As patiently, over the centuries, and through the pain of toil and torment, Eire learned to know itself and *accept* that self – the good and the bad, the strengths and the weaknesses, the perfections and the flaws, the whole ball of wax. And that simple, but sacred approval is as close as we come to truth, and love, and *home* on this very confused planet. So how about that?…" I ask, stunned by the entirely unexpected realization. "Yeahhh…like magic!" answers awe, the totality of the sudden awareness now sinking in to spin round and round inside my brain. "And that's why even I, a stranger, all alone in a foreign land, feel at home," sparks the afterthought, the spontaneous burst of energy then finally sputtering into silence.

One second. Two, three, four. In the restful quiet, a minute forms before my tongue can find itself again. "All right, W.B.," soothes my murmur, "I'll let you go back to sleep now. You take care…And be good to Georgie, ya hear? 'Cause Lord knows how well she supported you, and you sure weren't easy on her. Oh, and one more thing," I add, smiling. "If you happen to run into an angel named Patty, give her a hug for me, okay?…And while you're at it, if you happen to find yourself with a little spare time on your hands some day, and want to send a great poem my way, well, I'd sure as hell take real good care of it," I end, nodding my further assurance as I gently pat the headstone, then slowly drift away.

On the train to Sligo, just before he exited, my friend Tommy had asked me to bring greetings to his Aunt when I visited Drumcliffe. And finding her easily, just three rows into the cemetery, I honor my promise with a sweetly toned, "Hi, Aunt Mary. Tommy sends love," before ambling over to a short stone wall and leaning on it for a long look at the green grasses bearding Ben Bulben's face, while further celebrating the afternoon's revelation with an apple, and an even sweeter smoke. Then, trailing slowly back through the churchyard to the bus, as it pulls away, my misting eyes say so long to this small slice of Ireland that has become a part of me forever.

Having already been treated to a morning meal of lush landscape straight from heaven, and further satisfied by the telltale truth uncovered inside the pristine setting of Drumcliffe, I am totally unprepared for any-thing more. But more there is, and so much so, that Madam Mae West's whimsical words, "too much of a good thing is simply wonderful," take on new meaning. As with Enya and Mary Black crooning Irish ballads over the sound system, for a half-hour our tiny bus winds and weaves eastward along narrow roads and through farmhouse-dotted valleys that are green, to purple-green, to avocado-green, with a hundred varying shades in between. And when it seems as if the eyes can hold no more, we arrive at Glencar Lake, lying like a fine plate of silvery china in a valley hollow, with Ben Bulben serving as sentinel in the far distance, and for-ests of trees hugging the surrounding hills. The Land of Heart's Desire, indeed! shouts my mind, my tongue frozen by utter awe. For the glory is everywhere, it's around us, above us, and at every turn of the eye!

There's even a waterfall, gamboling gracefully from between the flanking evergreens to tumble over several beds of rock before settling into the calm-sure hands of the lake. And craning my neck to watch it tumble, twist, and turn one last time when our trusty guide places the bus back in motion and steers slowly and steadily westward, I simply sit and stare in silent wonderment. Not for long, however, as when we wind past Cope's Mountain, Ray the Raconteur interrupts the scenic concert with an anecdote about why the locals nicknamed it Protestant's Leap. It seems that in the 1800s, five British Redcoats on horseback were arduously pursuing several Irishmen in order to mete out some heavy punishment for having committed the heinous crime of staying out too late in their own country, a vicious violation of the curfew. Now, it seems also, that in their hot pursuit of these arch criminals, the Brits zigged when they should have zagged, and therefore plunged off the steep cliffs to a meeting with their Maker well in advance of what their years dictated. Related by Ray in such a lighthearted tone that the tale's sad and distant reality is like a small wave on the green sea of scenery spread out before us, our response is to chuckle as if it were an innocent fairy tale. Which is precisely the proper term to describe the locale that then floats into view just seconds later when we arrive at Parke's Castle.

A fine example of a seventeenth-century fortified manor house, located on Lough Gill's southern shore, with the customary hills of Paradise-green forest running in all directions as far as the eye can see, *picturesque* serves only to emphasize the boundaries of understatement. For while *perfect* comes closest to describing the great good fortune we are experiencing, even that effort fails to capture the full essence of the beauty parading before us. One simply says, There is a God!, and after trying futilely to inhale it all, and hold it, adjourns for tea and sweets at the Castle's snack bar. Olive and Nile join me, along with two Londoners, Alice and Jack. And seated around a table on the patio, munching bites of cookie and cake between mouthfuls of conversation about each other, and how lucky we are to share such splendor, it is an hour we subconsciously pray will last forever.

It doesn't, of course. But our wistfulness upon leaving is soon relieved by the miraculous view we receive upon reaching Rosse's Point on the sandy shores of Sligo Bay, just four miles away. With the sun starting to set, and huge, white, cotton-candy clouds blanketing the western horizon, we stand and gaze north to the Blue Stack Mountains some thirty-six miles away, then south across the bay to Strandhill, lying at the foot of our old friend Knocknarea. Accented by the lonely lighthouse on tiny Oyster Island, it is a picture of total tranquility. And as if to further emphasize the scene's Serenade of the Serene, an innocent question about the Celts from Olive allows Ray to add an exclamation point to the perfect peace flowing from our day. "Well, you're right. Absolutely," Ray replies. "It took about three hundred years, mind you. But once the Celts had fully merged with the earlier inhabitants, about 250 B.C., the next thousand years was an era of Basic Peace here in Ireland. Oh, there were some squabbles every once in a while between the tribes," he shrugs with a smile. "But you're right, for a thousand years, till the Vikings arrived, war was on holiday. People farmed, and lived their lives, and somehow, just got along with one another..."

Makes perfect sense to me, I muse on the ride back to the hotel. Hell, who'd want to make trouble in such a beautiful place, concludes contentment, oblivious to the harsh realities of the modern world. I'm last to be dropped off, so Ray and I enjoy a chat for a minute or two before he has to hurry home. With his wife and children down with the flu, he'll pick up Chinese food on the way. And when I offer to buy as a small token of my appreciation for the treasure this day has gifted, accentuated as it was by his kind hospitality and good humor, he graciously accepts.

"I'll never forget Sligo, or you," I tell him as we shake hands.

"I know, it's in your eyes. And you'll be back too, you'll see," he replies, handing me his card. "Travel safe. And when you get a chance, drop a line."

Then, he's gone, and I'm left alone with my thoughts and a trunkful of settling memories. Wow...What can I say? enters my mind and sits down as if to stay, the query then triggering the words of Portland poet Hazel Hall. "Today has held more than you can define," she had written almost a century ago. And while I understood, and felt her truth on my wedding day with Patty, and on the evenings when my kidlets had arrived, not until this moment did I fully appreciate the depth of her wisdom. For this day, so full of discovery, so rich with natural beauty, so utterly magical, is beyond definition, I muse, watching the dusk fall about me. Because wonderful as words are, and much as I love and treasure them, sometimes life is so special, so close to the Living Light, that what one learns and knows are beyond articulation, and can only be felt. "Like love," I whisper ever so softly, before slowly turning around and shuffling inside.

XI

RACHEL

OKAY. OKAY. I KNOW. I PROMISED YOU A ROMANTIC ADVENTURE when we reached Sligo, and to twist a phrase on your behalf: Turn up the heat, Hobman, or get out of the kitchen.

Well then, to begin, I am a widower. Twice, in fact. Oh, the first disaster, the proverbial marriage made in hell, technically ended in divorce. But believe me, the taste of death was everywhere, the only star in a black sky the sweet and sunny personage of my daughter Amy. Somehow, I survived. And because the Godperson rewards fools who dare to dance where angels run for cover, I was then blessed with the happy heaven of Patty. For 13 years I enjoyed a partnership of pure love, until just after our Bar Mitzvah cancer stole her away at only 38, leaving me at 48 with two little boys aged 6 and 9. During the pain and emptiness of the aftermath, reading regularly substituted for sleep. And when Tom Robbins hit me up with the idea that "for those with enough courage to see it through, disorientation always leads to love," instead of hitting back while shouting bullshit! I smiled wistfully, recalling that the prophecy had come true once. So, why not again? I queried the surrounding silence after heavy thought. Hell, it's legal, and if nothing else, it's a nice idea, ran the railroad of reason.

Nice idea? What it was, was absolute manna from the heaven of hope to a grief-stricken, sex-starved Romantic. Oh, yeah, in the highly unlikely event that you haven't already guessed, I confess: through the center of my soul runs a deep streak of romanticism. In fact, an analogy to the Grand Canyon is not inappropriate, which is to say that it could be filled up, but to date nothing or no one has.

All right, now, you have the picture: Lost Little Boy Innocent steps into the wacky world of dating after a prolonged absence during which all the rules changed. I mean, to one whose dating experience was founded in the nifty fifties and the pill-less sixties, the lonely and licentious landscape of the nineties was as mystifying as the mountains of Mars. Christ, during the dark ages when I began to experiment with love, the mention of STDs would've been greeted with a hearty, Huh? What's insecticides got to do with sex? But now, amidst the advanced society of today, you can die from making love. Oh, all right, maybe sometimes it's just plain old screwing, but in either case, death is a little harsh in the penalty department, don't you think? I mean, Jesus, but what a world – toss a little poetry into the salad bowl of sociology, and you get a dicey dictum indeed: Abstain, abstain, and you've got repression; keep it up and you'll suffer depression. Join instead in a union that makes you feel neat; here comes AIDS and your story's complete!

However, not to worry. You have to actually meet someone who presents the possibility of sex before this portrait of the penultimate problem paints itself with life colors. And in my case, both fortunately and unfortunately, the hallowed hues of energy remain on the palette, hardening into dust courtesy of an unending series of sorrowful dates with widows, divorcees, and old maids. Oh, I know, you're thinking, Can it really be that tough?

Well, dear reader, let me put it to you this way. What we have for middle-aged dating fans are two perilous pools of possibility from which to choose amorous activity. First off, are widows, who almost exclusively harbor a desperate desire to be with their husbands. Now I don't blame them of course, not one bit, 'cause I want to be with my Patty too. But on the other hand, if that's really all that's on your mind, then better to stay at home and watch TV – it couldn't possibly be any more dull, and that way you're free to yawn, belch, or fart whenever you want.

What? sneaks through your smile. I'm kidding? No, it's straight-skinny time all right. Why on just my second excursion into the wondrous world of starting over, the very first thing that Trisha said to me was: "You know, I don't actually consider this a date." Okay, lady, I thought, nouns aren't a problem, call it what you want: a chance meeting, two ships with broken radar passing in the night – a kidnapping even. 'Cause I want to go home anyway, I'm missing SportsCenter on ESPN.

What? you say a second time. I CANNOT be serious? Johnny McEnroeing into mind. Hell, they can't all be that way, jackknives your jargon – and you're right. But only because I gave'm up after the third non-date. I mean it was baseball season, and I figured three outs and the inning's over. I just moved on to cataclysmic category number two: divorcees and never-been-marrieds.

And no better? now tiptoes over eggs into your brain's backyard, the sad reality of my predicament beginning to seep into all your senses.

Well, the truth dictates, worse. Much worse! In fact, after a few of these Senior Sallies, I had to take a refresher course in CPR. No, really. I mean these ladies were all so old, tired, and defeated, that I was afraid they were going to die on me, and how the hell was I going to explain that to the folks at home. I mean, what do you say? Oh, I'm so sorry – we were just having this lovely little conversation about pets, bric-a-brac collections, and social security, when all of a sudden age simply reached its logical conclusion and she toppled over into her broccoli. I mean, how does that sound? Not too good, right?…See, I told you. And what else is there? 9-1-1 was busy? The doctors were on strike, 'cause health insurance doesn't cover an acute absence of life?

Right. I'm so glad you can see where I'm coming from. That way you'll better understand how pleasantly surprised I was to meet Rachel when I telephoned the Sligo Park Hotel last April in search of a room reservation. "No problem," she assured me, the musical lilt of her voice smiling away my accumulation of three prior unavailabilities. "We have a special room for you overlooking the garden. And I'll look forward to meeting you," she added after we had joked about the complexities of operating a computer.

Me, too, I thought after we hung up, a wave of sudden excitement sweeping a smile across my face as I underlined Rachel three times on my notepad. And when my confirmation arrived by fax several minutes later, accompanied by a map with hand-drawn notations to "ensure my safe arrival," Mr. Romantic rubbed the Rip Van Winkle cobwebs from his eyes, grabbed hope with one hand and desire with the other, and clapped them fast together in a rising crescendo of applause. Add a dash or two of imagination, or three or four or five, and inside of one happy hour a full-fledged fantasy was boogalooing across my brain, then slip-sliding cheek to cheek into both chambers of my heart.

Now, lest you think that your guide is totally nuts, Mr. Reason also had his say. With cold, calculated logic, he promptly advised that the hastily conjured conclusion was a stretch of significant proportion. That the facts pointed to nothing more than a courteous clerk simply welcoming a future guest. And that to arrive at the doorstep of a different judgment constituted a divorce from reality so sufficient as to warrant the assessment of punitive damages. However, Mr. Romantic had also attended law school, and immediately countered with the persuasive proposition that while all six of the previous reservation attendants had cheerfully assisted, only Rachel had added the personal touches of looking forward to meeting me plus a map to ensure my safe arrival. No, there are no accidents, Mr. Romantic argued to the jury of one. And to ignore what was obviously a sure and certain psychic sign would not only offend the paranormal powers that be, but would also result in a crime against self so monstrous as to amount to a self-inflicted capital punishment!

"Well, now, we can't have that," I chuckled, as I placed the confirmation into my travel notebook. "Besides, fantasies are fun, aren't they?" oozed my optimism. And when a letter from Rachel then arrived a week later bearing a second map, this one replete with noteworthy sights and restaurants, case closed, as our first date was all but set and Mr. Reason's appeal promptly denied. In fact, imagination had now married invention, and Rachel soon acquired flesh-and-blood attributes as well as a history. Aged 48, she stood five-foot-two, with blue eyes, silvery-blonde hair, and a shape that would catch one's attention, just in case you missed the high cheekbones that highlighted her pretty face.

Which, I most certainly did not. I told you that my romantic streak runs Grand-Canyon deep, and as you can seriously see I was telling the whole truth and nothing but. And as a result, in the fertile fields of my feverish psyche, no detail was omitted nor lost to oversight, from the slender slope of Rachel's ankles to the sweet-soft sound of her voice to the way she wrinkled her nose when she laughed. Add to this the accumulated knowledge that she was an only child of deceased shopkeepers, had ended her education after high school but read omnivorously, and had never been married after being abandoned by a fiancé in her late twenties, and you can fathom that for a blind date, I was relatively comfortable as I approached the front desk of the Sligo Park Hotel in the early afternoon of my fifth day in Erin.

The adverb *relatively* is used advisedly because once again the constraining commandments of truth compel the confession that during my sixty-year span of life, I have never, ever, not even once, approached an attractive woman without each and every one of my nerves snapping to attention to salute insecurity, the accompanying bugle corps blaring, Oh, I Hope She Likes Me, in the key of anxiety sharp. And so, therefore, it was only with relative ease that I inquired of Jeanette during check-in as to whether Rachel was about.

"No, she's not working today," rolled her reply. "But say – are you the one she sent the map to?" And when I quickly nodded yes through the sudden cloud of concern, "Oh, well she'll be here tomorrow for sure," sprinted assurance, alongside a matching smile.

You see, I encouraged myself as I strolled to Room 210, even the others know. So just have patience and enjoy Sligo, 'cause something special's about to happen.

To paraphrase Shakespeare, however: Alas, poor Hobman, it was not to be. Why not, I do not know. But when tomorrow arrived, Rachel didn't. At the desk, the explanation was simply, "Sorry, she's not coming in," and no more. And what happened to "tomorrow for sure" I don't know either. Even after the initial shock was absorbed, and the sharp pangs of disappointment had dissipated into a dull ache, I was companioned only by conjecture's confusion. Maybe she's only thirty-five, and you're too old? sauntered into mind first as I lit up my pipe outside the hotel and made ready for the day's explorations. Or maybe the ladies at the desk reported that you're not handsome enough? Hell, let's face it, Leonardo DiCaprio you're not – or make that Paul Newman to be more age appropriate, followed the sad stream of thought. Or maybe even, she just plain got scared? I mean, who's to say the would-be suitor isn't an axe-murderer in tourist disguise? And even if not, even if he's as cute and cuddly as a teddy bear, he's still a stranger on holiday who'll be leaving, so why invest time and emotion in what might have been but will never be? Like I said, I don't know. I just don't know. T.S. Eliot wrote that "place is always and only place, and what is actual is actual only for one time and only for one place," and I don't understand that either, though it somehow massages the question mark deep inside me. All I do know is that –

What?...You're disappointed?...You were eagerly anticipating a huggy-bear, kissy-face scenario with a happy ending, and now you're frustrated? Well, how do you think I feel? I mean, hell's bells, collect one more sad soul and we can form a corporation. You know, we can call it Failed Fantasies Inc., or Folded Fairy Tales Ltd. Add an equally sexy logo, and there's no telling how much stock we can sell. I mean, maybe fighting through disorientation doesn't *always* lead to love? Maybe only *sometimes*? I'm not sure. In fact, right this moment, like a shipwrecked sailor in a stormy sea, I'm just clinging to the half-mast of my beliefs that there are no accidents, and that romance's reservoir still permits the possibility for future dreams to be richly realized.

In the meantime, however, to demonstrate my gratitude for your having listened so intently to my torturous tale, then graciously commiserated with me, how about we travel on down the trail to gallant Galway and its fabled Browne Door. Step through it, and who knows what one might find? Maybe, even Rachel?

XII
BROWNE DOOR TO SPANISH ARCH

Sunday marks one full week in Ireland. And as if the day itself wants to join in my Anniversary celebration, it generously sets the table with a crystal-clear blue sky, and for fancy china, a great golden ball of a sun.

Wow, just seven days, but it feels like a lifetime, I muse as Bus #66 pulls out of Sligo's tiny, white and red-trimmed bus station and heads south along Highway N-17 toward Galway. Make that Gaillimh, if you speak Gaelic, teases my next brainwave as I settle comfortably into my seat by a window and begin browsing the countryside. It's only mid-morning, but the sheep at the base of Mount Knocknarea are already hard at work grazing, my silent "so long" to Queen Maeve wafting over their bowed heads, along with my vow to return one day and hike to the summit. Well, interrupts a flashback, I didn't find romance in Sligo, but neither did my bedtime companion Nuala, when she escaped to the countryside for vacations during her rise as a journalist with BBC. Hell, it ain't easy, I reason, recalling her struggles from last evening's read. However, I did find an important truth, and more beauty than several lifetimes could bargain for. So, who's complaining? Not me. And besides, who knows what's up the road? grins gratitude, tinged with hope. Then, pulling my map from my backpack, along with part of a candy bar, I survey the towns and villages we will be visiting during the two and a half hour journey, the ache of sadness at leaving Sligo giving way to the smiling promise of fresh sights, sounds, and adventures lying ahead and in Galway.

The village of Ballincarrow is first on our agenda, so small that we pass through it in seconds. Then, as miles of green fields dotted with sheep and cows parade into view, only to give way to sister scenes as the bus rolls southward, like chimes singing in the wind, the musical notes of Tobercurry, Curz, and Charlestown sound, then fade as we pass through narrow streets lined with flats and shops, and on by cottages trimmed with flower beds, small schools, and steepled churches. Postcards, whose letters are neat and tidy in their spelling of rural, slow and sleepy, pristine, and peaceful. Yeahhh, who would want to make trouble in such a beautiful place, echoes yesterday's thought, followed closely by Ray's observation that people farm, and live their lives, and, somehow, just get along with one another.

At Knock, a town with one street, we stop to stretch our legs, and find surprise: we've landed at a major site of Christian pilgrimage, equal to Lourdes and Fatima! And almost instantly, I spy an ancient Celtic Cross carved out of brown stone that rises toward heaven atop a five-foot pedestal. Called the Papal Cross since 1979, when Pope John Paul II visited the village to finalize official approval of the century-earlier sighting by fifteen locals of the Blessed Mother, St. Joseph, and St. John the Evangelist on the wall of the adjacent church, its weathered face speaks legions toward all that it's seen through the ages, as if somehow, strangely, inviting your curiosity to engage it in conversation.

For some reason, equally strange given my proclivity for talking to inanimate objects, I don't. However, five minutes later, it is precisely my like appeal to Mr. Henry Casey that causes him to initiate a chat after he climbs aboard and our journey to Galway continues. Not yet thirty, with nice-looking roundish features, and neatly dressed in slacks, sport shirt, and blazer, his friendly inquisitiveness, combined with his casual sense of confidence, makes him immediately likable. Then, when his highly developed sense of intuition prods him to inquire if I'm Jewish, and have ever been divorced, not five minutes into our dialogue, the adjective *interesting* also climbs on board, although *interested* should get equal consideration. For Henry is most definitely *into* the world. All of it. Everything! Although a dedicated teacher of mathematics at a college in Galway, his scope of interest is truly global. Which, for purposes of our colloquy is most fortunate, as my background in math is rather limited, to put it kindly. But, no problem. None. For history, politics, and travel will do nicely as subjects, thank you very much. Not to downplay for an instant, movies, books, the 1960s, Vietnam, and the Law. Talk?…Hell, I can talk, Lord knows. But Henry will keep the tongue of even the most avid gabber well exercised, and your brain snapped to attention and in a high state of alert, for good measure. What of Ireland have I seen so far? What lies ahead? And what do I think, and feel?…He's visited Seattle, so how's Portland measure up? And what was all that noise about Clinton's impeachment, and the recount in Florida?…Got a favorite movie? Harry's is Grace of My Heart, a must-see, and I need to read *City of Quartz* as soon as possible. Oh, and I write poetry, do I? And admire Yeats?… "Well," he enthuses as we approach the town of Tuam, an hour and fifteen minutes into our discourse, "let me point out Coole, the home of his friend, Lady Gregory. See, there's the tower Yeats built, where he lived and wrote *The Swans of Coole*," he shotguns, directing my eyes out the window. Then, in the fifteen minutes before we reach Galway, he asks for the secrets to a successful marriage, me presumably having knowledge of both the north and south poles from having visited heaven as well as hell. Talk about a crash course, all right, engineered by an unbridled romantic without notes. But I do my best, spinning out the basic recipe of careful selection, followed by a full measure of patience and prudence, all seated on a firm foundation of pure luck! And when we pull into Ceannt Station, he leaves me with a Gaelic blessing: "Giorian beirt bothan," he smiles out, shaking my hand. "Two shortens the road."

Indeed it does, I muse, shaking my head at how quickly the journey had passed as I begin my search for the Great Southern Hotel. Well, *search* may not be exactly the proper term. As after exiting the station and pulling Big Blue fifty yards up to the corner, I turn left, and there it is in all its stately glory. And this time I've got it correct, times two: Not only do I deserve a pat on the back for selecting an extremely convenient location, a more detailed review reveals that the reward of a pastry or two might be in order for having managed to add a palace to the package. For rising gracefully to a height of five stories, and occupying the better part of a block, with its name in gold letters accentuating the gray-white limestone from which it was constructed in 1845, *palace* is exactly what the Great Southern looks like. And when I then enter the lobby, with its plush carpet, marble columns, and chandeliers, *regal* pops into mind to seal the deal. Four stars?" I mutter to myself as I approach the desk. "Seems to me, we've got a whole galaxy here!"

A charming lady named Noreen checks me in, and offers sherry to ease the short wait till my room is ready. I choose coffee instead, which is promptly served with cookies on a silver tray in front of the comfortable couch I plop myself down on. And the ten-minute wait is just long enough for me to decide that sometimes regal isn't stuffy, and that elegant surroundings can also be functionally enjoyable. Which, fortunately, also proves to be the case when I reach Room 342. Of good size, with high ceilings featuring a chandelier over the king-size bed, the warm but muted colors instantly create an aura of livable comfort. The west-wall windows offer a lovely view of Eyre Square, and on a small table to their front, the large bowl of fresh fruit and the bottles of spring water are a very nice welcoming touch. "Okay, you're home. Now, let's go see Galway!" I enthuse, growing excited, then hurrying to ready myself for the dash downstairs and out the front door.

Time is approaching three o'clock as I walk across the street and enter Eyre Square, a mid-sized park that was originally a market area, but was donated to Galway in 1710 by its then Lord-Mayor, Edward Eyre. Now the City's focal point, with its pathways and benches lined by colorful flower beds and statuary, it has also become the City's playground, a fact readily supported by the large numbers of people taking a stroll, reading beneath a shady tree, or listening to live music in the large bricked circle located in its center. They're friendly, too, these Galwegians, I muse, returning smiles and head nods from several locals, the quaint nickname adding to the shared warmth as I wend my way to the Quincentennial Fountain situated to the front of the performing trio. Erected in 1984 to celebrate the 500th anniversary of Galway becoming a city, it consists of sheets of iron mounted to depict the area's distinctive sailboat, the Galway Hooker. And though impressive, with its orange sails and modern configuration thrusting upward toward the oceanic blue sky, it's the two landmarks on the opposite side of the center-wheel that call out to me. First up is a life-size bronze statue of Pedraic O'Conaire, a Galwegian who lived from 1882 to 1923, and who is recognized as one of Ireland's greatest short story writers. Seated on a stone fence, and dressed in a suit and tie, completed by a bowler hat atop his head, Pedraic looks eager for a smoke and some conversation, so I drop down next to him in an effort to oblige. A cheerful fellow, with a sharp wit, he is only mildly impressed with my resume of twenty-two poems and a tenuous relationship to Yeats and Shaw. But when he learns that I also published one short story, he warms up a bit, before then reminding me that at sixty, I've already lived half again as long as he did, and that if I want to amount to something, I'd better get on the stick.

Uh-huh…ya hear'em?" I chide myself after taking my leave and wandering over to the fabled Browne Door, some ten yards away. A full fifteen feet wide, and towering thirty feet above ground, this stone-arched doorway, with its huge window overhead, was once the entrance to the family mansion belonging to one of Galway's fourteen founding tribes. Now free-standing and framed in cement, it stands proudly as a staunch reminder of Galway's storied past, a history that then flows into mind as my gaze freezes on the cut-stone symbol whose shadow surrounds me. In fact, Galway's name in Gaelic, *Gaillimh*, means *stony*, I recall from my studies. And influenced by its remote location amid rocky lands at the head of Galway Bay and the River Corrib, this unofficial capital of West Ireland has a personality wholly unlike Eire's other major cities. Here, there are no Georgian streetscapes like Dublin, no castles like Limerick, no grand parades like Cork City, and no Viking towers like Waterford. For Galway was not conquered by the Norse invaders. No, instead it was invaded by the Anglo-Normans in the thirteenth century, with the DeBurgos founding a formal settlement beside a ford on the River Corrib. Then, by 1270, strong stone walls had been added, and inside them a great medieval city began to rise.

Because of its position on the Atlantic, the scribes teach, as the Middle Ages then unfolded, Galway emerged as a thriving seaport for wine, spices, and fish, developing as it grew a brisk trade with Spain and other European countries. In turn, this prosperity fueled Galway's further expansion into a powerful City-State between the fourteenth and the mid-seventeenth centuries, becoming known as "The City of Tribes" due to the influence of fourteen wealthy, merchant, Anglo-Norman families who settled here and proceeded to rule the town as an oligarchy. Named Athy, Blake, Bodkin, Browne, Darcy, Font, French, Joyce, Kirwan, Lynch, Martin, Morris, and Sherret, each family had its own mansion or castle, and from it a street flowed forth to join the others and form the core of what is still downtown Galway. "Well, how about that? The original Company Town, huh, ye clan of Brownes? I tease, my eyes finding two coats of arms carved into the doorway, dated 1627 and belonging to the Brownes and Lynches. "I mean, I read about these, they're marriage stones, and represent the union of two elite families, sorta like the Rockefellers and the Vanderbilts in my neck of the woods. Listen," I gibe, walking through the doorway, then back. "You guys ever hear of the anti-trust laws?…Right, I didn't think so," sounds the answer through a smile, Galway's more recent history beginning to trickle into mind. For the foundation of commerce laid down by these founding patriarchs is alive, well, and growing feverishly in today's Galway. In fact, ever since the founding of University College in 1848, and the establishment of a permanent rail link with Dublin in 1854, growth has been the City's buzz word, the first key opening Galway to an infusion of youthful vibrance as a college town, while the latter connection made it the true Trading Hub of the West. Happily it has been growth controlled by enlightened local government, allowing Galway to leap into the twenty-first century as Ireland's fastest growing city, while still preserving its rich heritage.

"Well, if Galway's on the move, how about we do likewise, and have a look-see?" issues an idea when the stream of information pouring into mind ends. Sounds good to me, smiles my answer as I head north for thirty yards to Williamsgate Street, then turn left. And having entered downtown's busiest thoroughfare, I am immediately struck by how narrow it is, not more than twenty-five feet from sidewalk to sidewalk. Motorized traffic can manage only a crawl, as pedestrians overflow the walkways to stroll in the street. And for a moment, connotations of Dublin's Grafton Street slip into mind, as lined on both sides with shops and cafés of every possible description, *action* keynotes the busy scene. In reality, however, far more reminiscent of Sligo's Castle Street, here, too, the two stories overhead house offices and flats, while the smaller scale of the street won't allow for a full-size department store. True to the area's geography, and setting the tone for its own identity, most of the buildings are constructed of cut-stone instead of brick, those in their natural grayish-white hue competing for attention with the rainbow of bright colors smiling from the faces of their neighbors. Again, Dublin drifts into view, this time the focus on the merry doors along Merrion Square, as after a block, when Williamsgate becomes William Street, I'm greeted by an entire collage of grey, red, blue, and goldish-yellow facades. And though the buildings in sight are clearly closer in size to those of Sligo, I further note that while they're not taller, they are wider, and the shops and cafés inside far more numerous. That makes sense, of course, I tell myself, as with a population of 60,000, Galway's over three times the size. And while its buildings are every bit as old, forms a conclusion, they're prettier, as in more stylish, with cleaner lines and greater detail.

Uh-huh, nods my head as the observation sinks in. And speaking of old, but most impressive, how about that beauty? carols confirmation, admiration welling up as my eyes pore over a stately stone structure located on the corner of where William now becomes Shop Street. Four stories high, with an arched entryway, numerous decoratively carved windows with matching overhangs, and projecting gargoyles peering down from just beneath the roofline, this splendid structure was once home to the Lynches, one of Galway's fourteen original Tribe families. Dating back to the late fifteenth or early sixteenth centuries, over the door, halfway to the roof, is a large carved roundel framing the Lynches' coat of arms. And as I stand and study the former castle, now occupied by the Allied Irish Bank, What would they think? dances up and down in a curious corner of my mind.

"They'd like it, one whole hell of a lot!" booms the Professor's answer, cutting into my reverie.

"Ohhh, is that right?…"

"Uh-huh. Those people were capitalists in the truest sense. So what better than a bank? I mean, pay low on savings accounts, charge high on mortgages, and foreclose in ten seconds flat if the suckers don't pay. And as for credit cards, why those annual fees are just l-o-v-e-l-y," he oozes sarcastically. "Wanna talk car loans?…"

"No…I don't," trickles my reply. "Instead, where the hell were you for the past two days?…"

"Well," he says slowly, suckering me in. "Maybe you struck out in Sligo, but I didn't! I mean, some colleens really go for us older guys with experience. So, sorry, little buddy, but while you and your friend Yeats were busy solving momentous philosophical issues, I was having a little huggy-bear, kissy-face fun! You oughta try it, might lighten you up a bit. I mean – "

"Hey, listen, Mr. Swinger-Man. I DID try, so no need to rub it in."

"Okay…all right…Don't go overly sensitive on me now," he urges. "I've got an idea. Since you're going to see a church next, how about we say a little prayer for you. You know, a selfish one. Then, maybe your luck will change."

Ohhh, yeah…sure, I think, shrugging him off as I take a right off of Shop Street onto Church Lane and head for the steeple one block straight ahead. Once I have arrived, my innate attraction to old buildings causes me to be instantly captivated by St. Nicholas' Collegiate Church, a relatively low-lying but handsomely designed stone edifice that is the largest medieval parish church in Ireland still in use. Built in 1320 on the site of an even earlier chapel, it was expanded during the sixteenth century when Galway's prosperity was at its height, and is dedicated to St. Nicholas, a fourth-century Bishop of Myra in Southwestern Asia Minor. Although he is best known as the patron saint of children, or Santa Claus, during the Middle Ages he was commonly revered as the patron saint of sailors – a curious synchronicity leading to the historical footnote that Christopher Columbus almost certainly worshiped here in 1477, thereby drawing inspiration from the celebrated tales of St. Brendan the Navigator, an Irish monk who is believed to have sailed to America in the sixth century. Inside, St. Nicholas' exquisite stained glass windows would indeed inspire prayers, albeit *unselfish* ones, and its interior showcases many medieval furnishings and fixtures, including the Crusader's Tomb, a twelfth- or thirteenth-century burial vault with a rare Norman-French inscription, and a late fifteenth or early sixteenth-century free-standing benitier or holy water stoup, highly uncommon for Ireland.

Returning outside, several studied minutes later, I need time to reflect. Only slightly more than an hour has passed since I left the Great Southern, but I've already talked shop with Mr. O'Conaire, met the pioneering Brownes and Lynches, and prayed in the ghostly shadows of Christopher Columbus and Galway's legions of ancient mariners. True, I had failed to ask for St. Nick's personal blessing, I consider, lighting up my Peterson from a curb across the street. But on the other hand, I'm already lucky beyond words just to be here, so why push it, concludes my defense. Then, just sitting and smoking, for several minutes imagination's eye is infused with watching the various Tribe families amble in and out of the Church, the *feel* of long ago seeping inside me.

When church finally lets out, and the Tribes break for lunch and leisure, I slowly pick myself up off the curb and return to Shop Street, where I continue traveling westward. One short block, and it turns into High Street, where I windowshop Thomas Dillon's Claddagh Gold Jewelry Store, noting that the sign against the warm red face of the shopfront advises that they've been in business since 1750. At Kenny's Book Shop across the street, I'm sorely tempted to browse the prints for which it is renowned. But with a whole city to see, and only this afternoon to meet it, I nod so long to the brightly blooming flower baskets accenting the green facade and push my feet toward Quay Street. It greets me, just one block further down the roadway, by tweaking a previous thought and forcing a quizzical smile. Williamsgate, to William, to Shop, to High, and now Quay, I review carefully, memory racing back to Sligo and its Street of Four Names. "Well, I'll be damned, but Galway's trumped the Trinity by two!" I mutter, suddenly seeing myself walking the less glamorous Castle Street and discovering that I miss Sligo. Yeahhh, I know, murmurs my confession. But Galway's special too, and the Spanish Arch is waiting, so what do you say we get on with the program?...

Okay...No problem, dribbles the answer. And just to make sure we're at full strength, how about a little nourishment? I mean, hell, Quay Street's at the heart of Galway's Left Bank, and with all these shops and cafés, there must be a bakery or two that could use an extra customer, especially one with my confectionary credentials, don't ya think?...And as if from my mouth to God's ear, halfway down Quay, I find one, on Kirwan's Lane, a surviving medieval alleyway off to the right. Then, refueled and retooled, I mosey on through the maze of curio shops, art studios, and restaurants to where Quay Street curves left toward the river. There, while still munching my pastry, I stop to admire the remnants of Blake's Castle, almost a replica of Lynch's, only about half the size, and with one highly unusual feature: the Jurys hotel, constructed in the 1990s, is built around it, so that while the Castle's facade juts out several feet to the front of the surrounding structure, it is nevertheless now incorporated into the hotel. I don't even have to ask the Professor what the Blakes think about this entrepreneurial endeavor, if the Lynches can migrate into banking, well then, what's wrong with hosting a hotel, for God's sake?...

Nothing. Absolutely, positively, nothing, resonates reason as I nod farewell to the gargoyles, and still smiling, proceed on around the bend in the roadway. Half a minute later, a large, cobblestoned square presents itself, flanked by the River Corrib on the west, restaurants with outside diners on the east, and to the south, a hundred yards in front of me, the fabled Spanish Arch. The centerpiece of a massive twenty-five by fifty-foot cut-stone wall built in 1584, the twelve-foot archway in the middle easily allows for passage between the residential area to the south and the commercial activities along the Street of Five Names. Once the focal point of the landing dock where Spanish ships unloaded cargoes of wine and brandy from their galleons during the sixteenth-century heyday of trading between Galway and Spain, today it faithfully stands guard over the Galway City Museum to its left, and the pedestrianized plaza to its front, with its restful view of the water. And after slowly strolling over to where I can pat its stone blocks, I then seat myself on a step near the river's edge and try to imagine the commercial commotion of yesteryear.

"It's pretty busy today, too," I whisper when my gaze sweeps back across the diners drinking wine in the warm sunshine, to the bevy of sunbathers stretched out on the grassy nubs nosing north along the Corrib. The river itself is beautiful, blue-green, with the sun welding silvery sparkles onto its rippling surface as it rushes toward the Atlantic. A hundred yards away, the Wolfe Tone Bridge arches lazily across the hundred-foot width, leading to the Claddagh, a residential neighborhood spread out along the western bank. Some historians, I recall as I light up my pipe, believe that in ancient times the Claddagh was a fishing village, possibly older than Galway itself. Well, I don't know about that, I muse, totally relaxed by the sunshine and the scene's serenity. Seems to me, a tougher question is: Why would anyone ever leave this spot?...

"Because if you don't, Mr. Can't Ever Get Enough of Nature's Wonders, you'll miss the rest of Galway. That's why!" interjects the ever faithful Professor. "Besides, the next part of your journey is along the river anyway. And who can tell? Maybe you'll accidentally bump into a dinner companion?"

Too content to jab back at him, I simply smile, and, after relighting my pipe, head north along the Corrib. My watch reads four-thirty as I settle into a moderate but steady pace. And once in groove, for the next hour and a half, my feet don't stop moving. First up is a residential neighborhood composed of three- and four-story flats lining both banks of the river for two miles or so. "Hey, you guys, need a neighbor?" I chuckle to the colorfully painted windowframes, some further brightened with hanging baskets of flowers. Then, as I approach the Salmon Weir Bridge, so named because from its vantage point one can watch salmon jump upstream, I slow to see if I can spot any leapers. "No luck," I commiserate with a lonely wisp of cloud overhead. "But hey, it is Sunday, the day of rest, and salmon have rights too, you know. I'm not sure about trout, 'cause they're not unionized. But salmon even have a delegate to the U.N., so don't be too hard on them, ya hear?..." And I do: the river gurgling, the whitecaps whooshing, the spray humming over the rocks, all in perfect harmony. And there's aroma too, the smell of grass mixing with the fragrance of flowers and fresh coffee in the hands of a passerby, to create a full bouquet and inspire a deep inhalation and slow, savoring release, so satisfying that it commands a repeat performance.

Fifty yards from where I cross over the Salmon Weir Bridge stands the Cathedral of Our Lady Assumed into Heaven and St. Nicholas. "Now, how's that for a heavy-duty handle?" teases a thought as I approach this 1965 addition to Galway's family of fine architecture. Must be that they tried to compensate for the lack of medieval history by adding a name that could stretch all the way to Dublin, sidles my cheerful sarcasm, my eyes scanning for details as I circle the Renaissance-style edifice constructed of limestone and marble. I can't fully appreciate the massive, turquoise-tinted dome that dominates Galway's skyline until I've recrossed the bridge and meandered two blocks away. "Yeahhh, she's queen of the mountain, all right, and a true beauty too," purrs my analysis to a soft close as I continue on through the neighborhood of small cottages, all well-kept, and looking sleepy in the late-afternoon sunshine.

And you know what? enters an offshoot consideration when I reach St. Vincent's Avenue. The people here look young too, just like in Dublin. And likewise, for the most part they're smartly dressed, especially the pretty young ladies. I mean, I know it's a college town, but still, it seems like it's illegal to be over thirty around here, idles my observation, before my train of attention is then diverted to a large and attractive building with facades facing both St. Vincent's and Newtown Smith Street. Classical in design, with a Corinthian-columned portico leading to the entrance, and a lemon-yellow front facing me, the Town Hall Theatre is Galway's major performing arts venue, and a most impressive edifice in its own right. "I wonder what's playing, Ponce de Leon's *Youth Springs Eternal in Ireland*?" I gibe as my feet again pick up speed. And after churning a couple of miles through the collection of shops and flats lining St. Vincent's Avenue, Wood Quay, and Eyre Street, they finally deposit me back in Eyre Square, just before Father Time strikes six o'clock.

Two soccer games are in progress as I revisit the Quincentennial Fountain, this time noticing the plaque to its right which commemorates JFK's visit in 1963. Hey, I was only twenty-three then, smiles an afterthought, I'd have fit in Big Time! Not only a fitting observation, no pun intended I assure you, but without warning, also a highly accurate prelude to the experience I was about to enjoy. For having decided that dinner was not only in order, but needed, upon reentering the Great Southern, I wander down to the basement, the site of O'Flaherty's Pub, "home to fine food, music, and drink."

And, on this auspicious occasion, *hurling*! As when I enter, the sport occupies center stage, courtesy of the largest big-screen TV I've ever seen, and supported as it is by a virtual mob of people who are alternately cheering and groaning as if the fate of the world were at stake. Turns out, it's only the finals of the All Ireland Hurling Championships, with Galway pitted against Tipperary. But to the hundred and fifty souls assembled, it is Armageddon itself! In color! I mean, Galway doesn't need a power plant, the electricity circulating in O'Flaherty's could light the whole city. Hell, maybe even the whole county! speculates second thought as I reach the bar and order a Guinness. Now, even though I'm a genuine, fully certified sports nut, for the moment I find myself at great disadvantage. For what I know about hurling can easily be placed on either the right or left side of one of the bubbles atop my frothing brew. Not to worry, however. Upon noticing the quizzical expression mapping my face, Liam, who was picking up a second round of liquid enthusiasm, invites me to his nearby table, where, after hurriedly introducing me to Mary, Ian, Christie, and Rory, he then undertakes a crash course in the game's basic rudiments. An obvious optimist, with a large store of patience, Liam explains that hurling is similar to field hockey, "only a bit more physical," from having originated with the Celts. "And it's for pride," he half-shouts over the din, "there's no pros here, it's not for money, but bragging rights!" A *bit* more physical? I consider, watching the non-stop, fast-paced action, bodies falling like bowling pins, only to bounce right back up and reenter the frenzied melee. Hell, how about a mixture of lacrosse and rugby? And while I don't exactly have a firm grasp of the game's finer points, or the overall strategies being employed, no matter. Armed with a teaspoonful of basics, and fortified with Guinness and my Galwegian compatriots, I am soon yelling and screaming as if it were the seventh game of the World Series and my Mariners were clinging to a one-run lead in the ninth inning. War?…Ohhh, no, as a famous football coach once philosophized. It's much more important than that! And one whole hell of a lot more fun, too!

Tragically, however, through direct intervention by the Devil, Tipperary prevails 118 to 115, and a pall settles over the pub. Until, that is, someone suggests that another round of Guinness is the only cure. And if one round revives breathing, well, two or three restore music, storytelling, and laughter, until finally the clock strikes eleven and bladders threaten to burst. So, after a round of handshakes and a chorus of so longs, the group disperses, and the newly crowned *Galwegian buddy* retreats to his room, where the silence is suddenly deafening. A shower seems in order. And then afterwards, telephone calls home, which bring good news to end the day. Amy is A-okay in Los Angeles. Nickels and Matty likewise in Tucson and Portland. And…my Mariners won, six to nothing!

Well, at least I'm fifty-fifty, I muse, sitting down at the table in front of the windows for a bedtime smoke, my eyes traveling to Eyre Square. Through the dim light provided by the hotel and several nearby businesses, I can make out the park's outlines, and my mind's eye passes over the Quincentennial Fountain to visit my writing crony Pedraic, before settling on the Browne Door. Ohhh, yes, Galway's got its own personality, all right, shuffles a thought slowly. Uh-huh, no doubt. It's got sixty thousand people, and is growing steadily, yet its core is still small and compact, and walkable. There's all kinds of businesses, an active theatre, the University, and a passionate love of sports, yet the centerpiece of life remains family and friends, with time for both ensured by a pace of living based on busy, but without the frenzy of go go go. And while Galwegians still keep ancient traditions very much alive, the youthful population is also full of energy and embraces innovation. Hey, let's face it: It's Renaissance City cool! ends my ruminations, the smoke from my pipe floating out the window, followed by a peaceful smile of satisfaction.

XIII

CUAIN NA MARA

N O SLEEPING LATE TODAY, DESPITE THE AGENDA'S MIDMORNING BUS
tour. Nope. At six forty-five, I awaken to the soft sounds of a Gaelic
lullaby, Cuain na Mara...Cuain na Mara, echoing into ear. Meaning
"Harbors of the Sea," and translating into English as Connemara, unlike
most place names this one does not refer to a city or town. Instead, it
identifies a section of County Galway lying west by northwest of Galway
City, and is synonymous with stunning scenery, featuring wide and open
vistas, with rugged terrain in its natural state. A remote region, I recall
while propping myself up against the pillows, Connemara doesn't have
any outstanding museums, landmarks, or national monuments. Rather,
it holds a treasure-trove consisting of a coastline indented with little
bays, inlets, and beaches, along with an interior dotted with small villages surrounded by lakes, waterfalls, rivers, and creeks, all dominated
by the Twelve Bens Mountains rising in the center to overshadow a bog-
filled landscape that is also home to gorse and heather, rhododendrons,
fuchsia, and wildflowers.

"Holy cockamolies, it's Rural Time again!" I announce to the chandelier overhead, then sit up in acknowledgment of my aroused sense of
anticipation. "Right up old Hob's alley," adds enthusiasm, a plateful of
eggs and bangers also jumping into contemplation's view on my way
to the bathroom to free the remnants of last evening's Great Guinness
celebration.

At ten-thirty sharp, with the sun still climbing into a bright blue
void marked occasionally with chalky smudges of cloud, the Lally Tour
Bus pulls away from the Tourist Center on Eyre Square and heads west

123

across the Salmon-Weir Bridge. Passing the nicknamed Cathedral of the Heavy-Duty Handle, I nod greetings, then crane my neck to fully gather in the cut-stone, Corinthian-columned buildings forming the campus of University College–Galway. Almost simultaneously with Martin the Bus Driver's commentary that the student body is twelve thousand strong, the thought, I wonder if my friend Henry is busy lecturing on logarithms, bolts from my brain, then passes with a smile as we cross the urban boundary and enter the countryside. Once again, I'm surprised by how quickly urban turns into rural, my eyes finding, then floating along the edges of Eire's largest lake, Lough Corrib, as the bus traverses its twenty-seven-mile length, beginning just outside Galway and stretching to Oughterard.

A charming little fishing village, which was once home to the ferocious O'Flaherty Clan, it now serves as the "Gateway to the Connemara," one we quickly pass through into a landscape that changes radically, as suddenly as traditional Irish music fiddles forth from the sound system. Gone is the peaceful, sky-blue surface of the lake, with its abundant green backdrop of gently rolling hills that seem close at hand. And replacing it, as fast as the click of a slide show, is a much harsher vista of wide-open space as far as the eye can see, with the horizon formed by the low-lying Maamturk Mountains that are strung out around the valley like a herd of humpback whales. "H-e-l-l-o, Cuain na Mara," I murmur in amazement, my eyes slowly but steadily searching the foreign scene for signs of welcome, and finding a majestic beauty, but no smile. Color and texture are the first factors to express their differences. For unlike the lush green blanket spread out before you by the Land of Heart's Desire, here one's greeted by an eccentric, green-and-brown patchwork quilt, with small pools of water interwoven ever so often. And instead of velvety soft and silky, the land is rocky, rugged, and raw, with occasional patches of heather softening its stark face.

"Wow!" whistles my continued sense of surprise when the bus stops on the far side of the village of Maam, and I can stand and stare, sweep and search. It's different, all right, incubates a thought as I peer at the Maamturk's mixed hues of gray, green, and brown. And it's absolutely beautiful, too, in its own forbidding way. It's so open and untouched, so empty, so...so...*lonely*, I finally manage to conclude after hesitating to allow the right word to surface. Yeahhh, here the solitary ghosts of

Connaught's ancient tribes can really raise the goosebumps. And here, somehow, the Spartan scenery wrapped inside the miles of silence strangely makes the past seem as close as yesterday. 'Cause this is the way it was in St. Patrick's time, and before, seeps understanding, a faint smile playing on my lips as I slowly begin to grow comfortable. A feeling further nourished by my discovery of several clusters of homes at the foot of one of the Maamturks – in turn, the sighting triggers into mind my long-ago midnight readings. Empty?...Well, not quite. For though sparsely populated, Connemara is nevertheless dotted throughout by small towns and villages, and remains proudly the region most like old Eire, where thirty thousand people still speak Gaelic, and stone fences, piles of newly cut turf, donkey carts, and sheep still abound. True, I recall, recent prosperity has made it possible to also see a TV antenna or two, and cars. But in the many tiny villages of seven hundred or less, tradition is still the watchword, and the pubs still ring with native song and dance, while cottage industries carry on ageless crafts, and the people still have time to stop and chat.

Right, sleepy little villages just like Maam, I confirm, flashing on the miniature downtown we had just passed through, with its single street, its few older but well kept buildings and storefronts, the pub in its center, and the sidewalks thinly occupied. Thirty thousand folks, huh?...Well, a few hundred here, a few hundred there, and it all adds up, I surmise with a smile, memory's record then playing on to focus on sheep. The region's primary occupation, due to the fact that the highly acidic soil renders it unfit for farming, courtesy of a fifty-fifty subsidy footed by the European Union and the Irish government, sheep roam the Maamturks in great numbers. Black-faced sheep to be precise, raised by the locals for their meat, not wool, and whose coats are marked with differing shades of red and blue dye to designate their ownership. A highly humane form of branding, the practice also symbolizes perfectly a simple way of life stretching back over a thousand years, and which, with some modification, still idles happily along today. Uh-huh, just like turf fires, I affirm, dropping my eyes to a bog not more than fifty yards away. A section of soft, wet, spongy ground created over thousands of years by decomposing trees and plants mixed together, bogs, also known as peatlands, cover roughly fifteen percent of the Irish landscape. And by carefully cutting out small strips of the bog, then drying them in neat stacks in the open

air, one derives peat, or turf as the locals have called it for eons, a sub-
stance which can be burned to heat a home or ground down to fertilize
a garden. Hey, not only is it cheap, I muse, but it's also environmentally
friendly, 'cause it's natural and releases no harmful chemicals. Now how's
that for a nifty product? chirps the Sierra Club compartment of my busy
brain. No losers, just winners! it hums happily as I climb back aboard
the bus and we head on toward the village of Leenane, the Maamturks
rolling alongside, my eyes then catching sight of yet another signpost of
Irish traditional life, the rock wall. A *dry* rock wall, my studies remind,
as no sand or mud was used to construct them. Instead, as a shepherd
or farmer cleared his land, the rocks were carefully piled on each other
so as to create a tight formation, but still leave holes for the wind to
pass through and thus avoid toppling. Practical, huh? offers the now
energized agents of ecology. You clear the land, mark its boundaries, and
fence the animals in, all with the same rock – sorta like *three* birds with
the same stone, purrs the Proverb of Pragmatism to a close, the miles of
seemingly endless open space lulling me into peaceful trance.

N-59, the one-lane road we've been following west from Galway,
narrows further as we now climb north, twisting and turning through
the mountain pass for half an hour, before suddenly leveling off for a
soft landing at the tiny village of Leenane. And when I say tiny, I'm
talking half an eye blink and you'll miss it, as in just one cluster of two-
story buildings on the north side of the road, and three singles on the
south. I mean, Maam is a virtual metropolis by comparison. But, on the
other hand, Leenane wins hands down in the Prettiness Department,
with its pastel-colored storefronts and blue-shaked sloping roofs. And
that's just for openers. As nestled comfy-cozy into a hollow between the
surrounding Maamturks, now dressed in their finest greenery, for a finishing touch that not even delectable Dublin can match, lovely, Lilli-
putian Leenane plays host to Ireland's only fjord, located providentially
in its front yard. A clear channel, shaped like a long, slightly crooked
finger, it wanders tranquilly from the frontal bay through a narrow gap
between the sheltering Maamturks for six miles, before finally flowing
into the Atlantic. And on this occasion, its violet-blue waters, running
to a depth of a hundred fifty feet, basket-catch the sun's slanting rays to
cast a dreamy spell of enchantment over the noon hour. For sure, and
then some! idles a confirming thought, floating gently in the warm air.

As seated dockside on a wooden bench, with coffee and pipe in hand, and looking lazily across to the eastern shore which resides in County Mayo, the Hobman is as perfectly content as the surroundings are serene. Even the Professor's efforts to engage in conversation about the locals harvesting mussels and oysters fall on deaf ears, as does the subject of Nazi submarines using the fjord to recharge their batteries during World War II. Not today. Not in this rhapsodic setting, I think, settling into my cocoon for several snoozy minutes, before finally rising to stretch, then freeze-frame one last look as I return to the bus.

Already stunned by the rough-hewn beauty of the morning's scabrous scenery, then mesmerized by Leenane's Etude de Fjord during noontime, as the bus now turns west and rolls onward, I am totally unprepared for the encore of idyllic that soon follows. Or, on second thought, make that Idyllic with a capital I, spelled Shangri-la! For as we gradually descend through the Twelve Bens Mountains, along the edge of the Connemara National Park, the multi-hues of green in which Eire ordinarily dresses return to form the customary backdrop of over-abundance. And when fifteen minutes later, we pass through the quaint village of Kylemore, then stop before Kylemore Abbey, perched like a queen on her throne at the head of a sun-sparkled lake, *unprepared* once again strains the boundaries of understatement – as with *sumptuous*, *splendid*, and *spectacular* tripping over each other trying to exit the tongue first, fairy-tale has to resurrect itself from the Parke's Castle setting on Lough Gill in order to accurately portray the feast feeding one's eyes. In fact, a castle fit for a fairy tale is indeed the proper phrase to sum up the palatial mansion originally built in 1864 as a private residence by Mitchell Henry, a wealthy English merchant. For though some two hundred feet wide, with equal depth, and augmented by towers, turrets, and battlements, its simple classical design, with Gothic overtones, nevertheless allows it to appear graceful despite its great size, and soft and delicate in spite of its stone composition, an aura further enhanced by the surrounding blanket of dense foliage and the placid waters lapping its doorstep. Initially presented by Henry as a gift to his new bride, its stately beauty and loving purpose stir a memory of the Taj Mahal, and, likewise, stand as an exquisite statement of architecture's tribute to love. Tragically, however, I recall while standing in the courtyard and continuing to survey with wonderment, in sad similarity to the Indian saga, young wife Margaret died suddenly shortly after moving in, causing Mitchell to add a Gothic church next door in her memory, before retreating broken-hearted back to Manchester.

"Boy...what a blow," I whisper, shaking my head ruefully, then shifting my eyes to one of the Twelve Bens standing guard in the far recesses of the Abbey's backyard. "Hey, are you Benbaun, Bencullagh, or Benbrack?" I quip, momentarily diverting my gaze to the rounded peak some two thousand feet high, before slowly letting it drop back down to readdress the Abbey. Well, at least now you're home to a highly respected all-girls prep school run by St. Benedictine nuns, offers consolation. Margaret would like that, don't ya think? adds hope as I stroll away toward the Abbey's café in search of a snack. Even though it's two o'clock, my appetite remains hidden, apparently overwhelmed by the day's discoveries. However, in that hunger bears no real relationship to my insatiable desire for sugar, I purchase a cookie to keep my coffee company, and after exchanging pleasantries with two lovely ladies from Italy, seat myself beneath a tree in the side yard to further view the lake. An innocent act. And certainly without criminal character. Unless, of course, the prosecutor is the Professor, under a full head of matchmaker's steam. "Well, I'm sure glad to see we're maintaining our addiction to junk food," needles his greeting.

"Hey, listen pal, I'm not really hungry, so knock it off," saunters back my aggressive defense.

"Why?...'Cause you struck out again, with the two luscious Italian babes?..."

"What?...Have you lost it completely? I mean, they don't speak English, *prego* summarizes my Italian, and you expect me to hook-up?"

"Uh-huh. If you can't pull off a dinner date in this romantic setting, then strike three, you're out! Hell, you don't need words, you've got the Garden of Eden on your side!"

Well, I'll give'm that, I muse, wandering back to the bus after he finally calmed down and we shared the second half of my cookie. Kylemore is as good as it gets, all right, an absolute heaven for nature lovers and honeymooners alike. And speaking of otherworldly vistas, still more awaits us. So – What? you say. Impossible?...Well, not for Connemara. For as the bus journeys farther west, the Atlantic now joins our tour, bringing with it a craggy coastline featuring countless chiseled inlets and bays, along with charming villages named Letterfrack and Sky Road, Roundstone and Screeb – tiny hamlets whose citizens fish for salmon, trap lobsters, and fashion musical instruments and furniture. In the grassy meadows on the inland side of N-59 graze the famed black and white Connemara Ponies, renowned for their intelligence, gentleness, and agility. Legendary jumpers, the label *pony* results from an ironic sense of humor dating back centuries, as the handsome horses actually measure up to sixteen hands high, their tall, proud silhouettes adding a regal touch to the rural geography flowing past my window.

At Clifden, the largest town and "unofficial capital" of Connemara, the steady stream of small villages is interrupted. For boasting a population of two thousand, and a downtown that hosts several blocks of brightly painted multi-storied buildings, this age-old marketing hub seems in contrast like a burgeoning metropolis. Uh-huh, this is where the *action* is, all right, I conclude when the bus slows to a creep, before then resuming its prior pace, the passing miles quickly regaining their flow until we reach halfway to the village of Costello. There, firmly reentrenched in the rural countryside, we halt to visit two small farmhouses which were abandoned during the Great Famine, and which are now being restored.

A historic highlight, long anticipated, for a moment the mixed emotions of curiosity and sadness hold me in my seat, before nudging me cautiously outside into the crisp air of late afternoon. Where, for a meandering minute, my eyes slowly survey what in 1845 were working farms. Both houses, one on each side of the road, are small, maybe a thousand square feet – and stretched out behind and to both sides of each is an acre or two, divided into sections and enclosed by rock walls. "We couldn't feed ourselves, Howard," Jerry Mac had said sadly, and Nuala had written of a "permanent inferiority complex" flowing from the 1845–1847 failure of the potato crop. And as their painful words echo into ear, my feet finally move, shuffling me over to the bright red metal gate of the smaller of the two homes. Who lived here? What were your names? floats a thought as my eyes slowly sweep over the matching red paint of the front door and windowpanes, then upward to the thatched roof and the lonely-looking chimney. And did you starve to death, helpless and unhelped, 'cause no one cared, not even for the children?...Or, were you forced to flee from *your* home, in *your* country, leaving behind loved ones and carrying only your clothes and an emigration permit? Is it possible, even, that I know one of your descendants? asks irony, an eerie feeling gripping me as I stare solemnly at what was once alive and fruitful, before blight and oppression co-authored one of history's most tragic chapters. "God, am I sorry…so sorry," I murmur after several searing seconds pass, pulling out my pipe for comfort, my eyes returning to the front door. It's what's called a half door, my readings remind. 'Cause the English taxed houses based on the number of windows, so the poor Irish tenant farmers devised a door whose upper half could be opened just like a window, but without being classified as such. Yeahhh, that's where the phrase *daylight robbery* comes from, all right, so good for you, you poor ingenious souls! musters the ache inside me, my gaze once again sweeping over the deserted fields and lighting on a third house in the far distance, its roof long ago collapsed, its heart bared to the elements.

"Well, at least it's sunny today," I crack, attempting to cheer myself up as I tap out my Peterson and make ready to reboard the bus, the tightening in my tummy loosening at the thought that this melancholy yesterday was long past, coupled as it is with the flashing panorama of all the prosperous farms I'd seen on our tour. And, to add further sunshine, the day's wide-angled lens still isn't closed down either. No, not hardly. For as the bus now wends its way back toward Galway along the increasingly rocky coast, for the next hour we are treated to breathtaking views of the Atlantic, with the Aran Islands winking from the far horizon, as well as glimpses of venerable villages named Rossaveal, Inverin, and Spiddal as they slip peacefully past, the miles lengthening, then growing shorter.

And as I snuggle up against the window, casually watching as the failing light turns blue into purple, from deep inside me a newborn well of contentment slowly bubbles to the surface. Something was learned today, hums its message, a lesson I cannot fully define, yet can clearly feel. Something I first felt back on O'Connell Street in Dublin, an urban-rural rapport, now somehow holding hands with Sligo's slower pace, and Galway's renaissance mixture of tradition and innovation. Something seeping into my heart from the gentle green hills leading to Ben Bulben, and as well from the craggy crevices of Connemara. Something so instinctive, so spontaneous and subconscious that words have trouble going there, leaving intuition to speak silently of *home*, and *hope*, fostering a smile from the inside out, like the peach-purple sunset casting its glow over Galway Bay.

XIV
CITY WITH A RHYME

WHILE I'M SHAVING EARLY TUESDAY MORNING, FOR COMPANY, WILLIE Nelson's "On the Road Again" hums happily inside my head. For a few bars, I sing along out loud. Then, recalling how good Galway has been to me, I clamp shut and turn my energies to a quick shower, then breakfast.

An apt theme, nonetheless, for get-away day to Limerick City, at nine-fifteen, when Bus 51 pulls out of Ceannt Station, the ballad's yearning refrain strums back into mind, in perfect harmony with my mixed feelings of sad to leave, yet glad to see what lies ahead. And after I crane my neck for a so-long, God-bless, last look at Eyre Square, the song's title turns into the truth of Highway N-18, the reel of green fields and rolling hills resuming its technicolor spin. Just like Sligo to Galway, we're traveling south, only this time a bit inland, indicates my map, a trip of sixty miles or so. And as I settle into my seat and glimpse the sleepy little villages of Oranmore and Kilcolgan as they drift past my window, the relaxed pace of rural life experienced in Leenane and Kylemore also slides into view, tugging along a replay of a story our guide Martin had related. It seems that an American with a couple of idle hours to spend wanted a quick tour of Killarney, and hired a taxi in order to accomplish this goal. Despite his instructions, however, the driver kept stopping here and there to chat with cronies, steadily increasing his charge's frustration. "What is this, the Irish version of mañana?" the American finally cried out, shaking with impatience. "Ohhh, yeah…for sure," oozed the cabbie's reply. "Only there's much less urgency attached to it."

"Right on," I chuckle softly, nestling closer to the window as if to

131

embrace the countryside that spawns the more gentle rhythms of rural life. It's an hour and forty-five minutes to Limerick, follows an equally relaxed thought, and I'm not in a hurry either. Nope, no problem at all, I repeat when we reach Gort a half hour later, noting the nice houses with sheep and cows corralled by rock walls as the village of eleven hundred flows on by. Thirty miles farther, and we stop for passengers at Ennis, a lovely-looking town of six thousand souls that appears larger than it is. On our approach to downtown, I spy several two-story homes that instantly contrast with Gort's smaller cottages, and when we near the town's center, a large cathedral sentinels a two-block square park that would make Sligo envious. You know, I'd like to know this place better, enters a thought while I quickly stretch my legs, the idea remaining fresh with appeal as our journey resumes. Someday, I promise with a carefree smile, then flash on the face of my friend Jack whose hometown is Ennis, Montana, before settling back into my seat for the trip's final leg. And after a halcyon half hour more of lush landscape waves past my window, our trusty transport reaches our destination, pulling into Limerick City's Colbert Station right on time.

Even though the taxi ride to the Royal George Hotel takes less than five minutes, it still offers an eyeful of welcoming Georgian buildings before I'm dropped off in front of a much more modern structure. Seven stories high, with windows forming the vast majority of the facade, at first blush the Royal George appears to be a nineteen-seventyish version of a Holiday Inn. Its pale lemon face however, softens its crossword-puzzle-like physique, and after I enter Room 409, with its light-wooded interior, king-size bed, and comfy couch, I feel right at home.

Not enough to stick around however. No, not even for a further chat with Fionna, the charming and curvaceous colleen who checked me in. If she were even forty, one would be compelled to take a shot at dinner for two. But, in that she is not quite in sight of thirty-one, my date with the sights, sounds, and smells of Limerick looks wiser, though most certainly not prettier. And after stepping hastily outside, my discretion is further validated by the chimes of a nearby church, advising that it's noon and time to tour. So turning south from the hotel steps, as my feet begin to warm to their task, facts and figures from my studies at Hobman's University of Travel flow into mind. Limerick, they inform, was founded by the Vikings in A.D. 922, and today is Eire's third largest city, its seventy thousand residents outranking Galway by roughly fifteen percent. Long associated with a five-line rhyme bearing its name, no one knows for sure if the poetic form actually originated here. But without question, the City is a busy seaport and manufacturing center, as well as an important market and communications hub. Like Galway, it is also home to a university, and is relatively small, compact, and walkable, spins memory's record, my feet picking up pace, my eyes beginning their search.

O'Connell Street, yet another tribute to the Great Liberator, is downtown's main thoroughfare. And lined as it is with four-story structures fashioned from the orangish-red-to-brown brick that is the hallmark of Georgian architecture, one is instantly reminded of Dublin, albeit on a vastly smaller scale. Home to an infinite variety of shops, with offices and flats overhead, this family of buildings, which runs for four blocks on either side of the centrally located Royal George, forms a downtown that gives rise to mixed feelings upon first impression. It's not nearly as beautiful as Dublin, nor as distinctive or colorful as Galway, I conclude after strolling the southern section to Hartstonge Street. But it is clean and neat, and solid looking in a sturdy, functional way – nothing fancy, sorta blue collar. I mean, it looks like it's seen a lot of living, and is ready for more, but it also seems a wee bit tired around the edges. "Hey, what do you think, Daniel, my man?" I suddenly shoot out to the life-size bronze statue of the Great Liberator standing in the center of an oval-shaped island sculpted into the middle of his namesake street.

Known as The Crescent, this artful ellipse marks the entryway into the Georgian sector of Limerick, the City's newest neighborhood, which was built between 1760 and 1840. And in that Mr. O'Connell has declined my invitation to engage in conversation, not even commenting briefly about the classically designed Jesuit Church to his right, I slowly remove my eyes from its orange-brick facade, complete with an intricately carved pediment, and move on to explore Newtown Pery, as the locals call the Georgian quarter. Turning left on Barrington Street, just past the block-long Crescent, I discover a row of lovely looking townhouses, one of which hosts a bright-red front door, and an equally colorful garden one floor beneath street level. Still smiling from the surprise encounter with nature when I reach St. Michael's Church at the end of the block, my grin widens further upon finding yet another row of two-story brick beauties, each with richly hued front doors reminiscent of Merrion Square's rainbow. Having been converted to offices for doctors and solicitors, they form the western edge of Pery Square, with St. Michael's stone frame serving as the northern boundary, and People's Park adding a generous belt of greenery along the eastern side. And *generous* is the appropriate adjective too. For some two blocks square in size, this commons truly honors Limerick's citizenry with tree-shaded pathways, benches beside the numerous flower beds, a Victorian-style drinking fountain, and a graceful, fifty-foot stone monument crowned by a carved figure, presumably Edward Sexton-Pery, the local gentleman who inherited a large estate in the mid-eighteenth century, and worked ceaselessly to beautify Limerick through developing its Georgian district.

"Good job, Eddie, old boy!" airs my admiration as I leave the park and continue ambling southward down Pery Street. Then, just before I reach its intersection with Davis, I'm stopped by the attractive Romanesque-styled building which is home to the Limerick City Gallery of Art. Noting that one enters through a Celtic-patterned door with a stained-glass fanlight incorporating the City's Coat of Arms, and recalling that the gallery houses a permanent collection of eighteenth-, nineteenth-, and twentieth-century Irish art, including works by my old friend Jack Yeats, I'm sorely tempted to treat myself to a browsing session. But ever mindful that there is an entire city to explore, I shake my head at hard choices and move on to visit the Tait Clock, fifty yards further south. It doesn't disappoint. For seated atop a Gothic octagonal tower some fifty feet tall, the decoratively styled four-faced clock, crowned by a steeple, is strikingly beautiful. And like a cherry topping a hot fudge sundae, it fits perfectly into Newtown Pery's Georgian scheme, I muse, then chuckle when it chimes to announce one o'clock. "Oh, so you're the nebby-nosed curmudgeon who consecrated bypassing Fabulous Fionna," gurgles my realization. "Well, no problem, 'cause you're kinda fabulous yourself. And I know, no need to harp. Gotta keep moving along, 'cause there's lots more to see and time's a ticking…."

It's true. So after saluting so long, once again I pick up the pace as I pass Our Lady of Limerick Dominican Church and head down Glentworth Street on my return to O'Connell. For history lies ahead, I remind myself: Limerick's medieval quarter, filled with ancient buildings and cobblestone streets that tell the tale of a bygone era to which I am so strongly attached. To reach it, I turn right when I reach O'Connell, then traipse northward. Nodding hello to the Royal George when I pass it four blocks later, two surprises await me. First, is the Arthur Quay's Shopping Centre, and it slows me to a stop just after O'Connell has merged into Patrick Street. Fronting a pie-shaped parcel of land for the better part of a hundred yards, it is a magnificent, multi-storied, enclosed shopping complex with over thirty different shops and restaurants. Constructed of red brick, with a pyramid roof and arched entryways, its today-meets-yesterday architecture argues most persuasively that great care was exercised to ensure that the Centre blended in homogeneously with the Georgian flavor of the surrounding neighborhood. And, boy, did they ever pull it off! bounces an enthusiastic brainwave as my eyes sweep across the sizable structure's soft lines, then criss-cross back and forth between the facade with its flanking towers and the harmonious features of its neighbors. A class act. Totally! I confirm, only to be further impressed after entering inside, then exiting off the mall into a park that serves as a backyard. For where most shopping centers would have a parking lot, here one finds a full-fledged commons of several acres, complete with flowers, trees, and a large, centrally located paved space for bands and outdoor festivals, all overlooking the River Shannon. "Well, talk about the Devil converting to Christianity!" cackles my astonishment. "What's next, an Irish King of England?..." Well, maybe, I consider, still chuckling as I amble over to the river's edge, then gaze across to the Thomond Bridge and St. John's Castle. That's where I'm going, that's the medieval quarter, follows a thought slowly, the keenness of my desire to see it, to touch it, momentarily dulled by the silvery beauty of the Shannon and the gentle green hills forming the far horizon.

Maybe, not so blue collar after all, huh? buzzes a question, when ten minutes later I return to Patrick Street and resume my trek northward. Yeah, you got that right, mister, trickles my answer as Patrick Street merges into Rutland, and surprise number two jumps out to offer additional evidence. For standing proudly inside Limerick's former Custom House, a handsome eighteenth-century Palladium-style edifice, is the Hunt Museum, the City's cultural centerpiece. Aware from my reading that it contains a world-class collection of historic and archaeological artifacts, as well as three thousand art objects, including paintings by Picasso and Leonardo Da Vinci, once again the temptation to browse is strongly aroused. A glance at my watch, however, reveals that it's already two-thirty, thereby resurrecting the merciless Doctrine of Hard Choices and moving my feet forward.

Still contemplating the unfairness of Father Time's refusal to expand per my greedy aspirations when I reach the end of Rutland Street, a smile slowly emerges over my frown as I cross Matthew Bridge onto Nicholas Street, my sons' sweet faces suddenly joining me to grin at the coincidence attending my entry into Limerick's medieval precinct. Known as King's Island, it was here that the Vikings landed in A.D. 922 to found Limerick. And it is here, I tell myself as my feet round the curve of Nicholas Street in the heart of the *Old City*, that two centuries later Donal Mor O'Brien, the King of Munster, built his palace. Uh-huh...then later he donated the site for use as a church, and...and..."there she is," finishes my follow-up thought out loud as the Cathedral Church of St. Mary The Virgin erupts into view, the massive stone edifice stopping me in my tracks and muting my tongue.

Only momentarily though, a soft "Wow" soon escaping as I drift across the street to gain distance for a broader view. Primarily Romanesque in architectural style, but with distinct Gothic features added, St. Mary's limestone frame muscles out some two hundred feet in width, and hosts a one-hundred-twenty-foot tower on its northern flank. And seated behind a wrought-iron fence, encircled by lawn and trees, the predominant plainness combines with its great size to instantly create an aura of subdued importance. Beautiful is not the first adjective to enter into mind. Instead, *ancient* and *venerable* flow forth, with *impressive* following close behind. All true, very true, I reflect as I enter the grounds through a stone archway, then wander around the western boundary to the cemetery in back. For completed in 1194, St. Mary's is eight hundred and seven years old, and after serving so well for so long is time-honored indeed. Yeahhh, that's impressive, all right, and you're important for sure, I muse, seating myself on a low stone wall and turning my gaze to a grave planted with a rosebush. Now, how special is that, murmurs an innocent observation in the relaxing sunshine. The plant doesn't die like cut flowers, but instead re-blooms to celebrate life!

An idea that wears a wide smile, its cheer is still mapped across my face minutes later when I approach St. Mary's sandstone-arched entryway, the huge oak door, believed to have been part of O'Brien's palace, standing open. Just inside, there's a small table attended by a woman. And so pleased am I to discern that her pretty face belongs to one over the age of thirty-five, that my "Hello" is even warmer than usual. "Ohhh, you're so welcome here," she returns, rising to shake my hand. "But have you heard your country's been attacked?..."

Nodding a disbelieving no, the quickly supplied details of three hijacked airliners striking the World Trade Center and the Pentagon slowly sink in as I step further inside and slump down onto a wooden pew facing the altar. And what did I feel? Alone, six thousand miles from home?...Nothing. Absolutely nothing, so severe was the shock, so numbing Novocaine's needle. I just sat there like a lump that was strangely absent from my throat, the thought, Could this possibly be real? circling my brain like a slow-motion merry-go-round.

It stops, only when a sisterly concept carves into consciousness. Maybe you can't *feel* it, 'cause it happened so far away? the interloper poses, a curious question I then share with Gloria, who has left her entryway post to offer comfort. Well, look around, our conversation concludes, there's pain everywhere. In Northern Ireland, Kashmir, and Somalia. In North Korea, Colombia, and Palestine. Guns fire, bombs explode, and hunger and disease devastate millions. But all at great distance, because it's not happening to *you* or even *nearby*. And even when we do stop still in our tracks, the pain is so collectively great, and we are so individually small and helpless that What to do? appears as far away as the tragedies themselves, lost inside the steady stream of overwhelm.

Still, despite the differences that divide us, the overriding truth is that we are all in this world together, just as Gloria confirms with her soothing, "You are not alone. What happened to America today, happened to us Irish too." A heartfelt human-to-human touching, its warmth kindles a thawing of shock's outer shell, freeing a faint urge to pray – a small stirring, which soon swims upstream to find both purpose and passion. Knowing loss from cancer's theft of Patty, I pray for those who died and for their families and friends. I pray for my country and that we will not overreact and add countless other innocents to the terrible toll. I pray for understanding and forgiveness, for peace and for love. And, I pray loudest of all for those who suffer far away and lost from view.

Then, suddenly, I chuckle softly into the silence. Catching sight of myself – an American, davening in Hebrew inside a Protestant cathedral, in a predominantly Catholic country – humor strikes, leaking "This oughta work, big time!" while crafting a consoling smile as *lonely* slowly begins uncoupling from *alone*. Sharing with Gloria that Lincoln once said, "I laugh to keep from crying," the grave threads of anxiety which have gathered into a knot loosen further to allow a chat about St. Mary's. Gloria, whose knowledge is extensive, points out that the pre-Reformation altar we are facing is made of stone, and that, at thirteen feet long with a weight of three tons, it is the largest in all of Ireland, and Great Britain to boot. The exquisite stained-glass windows behind it are also original, and most interestingly, the set of twenty-three misericords, medieval carved seats situated only a few feet away, are the only examples of their kind preserved in Eire. Pleased to be focusing on aesthetic treasures instead of the day's tragic events, I reach out my hand to finger one of the interior pillars. Also composed of stone, and six feet thick, it both looks and *feels* old. In fact, as my eyes wander from the altar to the ceiling, then back to the pillar, the overwhelming feeling is one of great age. And when I mention this to Gloria, she confirms that here, inside St. Mary's, one can somehow *feel* the Middle Ages. "More so than in St. Patrick's or even Christ Church," she adds, before walking me back outside and saying so long with a hug.

Across Nicholas Street, I spy a red-and-white Coca-Cola sign over a small market, its homespeak drawing me like a magnet. Upon reaching it however, it is the red plaque on the plain-looking, three-story office building next door that occupies my attention. For this simply styled structure once served as the residence of the O'Brien Clan after Donal Mor had donated his palace for the construction of St. Mary's. And after patting the front door and thanking him for his generosity, I head on up Nicholas Street in search of the Old City's second medieval treasure, St. John's Castle. The sad news learned in St. Mary's still hangs heavily in a corner of my mind, but having reasoned that there was nothing I could do for anyone, logic also argued that interrupting my Irish Experience served no purpose. So, with as much cheerfulness as I can muster, I continue moseying on along Nicholas' cobblestones for two blocks, until it bends slightly leftward and an enormous round tower greets me.

Two very sweet, older ladies are in charge of the Visitors Center, and immediately recognizing my "American accent," want to waive the five-dollar entrance fee. Knowing that the funds are used to preserve the castle, I warmly express my appreciation, but decline their gift, leading to a compromise admittance as a discounted senior, even though I'm sixty-one and Ireland's seniors have to be sixty-five. And with their kindness further buoying my dampened spirits, I easily shrug off the Professor's tease of "Boy, they should only know how this 'senior' ogled Fabulous Fionna, huh, old buddy?..."

"Hey, listen pal. My age is sixty-one, not dead. And I didn't ogle, I admired," I shoot back at him, before ambling over to view a life-size exhibit of King John seated on his throne. The Anglo-Norman King who ordered the Castle's construction in A.D. 1210 in order to protect the settlement beside the River Shannon, for several steely seconds his stern countenance stares back at me, until with a wink, I take my leave and stroll outside into the courtyard. Recalling that his Highness's solid stone fortress sprawls over an acre and a half, and incorporates some unique features for its time, such as curtain walls and D-shaped as well as rounded gate towers, I am still surprised by the football-field-sized quadrangle which is cobblestoned, and the surrounding twenty-foot walls which are anchored by the considerably taller towers. Major Massive! is the indelible impression that accompanies me as I wander around the perimeter, then climb the twisty steps of a tower to enjoy unsurpassable views of the Shannon. Dropping down to a station on the battlement walls, my gaze is further directed across to Arthur Quay's Park where I had strolled just over an hour ago, one part of my mind trying to imagine the medieval soldiers who had manned this very wall, the other trying to better comprehend the painful events of today. "Funny, isn't it?" I whisper into the gentle breeze blowing off the river. "But here I am surrounded by the Middle Ages, while brand new history is happening right at the same moment. Though come to think of it," furnishes second thought, "it seems like the same old story of war, war, war. I mean, new place. Fresh bodies. But the same sad story nonetheless. And funny, too," follows after a slow sigh, my mind's eye now suddenly retreating to scan today's visits to Newtown Perry, Downtown, and King's Island, "that while the world just got smaller, somehow Limerick seems to have grown. I mean, it just seems larger to me. Larger than my mental map. Larger than it was this morning. Larger even than its sister Galway. Still compact. Still walkable. But a bit larger all the same. And why?...How come? asks a stranger surfacing from the subconscious. And moreover, what's going to happen next after the hijackings? Are we going to attack some distant fortress, just like William of Orange did, when after defeating the Irish-Catholic forces at the Battle of the Boyne, he then laid siege to this very castle in order to crush the remnants of the Irish army? Huh? What do you think?…

It takes a minute or two. But after a testy tussle, me, myself, and I finally manage to suppress the tangled mass of thoughts beleaguering my brain. And to celebrate, I linger at my post for several minutes more, simply savoring the peaceful view with a smoke, until just before five o'clock hunger puts in an appearance. Recalling that upon my approach to the Medieval Quarter, I had spied a quaint-looking restaurant named the Locke Box, just off Matthew Bridge on the banks of the Shannon, like Limerick, its appeal grows larger. And after bidding farewell to King John and his legions, I return to the white-faced eatery with the green awnings over the flower-centered tables out front. The first floor is a pub. And it is here, over a pint of Guinness, that TV brings me my first actual view of the firestorm that was once the World Trade Center. Stunned afresh, when I see men and women jumping to their deaths rather than be burned alive, for the first time anger scorches through me. A raw fury, which is subdued only by the considerable chorus of hugs and handshakes accompanying "We love America!" from the Irish, English, Dutch, German, and Croatian strangers I'm sharing the moment with, the depth of their sincere sympathy soothing the pain, allowing me even to feel proud, though tinged with guilt for having garnered such affectionate attention due to my victimized countrymen.

After the hour of unexpected comradeship subsides, I climb the stairs to the second floor and a small table on the balcony overlooking the Shannon. There, trauma's tension having been eased by the Guinness and the warmth of my well-wishers, I enjoy an absolutely delicious dinner of fresh salmon baked in breadcrumbs, accompanied by rice and beer-batter–encrusted mushrooms. Tasty?…It was a feast fit for King John himself! And momentarily freed from reality, I eat like I was King and all was well in the world.

Still relishing my meal on the stroll back to the Royal George, my Peterson flag pipe sowing rings of satisfaction in the evening breeze, my musings are of how truly excellent the Irish cuisine is in general. From the sumptuous breakfasts, to the rich roast-beef sandwich I'd shared with Strongbow at lunch, to the sweet lobster in cream sauce for dinner in

Galway, these Irish most definitely know how to cook! records reflection. And let's not forget bake, either. No, not even for a split second can one fail to pay proper tribute to the cookies, cakes, and pastries provided by Dublin's divine bakeries. And as for the Chocolate Bar created by The Gourmet Parlor, well, suffice it to say that most fortunately, genius knows no bounds! croons my admiration, rising to Mt. Everest heights as I reach Arthur Quay's Shopping Centre. And with food occupying center stage, I promptly detour inside upon spotting TESCO, a full-scale super-market along the lines of my favorite Safeway back in Portland.

Like the Coca-Cola sign earlier, the tie to home pulls back into view the day's terrible tragedy, the strange feeling of dread returning knots to my stomach, and me back outside into the park. Where, as I gaze once again across the Shannon at King John's Castle in the gathering dusk, my mind meanders back over the unanticipated sights and sounds which had erupted so sorrowfully into consciousness, this time with the added concern that my cousin Karen or dear friend Noreen might have been in Manhattan. And having gained a firm foothold, Mr. Worry immediately expands his theatre of operations. As returning to my observation in St. Mary's, that there one could actually feel the weight of the centuries past, now I wonder if the *aging* I had sensed, so strongly, was really the melting away of America's last vestiges of *innocence*? And if so, what does this mean for Matt and Nick and Amy?...

Reeling from the fresh electric charges coursing through me, when the image of learning to live with fear then surfaces, I squeeze it off by clamping my eyes shut. And when they reopen, several sighing seconds later, the music of *We love America!* sings back into ear, the steady cadence of the chorus finally loosening the iron ache of anxiety anchoring my sorrow.

"Me too," I whisper, flashing from Valley Forge to Gettysburg to the beaches of Normandy. "And somehow, we'll be okay," adds hope wish-fully as I stand still as the Statue of Liberty, watching the sun set softly over the Shannon, the hour of dry tears slowly turning bittersweet.

XV
PICTURE POSTCARD

Ten miles southwest of Limerick City lies Adare, billed by many as "the prettiest village in all of Eire." A claim to fame I'm dubiously mulling over as the local bus pulls out of Colbert Station to begin its half-hour journey, after all the beauty my eyes have been treated to, my mind's microscope quickly clouds over trying to catalogue pretty-one, pretty-two, and the numerous others. Well, I conclude after flashing on Leenane with its fabulous fjord, Adare's got a better shot than some lovely lass does of being the prettiest colleen. I mean, that contest draws a new entry every hour, and frequently more than one, bubbles my good humor as my eyes begin surveying the lush countryside flowing by my window.

With nature's show further enhancing my cheery mood, after a minute or two, I pull from my backpack the box of mini-wheats I'd purchased at TESCO last evening, and while munching several, simply savor their sugary tops along with the sea of soft greenery, an inner smile widening as I recall my kidlets' concerns for me when I had finally reached them late last night. I couldn't be amongst better friends, I'd assured them, opining that only technically was Ireland a foreign country, and undoubtedly last on Al Qaeda's hit list. And when just a short time later, Bus Eireann rounds a bend in the country road we've been coasting along and crosses a tiny bridge into Adare, a matching grin jumps across my face as Pretty!...Pretty!...Pretty! sounds inside my head like a symphony of welcoming wind chimes. For even under the blanketing gray skies, *pretty* easily hops over slow and sleepy to dominate the wordscape of adjectives. As set amidst a flourishing array of trees and flowering shrubs, right alongside the River Maigue, is an exquisite village lined with ornate thatched cottages, colorful walled gardens, distinctive Tudor-style stone buildings, and the ruins of historic abbeys.

"It may not be THE prettiest, but nothing could be prettier," I enthuse after exiting the bus, my eyes quickly filling to overflow. "As in, wow, and then some!" streams affirmation, my feet beginning to move northward on Main Street. Aptly named, as Adare's sole thoroughfare, the wide, flower-rimmed road is lined with an equally wide variety of commercial shops, art and antique stores, restaurants, pubs, and hotels. Housed mainly in single-story stone structures featuring mixed brick and stucco facades, with most sporting well-stocked flower boxes beneath the windows, to say that the picture parading before one's eyes is quaint is like concluding that the North Pole gets a mite chilly in Winter. *Quaint* is for openers. Add *adorable, picturesque,* and *kidnapped straight out of a fairy tale,* and words finally begin to warm to the task of description. And most striking of all, the step-back-in-time aura emanating from yesteryear's authentic architecture is so naturally accentuated by the simple, slow-paced lifestyle of the residents, that there's hardly a trace of the twenty-first century marring the village's "Old World" image. "Call it Heaven's Hamlet, and that'll do," I muster in an attempt to synthesize the cheerful scene surrounding me. But, with a sizable serving of medieval history too, which also provides a serious side, follows my next thought as I stop before the Augustinian Priory, having reached the north end of the village in less than ten minutes.

Founded in 1316 by the Fitzgeralds, and known locally for centuries as the "Black Abbey" due to the dark robes worn by its monks, the Priory is constructed of limestone, and features a fifteenth-century tower that houses a cloister at ground level, while rising up through the slanted roof to an outside height of a hundred feet. Contrasting the austere appearance of its large frame, the interior showcases intricate stained-glass windows behind the altar, a graceful sedilia – a carved triple seat – located to its left, and a sizable pipe organ off to the right. Recalling that the Black Abbey was suppressed by the forces of King Henry VIII in the mid-sixteenth century, and thereafter fell into disrepair, as I stroll from the main sanctuary into the buildings attached to the Abbey's right flank, memory reminds also that it was restored in 1807 and converted to its present use as a Protestant place of worship and school.

Minutes later, when I return outside, a light drizzle begins falling. And through the fine mist, the stern face of the Abbey seems to soften, looking snug and cozy inside its shawl of seven wooly centuries. Saying so long with a smile, I then wend my way fifty yards farther north to the banks of the River Maigue. Where, after focusing for several seconds on its smooth and silky flow, I shift my gaze across its fifty-foot width to the ruins of Adare Castle spread out along the far bank for a couple of hundred feet. Known also as Desmond Castle, history further tells us that it was built in 1227 by the Normans, then dismantled four centuries later by Cromwellian forces in 1657. Most unfortunately, unlike the Black Abbey, which is still fulfilling its purpose, this remnant of the Middle Ages looks sad and serves only as a reminder of the destructive force of war, causing me to flash once again on the collapsed towers of the World Trade Center. Will we *ever* learn, I muse as my eyes wander further upstream to settle on a second set of ruins. Also medieval, having been dedicated as the Franciscan Friary in 1464, then burned in 1646 by Parliamentary forces, only its one-hundred-foot tower is fully intact, staring forlornly back at me from its ancient perch amidst a host of trees and looking very alone and lonely.

In stark contrast to yesteryear's ruins, however, several hundred yards to their left stands the Adare Manor, once the residence of the Earls of Dunraven and the centerpiece of their eight-hundred-forty-acre estate. And after ambling up the long driveway, puffing on my pipe against the dampness, I enter the finely manicured grounds and am stunned to a stop by its sheer size and magnificence. Now the home of a five-star hotel and golf club, this Tudor-Gothic mansion was built from 1832 to 1862, most fortuitously providing work for Adare's villagers during the Great Famine, and thereby shaping Adare into an "estate" village in the process. Composed of stone and brick, the Manor is host to a bevy of unique features, beginning with a turreted entrance tower, then following with fifty-two chimneys to commemorate each week of the year, seventy-five fireplaces, and three hundred sixty-five leaded glass windows. Not to forget for an architectural second, the elaborate decorative stonework in the form of arches, gargoyles, and bay windows and frames. An eyeful?…"Holy cockamolies, yes! And no wonder it took thirty years to complete!" whooshes awe's emotion as I stand and stare, then move to a different vantage point to gaze for several minutes more.

On my return to town, amazement tags along. Can you imagine trying to keep it clean? I muse, reflecting on my housekeeping chores at my "slum" back in Portland. Why you'd need an army of help just to dust, runs my reasoning as the Dunraven Arms Hotel slides into view. A much more humble hostelry, founded in 1793, its pale yellow facade, wearing a full beard of ivy, has been generating a warm welcome to visitors for over two hundred years. And across the street, inside a row of red-brick cottages with thatched roofs, each with a separate yard and walkway, sits a collection of the cutest shops imaginable. So absolutely adorable, that even casual shopper Hob is drawn inside The Gift Box, where a totally fun conversation with the proprietor, Liza, leads to the purchase of the perfect birthday-greeting postcard for my sister Frenda, who is celebrating fifty-eight this very day. Still smiling when I emerge a half hour later, the warm feeling fueling my satisfaction lasts the entire three-block walk to the Trinitarian Priory.

Incorporating the nave, chancel, and north transept from the original monastery built in 1230, and officially named the Holy Trinity Church, this house of prayer emulates its northern brother by being locally nicknamed the "White Abbey" in response to the contrasting white habits worn by its founding monks. And as I stand before its sizable stone walls and tower, noting the manicured lawn and flower beds which surround it, memory also reminds that its originators, whose work was the ransoming and liberation of Christian captives during the Crusades, were the only order of its type in all of Eire. As was the case with the Black Abbey, this monastery too was suppressed in 1539 during the reign of King Henry VIII and fell into disrepair. But restored in 1811 by the second Earl of Dunraven, and then given to Adare's Catholics as their parish church, in further emulation of its younger brother, it too is still proudly serving this function. "In fact, quite beautifully," I murmur, gently patting the almost eight-hundred-year-old walls before ambling across the street and southward a short distance to the Adare Town Park.

A lovely square block of lawn harboring numerous trees and flower beds, for a lazy minute I stand and stare up a stone pathway leading through a treed archway to a wishing pool a hundred and fifty feet to my front. Then, after adding my hope that everyone could claim the peace offered by Adare, I turn slowly away and head back across the street to the Heritage Center.

Built in 1994, but brilliantly designed to blend into Adare's ambience as if it had been constructed by the monks responsible for the village's architectural centerpieces, this stone structure, with its bright red window panes, welcomes one with a capital W to its historical exhibition, as well as its crafts shop and restaurant. Having already visited the Middle Ages in three separate locations, and ogled the handiwork of the Earls of Dunraven in abject wonderment, I pass on the exhibition, and instead wander inside the Black Abbey Crafts Shop and into unexpected quandary. For immediately upon entry, I spy an oversized green coffee cup embellished with a hand-painted cow that not only is the perfect addition to my daughter's collection of cow mugs, but also raises the critical question: Is it one step short of insanity to pay roughly twice the amount of the gift to ship it?…The evidence for the prosecution springs forth instantly, in the form of the look on the saleslady's kind face, reading, He's nuts, but doesn't appear dangerous, followed closely by the Professor's officiously intoned, "Never mind reasonable doubt, lunacy fans, this silly person has flipped his cookies beyond ALL doubt!" Fortunately for the defense however, besieged as it is, love conquers all with its awe-inspiring argument that life is short, and the supply of unique cow mugs even shorter. And with the teasing threat of a straitjacket now successfully defused, I further celebrate by adjourning to the Dovecot Restaurant to reflect on love's triumph and Adare's many charms.

Three hours have passed. Three sumptuous hours, whose menu offered a doll-house village filled with commerce and art housed in every shade of quaint, along with history, from the nineteenth-century Earls all the way back to the Middle Ages. Months ago, reading in bed late at night, I'd come across an observation, "that the best part of the fun, was simply 'being' in Adare." And now, seated at a tiny table with a warm sweet roll and steaming-hot coffee, looking out on yesteryear's relaxed pace of life, still alive and breathing slow and soothing, I agree with my whole heart. It's a picture postcard, all right, crawls my contemplation to conclusion. In fact, for this wonderfully peaceful and happy moment, picture-postcard perfect!

XVI
MOONSCAPE, CAVE, & CLIFFS

I<small>N</small> W<small>EDNESDAY'S</small> *E<small>VENING</small> E<small>CHO</small>*, L<small>IMERICK'S</small> <small>NIGHTLY NEWSPAPER, SEV-</small>eral sympathetic columns appeared in strong support of America after Tuesday's titanic tragedy. And while waiting for the Barrat Tour Bus the following morning, my relief at the enormous number of countries rallying round escapes through a wide smile as I scrutinize the details from my perch just outside the Royal George. After finishing my read, then tucking the paper inside my backpack, I gaze out lazily upon O'Connell Street and its nine o'clock bustle, my pipe tasting as sweet as the sugar in my breakfast coffee. It is a moment of layered satisfaction: the recovery is under way in New York, snapshots of all I've been so lucky to see in such a short but fulfilling time flicker into mind, and the day ahead promises yet more. Call it a quiet moment, filled with gratitude and undefined hope. A moment that whispers softly: Just relax, and enjoy the people parade.

I do. But only for a handful of minutes. For at five after the hour, the horn from the tour bus beeps me from my reverie and beckons me toward new adventure – a day of discovery, in fact, that begins almost immediately. As after climbing aboard to the cheery welcome of "Glad to have ya," I've no more than settled into my window seat, when I spy "HARTICIANS HORSE REPOSITORY" carved into a massive stone archway leading to an alley between two buildings. And smiling at the proud relic of a bygone era as our bus heads out of the City, my grin soon grows full upon sighting both a mini-market and shoe repair shop, each bearing the name, FRANKLIN'S, in big bold letters on their signage. Well, that's certainly a good omen, I hum to myself as the bus now crosses over the Sarsfield Bridge and heads north on Ennis Road. I mean, you see? aims my next thought upon sighting the Professor out of the corner of my eye, I told you I was Irish. Then, smugly content, I settle back in my seat and snuggle closer to the window.

The journey to The Burren, Ireland's Rock Desert, requires roughly ninety minutes, and begins by taking us past a row of highly impressive three-story, red-brick Georgian homes on large lots, before Limerick is left behind, and we travel next to Bunratty Village, with its restored thirteenth-century castle and Dirty Natty's Pub, which dates back to 1650. Then, as the lush green countryside once again appears to flow by my window, we retrace Tuesday's steps back through the towns of New-market-on-Fergus and Ennis along Highway N-18, before turning west a degree or two. Fittingly, an Irish folk song, "On the Road to Galway," is strumming over the sound system when we enter County Clare, and as the bus approaches the village of Corofin, Christy, our guide, and the wife of driver Richard, begins filling us in on what we are about to see.

Geographically covering a one-hundred-square-mile area, she informs, *The Burren* is covered with a barren, lunar-like landscape that began millions of years ago when layers of shells and sediments were deposited under a tropical sea, only to be thrust above the surface years later and left exposed to the erosive power of Irish rain, wind, and sun, thereby producing the limestone landscape that appears today. However, Christy keynotes, while we will be viewing only one of the rockier sections, there are other areas that contain pocket lakes and streams set amid hills, tur-loughs, valleys, and mountains, which in turn host an amazing variety of wildlife and greenery. Okay…rocky place, I get it, lazes a thought as the bus snakes past Corofin along a corkscrew road, then stops as suddenly as the landscape changes.

Now, maybe, it's because flourishing greenery envelops most of Eire, and this morning's travels had thus far served only to polish this image to a fine shine. Or maybe it's because I've visited the Connemara, and think I understand what open, empty, and craggy topography is all about. Or maybe even it's because the sun has ducked behind the hovering blanket of dark gray clouds, casting an eerie light over the current setting. But nothing, not my readings, not photographs I've studied, nor Christy's commentary, even remotely prepared me for what my eyes were now trying to comprehend, I mean, my "I get it" couldn't possibly have been more wrong. SURPRISE, Hobman. And Big Time! As stretched out before me for miles, are massive sheets of rock, jagged boulders, and pot-holes, with dolmens, wedge tombs, and hundreds of stone forts known as cahers interwoven throughout. Why, it's as if somehow, without warning, one has been kidnapped and rocketed to the moon! blasts a brainwave as I stand transfixed in place, my eyes wandering in amazement in all directions.

One of the most famous of the prehistoric burial tombs, a portal dolmen named *Poulnabrone* is located about fifty yards away. And after the initial shock of awe has diminished sufficiently for my feet to work again, I slowly but surely begin making my way towards it, stepping ever so carefully from one sheet of limestone to another, until finally, I reach the prize. Then, while I'm triumphantly inspecting the two huge stones that support the slab canopy, my mind's eye trying to picture the hunter-gatherers who managed to build it over four thousand years ago, rain begins falling. Notice, please, I did not say drizzle, I said rain. For a full-fledged downpour it is, the heavy heavens relieving themselves as if a thousand angels had drunk too much Guinness in too short a time. "In fact, way too much, and way too short!" I chuckle out into the wind which has also entered the scene, quickly pulling the hood attached to my coat over my head. Then, after muttering a hasty, "Peace be with you," to the ancient occupant, while wondering if my close proximity might have angered a primeval Rain God, or two or three, I begin the painstaking process of returning to the bus.

Now, if getting there was tricky, getting back is a true test of gym-nastic ability. And if you'll kindly consider that my idea of gymnastic endeavor is limited exclusively to trying to move my feet into the proper position to hit a tennis ball, with the clear understanding that tennis courts are both flat and dry, then you can better appreciate the degree of difficulty facing me in attempting to traverse stones that were not only slippery, but in some cases, sloped. Suffice it to say that to the casual observer, it now appeared as if I was the one who had consumed too much Guinness, and that thereafter, it was a true miracle that I arrived back at the bus without any broken bones, and without drowning.

Most fortunately, this good fortune proves to be the case. And when the hobbling Hobman and three other foolhardy explorers finally reach solid soil, our fellow tourmates treat us to a warm welcome of applause.

Having themselves chosen to view the Poulnabrone from the safe distance of just outside the bus, thereby easily securing shelter when the replay of Noah and the Great Flood occurred, their enthusiasm is both spontaneous and steady, as one by one the soaked sojourners straggle in, with special cheers reserved for a fellow American from Chicago who wasn't wearing a coat, and whose appearance now resembles that of a drowned rat. In fact, so total is Jim's state of disarray that it manages to dwarf my own Comic Ballet on Limestone, allowing a sheepish smile to slide across my face as Driver Rich slips the bus into gear. Somewhere, I'd read that The Burren is also home to thirty-three species of butterflies. Well, make that thirty-four, teases a thought, my grin widening further at the instant replay of Hobman's Jitterbug Juke amongst the dolmens, the bus gaining speed as the running reel also recounts my surprise at having discovered small purple flowers growing in crevices between the omnipresent rocks.

Thirty minutes later, and twenty miles further north, Richard guides our trusty transport into the parking lot near the entrance to the *Aillwee Cave*. One of Ireland's oldest underground sites, with an age of one and a half million years plus, the Aillwee contains almost a mile of passages and hollows that burrow straight into the heart of its harboring mountain, reaching in some places combined depths and heights of up to three hundred-fifty feet. And trailing single file after Christy through its gaping mouth, then along the narrow, dimly lit passageway, over the next half hour we are treated to the stunning sites of subterranean rivers, bridged chasms, and deep caverns, along with a frozen waterfall, and a varied assortment of stalactites and stalagmites. Some of the latter have been given names such as "The Praying Hands" or "Bunch of Carrots" in order to highlight their intricately water-carved shapes, and the frozen waterfall looks like a Jack Yeats watercolor, pressed as it is against the face of a rock wall that glows gold to pale orange. Moreover, nature has painted even larger murals on neighboring surfaces, striating multiple shades of white, brown, gray, and gold into lumpy figures and impressions that cater openly to a free-flowing imagination. Think Picasso. Or Salvador Dali. Or even Rorschach, in technicolor!

Next up are several hollowed pits where the bones of bears, horses, pigs, and badgers have been unearthed, revealing that the cave has provided shelter to both man and animals over the centuries. A somewhat spooky discovery, when viewed through the gloomy shadows cast by the flickering light, the creepy effect is further bolstered by the lady behind me, who keeps bumping into me each time the group halts to inspect a different display. And to make matters worse, after the fourth bump, which includes the clipping of my right heel, the Professor, who had somehow managed to restrain himself during my slip-and-slide routine in the Burren, now chooses to make light of the darkening situation. "Hey," he chuckles after her southern-accented apology echoes away. "Getting kinda chummy with the Louisiana Lovely, aren't we?..."

"Wwwwhat?" I stammer back incredulously, recalling the considerably overweight condition of my clumsy companion.

"Uh-huh. Looks to me like you've finally found a friend who wants to get close to you," seeps his sarcasm.

"Oh, yeah?...Well the only thing that's close to you, old buddy, is senility. Or have the bats simply grabbed your brain?..."

"Bats?...I don't see any bats," he returns quickly, sudden concern swiveling his eyes about.

"Well, that's because you're so old, your eyes don't work either!" I jab triumphantly, my thin grin growing upon the appearance of daylight as the trail ends and we emerge from our adventure.

And how do you spell relief? borrows my next brainwave from an old ad as we reboard the bus. Daylight! Daylight! Daylight! echoes rescue's refrain. Then, in further celebration of my escape from the Baton Rouge Bumper, the bus now proceeds past the village of Ballyvaughn and along the southern shore of Galway Bay, treating me to a panoramic view that stretches out over the blue-green water to the Connemara, where I had toured just three days earlier. The sun has reappeared, shining brightly on the lapping whitecaps, and in the far distance I can make out my old friends, the Maamturk Mountains, rising gently behind the sandy beaches fronting Spiddal. An absolutely glorious scene, for five full minutes I simply savor it, until gradually the remote fishing village of Doolin floats into sight.

Time doesn't permit a visit to this famed haunt of traditional Irish musicians, but the sweet tune fiddling forth from the overhead speakers in their honor most certainly adds a dash of spice to my soaring mood. In fact, having experienced the barren beauty of the Burren, and nature's equally unusual and fascinating artwork inside the Aillwee Cave, as I sit comfortably gazing out the window at the miles of sparkling sea and multi-shaded greenery flowing by on opposite sides of the road, my cup feels full indeed, and I would have been perfectly satisfied to simply relax and follow the fabulous vista all the way back to Limerick. Our guide, however, adhering to both the biblical truism that it's okay for cups to runneth over, and the more modern axiom that good things come in threes, has a grander idea, and steers a steady course to a vantage point several minutes south of Doolin. Where, along a five-mile stretch of open and windswept coastline, the Cliffs of Moher rise majestically out of the Atlantic to a peak of six hundred-sixty-eight feet, little bays lolling lazily at their feet.

And is *majestic* a wise word to meet the considerable challenge of communication?…Well, at the risk of once again threatening the record for understatement: For sure, and then some! As having jutted nobly out of the silvery sea to a height that's truly regal, then capped themselves with a crown of kelly-green moss, these giants sit on their limestone thrones like kings ruling a realm of beauty that is beyond enormous. And struck dumb, I simply stand and stare in abject awe, looking, and looking, and looking some more, until one minute piggybacks upon another to reach thirty, and the weight of wonderment threatens to burst my eyeballs.

It doesn't, of course. No black magic here. Only nature's. And after taking a brief hiatus to buy a hot coffee at the nearby Visitors' Center, I return to my perch to watch their Highnesses for a second half-hour, this time seating myself, the wind whipping away the smoke from my companioning Peterson, the charmed minutes ticking slowly by. "Lord…You sure were in a good mood when you made Ireland," I whisper, nodding at the handiwork holding my eyes hostage, the wind now dying down as the sun tilts toward early evening, me, totally at home, wanting to just sit and watch forever.

XVII

CAMELOT

I DON'T KNOW WHERE WILLIE IS, BUT EARLY FRIDAY MORNING I'M ON the road again. No music. Just a pleasant conversation with Calum the Cabbie during the short ride to Colbert Station. And after exchanging "All the best!" farewells, I'm left with just enough time for a second cup of coffee, savored with rambling reflections about Limerick, before Bus Eireann pulls out of stall number three, and once again we're traveling south, this time toward the town of Killarney.

The pictures that begin flashing back into mind from my long-ago midnight studies highlight a tiny town with Adare-like charm, seated in County Kerry, whose inhabitants refer to it as "The Kingdom" in succinct tribute to the area's legendary catalogue of glistening lakes, cascading waterfalls, majestic mountains, and lush foliage. And as I settle into my window seat, with my excitement level gently rising, in like fashion to my travels from Sligo to Galway to Limerick, nature's signature Green Parade begins as if on cue, and flows by seemingly without end. There are brief interruptions of course, as we pass through a string of quaint villages along our route. At Rathkeale, the narrowness of the streets draws attention, and at Newcastle West, a church steeple poking its nose up through the damp drizzle contrasts the coziness wrapped around me like a warm blanket. In turn, Listowel presents a pang of disappointment, at not being able to disembark and go in search of John Keane, then share in his winsome wit with cronies at the local pub. And at Tralee, our driver halts the bus for three minutes of silence as part of Eire's National Day of Mourning for the victims of 9-11. Still, nonetheless, for the vast majority of our three-hour journey, Mother Nature's magic show dominates the field of vision, carefully caressing our collective consciousness through each bend in the road, and delivering us safely and serenely to Killarney's doorstep.

Drowsing in a rear compartment of my mind, the town's claim of being Eire's Camelot slowly stirs awake when just before noon I touch terra firma in front of the small but extremely cute bus depot. Well, there's exhibit number one, I observe, winking back at the recently constructed but old-fashioned-looking stone facade, before going in search of my hotel. And when to my surprise, I bump into the McSweeney Arms, just a quarter-of-a-block later, the proof gains momentum, big time. For three stories high, and painted bright red with a white trim, each window in its two rows of eight bedecked with hanging flower baskets, the McSweeney smiles out over the sidewalk like a rosy ruby in a castle's coat of arms, saying sweetly: Welcome to Special!

Outside, near the entrance, a pretty young lady is changing the menu in the glass box affixed to the fascia, and turns toward me as I approach. "Mr. Franklin?..." she queries, bright blue eyes sparkling.

"Uh-huh. How'd you guess?" squeezes my answer through a growing grin.

"Oh, we were expecting you. But wondering too, if you'd come, or maybe go home 'cause of the trouble."

"Nooo...They don't need me. And besides," I tease, meeting her steady gaze. "I kinda feel I am home, here in your wonderful country. Don't I look a little Irish to ya?..."

"Oh, for sure you do, especially with your pipe," she chuckles without missing a beat. "And we're very glad to have ya. My name's Linda. And if you'll follow me inside to register, I'll show you to your room."

The lobby is small, but comfortably furnished with two large black couches and matching chairs, seated to the front of a fireplace. And Room 108, following suit, is equally small and homey, with its pale gold wallpaper, and the patchwork-quilt bedspread fronting the queen-size bed's wood-slatted headboard. Like home, indeed, I muse, glancing at myself in the full-length mirror on the wall near the window, before heading back downstairs for lunch. Unlike the lobby, the adjacent LaScala Café is good-sized and paneled in rich dark woods, with an island bar, sporting a shiny brass railing, in its center. Having skipped breakfast due to my early departure from Limerick, my appetite is standing at attention and saluting, a powerful plea that the hotel's chef promptly rewards with an absolutely fabulous feast of chicken with rice and mushrooms in a cream sauce, accompanied by salad and fresh-baked bread. The portions are so generous as to leave no room for dessert, even for a full-fledged sugar-holic. So, after reserving one of the luscious-looking chocolate tarts for my return, and with my after-lunch smoke in full billow, I set out to explore Killarney with renewed energy and ever rising expectations.

First up is the Franciscan Friary, only a quarter-block east of the hotel. A large structure, seated on immaculately manicured grounds behind a four-foot iron-spiked fence, its classical lines combine with the light-hued limestone to cast an aura of warmth and welcome. Dating only to 1860, and designed by Eugene Pugin, whose father designed the famous cathedral on the opposite end of town, its soft, almost sweet-looking appearance despite its size, draws a "Well done" before I mosey on across the street to meet an interesting statue.

Carved from white stone, and standing atop a two-tiered pedestal, is Speir Bean, which translates to Spirit Woman. A local landmark, with her left hand over her heart, and her gaze fixed on the far horizon, this lovely lady represents the spirit of Ireland, and also commemorates four Kerry poets of the Irish language from the seventeenth century. Smiling once again, at the marriage of Eire's spirit and the written word, this time I murmur "God bless" before moving on.

Not far, however. As standing only a short distance east of the poets' nook is the younger sister of Galway's Great Southern Hotel. And bearing the same name, while sharing also a like elegance of design, its heavily ivied facade adds further to the growing atmosphere of charm first experienced at the bus station and the McSweeney Arms, then strengthened by the Friary. In fact, once released from my bag of adjectives, *charming* becomes the watchword for all I'm about to see when I reach East Avenue, then turn right toward the center of town. For not more than fifty yards into my journey, I arrive at the Killarney Cultural Centre, dressed in pale pink with an aqua-green trim to match its front door. Cute as the pro-verbial button, and host to the town's artistic history, this colorful single-story cottage proves to be the perfect prelude to the rainbow which lies ahead. For after passing the orange-tinted Cineplex, a half-block later, and reaching Main Street, I am greeted by the Tourist Centre in red, the International Hotel in light yellow, the Town Hall in emerald green, and a slew of shops, restaurants, art galleries, and pubs wearing blue, brown, gold and white. Moreover, flowers appear everywhere. From a woven brocade across the fascia of the hotel, to window boxes over the entrance to the Tourist Centre and the Town Hall, to hanging baskets on the backsides of buildings in a narrow cobblestoned passageway connecting two sidestreets.

Adare-like?...Ohhh, yes. For sure. True, the buildings aren't nearly as historically old, and one doesn't feel as if one's stepping back into the Middle Ages. Nor are the structures as architecturally picture-perfect as they are in Hamlet's Haven, all stone and brick with thatched roofs. But, nonetheless, the general qualities of quaint, slow-paced, and friendly, with strong ties to Mother Nature and rural life, are strikingly similar. Killarney's larger of course – after all, its eight thousand citizens are ten times Adare's populace. But even so, it's not even close to being crowded, and the fairy-tale ambience is still present and fully accounted for. Its buildings may be more sizable, but they too are clustered like a village along only four major streets, and gaily festooned. And even though the pace is more lively, it still remains slow and easy, with time to stop and chat – as central to daily life as Catholicism. In fact, if pretty, old-world, and lively are of equal importance, if one wants a village lifestyle, but with a tad more *action*, then Killarney is the perfect combination of Adare and Sligo.

And speaking of yesteryear, right off Main Street, on Church Place, stands St. Mary's Church. Built in 1870, this brown-stoned, neo-Gothic edifice is revered for standing on the site of the original Cill Airne, the Church of the Sloe Woods, which occupied this location during the ninth century. And as I survey its traditional features, memory calls to mind that Killarney, in Gaelic, is also Cill Airne, meaning that the town germinated as an offshoot of the original religious site. "Early urban planning," I chuckle, nodding so long as I return to Main Street and amble two blocks to where it becomes High, then also joins with New to form a three-way, T-shaped junction.

This is the very heart of town, known as Market Cross because a century ago many different markets were located here, selling everything from butter to turf. Well, sometimes we change, just to stay the same, strums a thought as my eyes wander over the myriad of shops engaged in the same basic activity, a smile sliding across my face when I then narrow my focus onto a good-sized, red-brick building that harbors a uniqueness all its own. Known as the *Old* Town Hall, to distinguish it from its newer namesake a block away, which actually houses the local government, Oldie was built in the 1720s by Lord Kenmare with bricks left over from the construction of his mansion, and adds both age and tradition to the mix of charms circulating through the district. In addition, in a bold effort to claim the title of Killarney's commercial centerpiece, with the clock on its second-story fascia facing New Street, Oldie then stretches each of its arms out north-south, so that one is situated on High Street and the other on Main. Now, how about that, togetherness fans? surfaces my amusement. One building, two addresses, and a view of three streets. I mean, talk about a central location and a little convenience. Hell, you can buy a burger and fries on Main Street, Maalox for your upset tummy on High, and say a prayer for prompt relief while facing St. Mary's Cathedral at the end of New – all without leaving the building? cackles the follow-up as I slowly turn away and head west toward the steeple rising like a pyramid on the far horizon.

Three blocks later, New Street curves into Cathedral Place, and the steeple now rises two hundred and eighty-five feet to pierce the sky. And below it, spread out royally across a vast expanse of lawn, like a cathedral fit for a kingdom, is St. Mary's. Unlike her much older, Middle-Aged namesake in Limerick City, this St. Mary's dates only to 1855. And also unlike its medieval chaperon, revered for its storied history, this holy edifice is admired primarily for being one of the most beautiful Gothic-Revival cathedrals in all of Europe. Designed by the noted architect Augustus Putin, whose son's handiwork with the Franciscan Friary we admired earlier, this stately structure, while also built of limestone, is uniquely molded into a cruciform shape, then accented by a myriad of spires situated on its slender flanks and the base of its splendid steeple. And at the risk of once again threatening gross understatement, it is simply magnificent! Moreover, despite its relative youth, St. Mary's of Killarney did manage to garner a small role in Eire's more recent history. For when its initial construction was interrupted by the Great Famine, she served proudly as a hospital, and near the western doorway stands a great redwood tree to mark the mass grave of children who unfortunately succumbed. Today, however, a wedding is taking place. And just as I finish a prayer for *never again*, St. Mary's great bells peal with joy, and the happy couple exit and depart amidst the cheers and good wishes of their families and friends. For the second time inside an hour, Now, how about that? suddenly sprints into mind, this time sweetly contrasting the sad news of 9-11 received in Limerick's great sanctuary to the happiness and hope just launched before my smiling eyes. It's not exactly a complete comeback, I muse, still watching as the bridal limo turns a corner and vanishes. But it's a little love-step in the right direction, all the same.

And following with a series of my own meandering steps, for several minutes I leisurely explore the grounds adjacent to St. Mary's, noting first the picturesque stone structure known as the Bishop's House, then pushing farther west to view the ivy-covered walls of St. Brendan's College, whose steepled stone buildings are surrounded by tall trees and verdant hedgerows. Then, returning to the cathedral, I cross the street and enter the Knockreer Estate, once the fiefdom of Lord Kenmare, and now home to the 91,000-acre Killarney National Park.

Just inside the gate, a narrow pathway leads to a small wooden bridge over the Deenagh River, a shallow stream no more than fifteen feet wide. Then, fifty yards farther north, I stop in front of a thatched cottage which looks exactly like a freshly baked gingerbread house at Christmastime. Surrounded as it is by a two-foot hedge, behind which rows of roses smile, the only thing necessary to perfect its fairy-tale aura is for Hansel and Gretel to emerge hand-in-hand with greetings of welcome. Once the gatekeeper's home, it now serves as the official entrance to the Park. And after basking in its warm glow for a full minute, I smile so long and continue farther up the beckoning pathway.

Narrowing further to a width of six feet as I pad steadily along, Nature's Path, as I quickly nickname it, gently twists and turns through a forest of two-hundred-year-old trees and flowering shrubs for the next half hour. Then, just as I begin to wonder if I should have marked my trail more carefully than Hansel and Gretel did, I emerge onto a vast green plain, with the Tomies Mountains forming the far horizon, and Lough Leane lying like a shiny silver plate at their feet. For a slow-motion moment, I can't think, I can only feel, an inner voice wanting to but unable to scream Hallelujah!, settling instead for the prayerlike whisper of Dear…God.

Several minutes later, when I have sufficiently regained control of my senses from splendor's kidnapping, and am able to light up my pipe and scrutinize the Eden-like scene, details visit me. First is the observation that my vantage point is slightly above the lake, and a half-mile or so away, with the sea of green in-between dotted with a full variety of trees, several of which are sporting Autumn's colors. Then next, I note that speckling the serene surface of Lough Leane are several islands, all densely foliated and glowing in the late-afternoon sunshine. And finally, my eyes settle on a spit of sandy beach just beyond a large grove of trees to my right, its narrow form shaped like a child's finger, stretching to gently touch the sparkling water. "It's perfect," escapes my conclusion into the surrounding silence. "Absolutely…positively…perfect!" sounds my affirmation more loudly, sparked by my sudden awareness that I am totally alone in Paradise, the further observation that Eve is nowhere in sight pulling me back to the edge of reality.

But only the edge. For the beauty before me is so great that it continues to appear unreal. And even an hour later, when the approaching dusk once again forces me back from the brink and onto the pathway toward town, *unbelievable* is the adjective that echoes and re-echoes alongside. A long time ago, aged thirteen, I had read that while gazing at the stars, Lincoln had wondered how anyone could see such beauty and not feel the presence of a divine being. I had agreed with Old Abe then. And now, strolling along with yet another miracle engraved into memory, keeping close company with the Land of Heart's Desire, the Connemara, and the Cliffs of Moher, my own observation that God must have been in a very good mood at Creation-time also reverberates into ear.

"Uh-huh…For sure," I murmur contentedly to the trees and flowers. "And God must love Eire, with a whole heart!" follows the corollary, a grateful smile lighting my way home.

XVIII

FINDING FRIENDS IN THE GAP OF DUNLOE

DINNER LAST EVENING AT LA SCALA CAFÉ WAS SCRUMPTIOUS. SERIously scrumptious. As in pan-fried fillet of salmon on a bed of angel's-hair pasta, garnished with a poached pear! And the "reserved" chocolate tart that followed was so divine that I feel confident the cocoa beans were harvested in the paradise from which I had just recently returned. A totally tasty ending to an already exquisite day, its sugarsweet afterglow even inspired like-natured dreams.

In fact, when ten o'clock Saturday morning arrives, it finds me still fully contented from yesterday's blessings, and equally relaxed as I stand in line at the Tourist Centre, waiting to board the bus for a more extensive tour of Killarney's National Park. My carefree mood is further warmed by the friendly smile of Mary, a lovely-looking lady I engage in conversation, and we are soon laughing and chattering away as if we were old friends. And when Brian, her hubby, then joins us after purchasing their tickets, the infant bond between us instantly accelerates. Sharing with me their secret of having returned to Killarney to celebrate their fortieth wedding anniversary, with a redo of their original honeymoon, once aboard the bus, Brian, a tall, strapping fellow with bright eyes, queries me about my plans to navigate the Gap of Dunloe, a six-and-a-half-mile trail between two mountain ranges that leads to Lough Fada, the Upper Lake. I'd read that one could traverse it on foot, or by horseback, or via a horsedrawn carriage called a jaunting cart, and indicated the latter choice was my preference because I'd heard that the drivers, called jarveys, were legendary storytellers.

"True…True," Brian nods in agreement. "But you don't want to do that."

"I don't?…How come?…"

"Well, for two reasons," he returns. "First, it's really not the best way to see all the beauty. And secondly," he chirps cheerfully, the twinkle in his eye now dancing: "You seem like a regular fella, and I'd like to know you better. So I'd be pleased if you'd walk alongside me, we'll have a fine time of it for sure."

"You got it, pal," I hear myself saying without serious consideration, the good and gentle nature which fathers his smile shaking hands with intuition's feeling that something special was about to unfold.

And with my innate ability to transform gross understatement into an art form which rivals Michaelangelo at his best, *something special* begins to occur the very minute we exit the bus at the Kate's Cottage staging area. For Brian and I have no more than bade Mary, who has a bad back, a cheery farewell as she rides off in a jaunting cart than we're suddenly surrounded by the genial tones of, "Hey, fellas, I couldn't help but hear you say you're walking. Could I join ya?…" And turning round to meet the sweet smile on the pretty face of Maivor, who's tall and slender, and hails from a village south of Stockholm, as handshakes are exchanged, the newsome twosome is instantly transformed into serendipity's threesome, courtesy of Dame Fortuna. In fact, a minor miracle is occurring, although none of us are yet aware of it. As after a brief salute to the fabled Kate Kearney, the very beautiful local, who survived five marriages to organize the first tours of the lakes, the intrepid trio begin their trek. And as fate then stretches forth her fortuitous hands, inside of two miles, three total strangers, from three separate countries, with three disparate life histories, unconsciously forge a fast friendship. For as the trail gradually twists and turns uphill between the Tomies and Purple Mountains to our left, and the MacGillycuddy's Reeks on our right, conversation flows as openly and honestly and naturally as the scenic wonders we oooh and aaah over at every bend of the path – and magically, one Catholic son of Ireland, one Protestant daughter of Sweden, and one Russian-Lithuanian Jew from America's melting pot each create a separate stream which then merges into a river of joined lives, with currents of occupation, hobbies, and politics blending with those of family, church, and dreams, the past and future mingling inside the present, waxing, then waning, with hope shadowing worry, and laughter propelling instantaneous *like* for each other into a casually toned but nevertheless serious *sharing*.

Brian, who was born in Tipperary one month before I made my debut in St. Joe, Missouri, served twenty-three years on the Dublin Police Force, during which time he became an empathetic student of the human condition. The softness around the edges of his Irish brogue is a sure clue to his sensitive world outlook, and the pride and joy derived from his family gleams in his eyes like a thousand candles inside a cathedral. A good ten years younger than our sixty-one, Maivor, who is single, but hints at a significant someone, is easily the most adventuresome member of the club, having traveled seemingly everywhere, and amazing her male cohorts with how, having recently dreamed one night about Iceland, then received a request to lecture in Reykjavik the following morning, she promptly picked up and left for a visit the same day. I mean, doesn't everyone? implies her tone with a matter-of-factness that generates a hearty round of chuckles.

"Well," I gurgle back at her: "I have that response too, if I suddenly run out of cookies and dash to the market. But Iceland?…I don't think so. How about you, Brian?…"

"Not yet," zooms his instinctive reaction. But equally unequivocal is his strong interest in her work as a naturopathic physician. And as I listen to her effortlessly but passionately explain the workings of natural healing, it enters my mind that I have never been in the presence of a more intelligent or better educated person. Add to that quality those of an obvious sensitivity, a deeply caring worldview, and a keen sense of humor, and simply put: the lady is something else!

A perfectly apt description, courtesy of a serious application of slang, the connotative concoction also serves equally well to summarize our communal conversation. Which, having swelled to full force via the energized flow from all three tributaries, now gushes in rapid torrents, with any and all subjects fair game. In fact, the only requirements for admittance to the churning channel of discussion are curiosity, gusto, and humor. And governing from this pluralistic platform, the Fun Party proceeds to explore books, travel, and life in small towns versus big cities, music, art, and athletics – all without preface, or any particular order. An old caretaker's cottage we pass by instigates a lesson from Brian on how to build a thatch roof, and why they're more affordable. And after the dialogue has danced around architecture, it jumps to books, with Maivor introducing a current favorite, *Conversations With God*, that somehow gets Jean-Paul Sartre and his brilliant band of existentialists involved. Then, when our brief but intense analysis of man's search for the meaning of life is foreclosed by the circuitous conclusion that maybe the warm-hearted experience we're nurturing is as close as we can get, the Hobman holds forth on why baseball is as central to American culture as soccer is to Europe's. In turn, this ticklish tangent leads mysteriously, to world affairs, and how best to respond to the events of 9-11. And when, despite our best efforts, we are unable to solve the sad chaos of failed human relations, our only slightly diminished enthusiasm guides us to a stop beside Black Lake, where fresh chatter surges anew, this time about whether or not St. Patrick actually drowned the last snake in Ireland here? And is the surrounding scenery absolutely incredible, or what?...

The answers come easily. For there's not a snake in sight, and the view is positively unreal. In fact, overwhelmingly so. As having hiked almost three miles, we can now look both forward and back down toward Killarney. And as far as the eye can see in either direction are mountains and valley, the Tomies and MacGillycuddy Reeks standing like gentle giants that smile down upon us in our childlike wonderment, the verdant valley catching the sun's golden rays and painting the trees countless shades of green, yellow, and ochre, its floor dotted occasionally by a tiny silvery lake or distant farmhouse. "Beauty is truth, truth beauty," Keats had versified. And the weight of his wisdom only grows heavier as the three comrades resume hiking, their eyes continuing to eat and drink from the heavenly feast spread out around them.

And if, by some strange machination of the mind, you're thinking that the Godperson forgot dessert, stop immediately, and reconsider. For there's more. Much more. Chocolate cake. Apple pie a la mode. And a hot-fudge sundae, with not one, but three cherries on top! For at two o'clock, when we finally reach St. Brendan's Cottage at the end of our three-hour trek, awaiting us is a boat trip back to Killarney that gently descends over three of the loveliest lakes on Planet Earth, each one hand-carved and caressed with charm by the loving Lord. And now reunited with Mary, and morphed into the friendly foursome, we're soon seated in a bright-green dinghy powered by an outboard motor, and slowly cruising up a narrow channel and into Lough Fada.

Known also as the Long Lake, because it's shaped like a finger, as well as the Upper Lake because it enjoys the highest altitude, this smallest cherry on the divine menu is arguably the sweetest. For encompassing as it does four hundred and eighty exquisitely serene acres, with Eire's tallest mountain, Carrantuohill, sheltering her from a height of three thousand-four hundred feet, *awe-inspiring* is indeed a humble base off which to futilely try to build an accurate picture of the enormous beauty now radiating from the surrounding naturescape. A simple "Wow!" escalates into an even louder "Holy cockamolies, it's unbelievable!" before finally, simple vocabulary feels fully its inadequacy and falls silent, the thought which arose beside the Cliffs of Moher that God loves Ireland with a whole heart then returning in the form of a prayerful smile.

A heartfelt offering of both praise and thanksgiving, this adoration cannot help but repeat itself when fifteen minutes later we reach the *Meeting of the Waters* and enter the Middle or Muckross Lake, where the Rhapsody of Scenic Splendor is then replayed on an even grander scale. As fifty percent larger than its shimmering sister, the virginal vistas are even wider, and beneath Golden Eagle Mountain, several small rock islands appear, their flanks blanketed with moss, stalwart trees standing sentry on their craggy bluffs. And when several enchanting minutes later, we then glide into Lough Leane, the magic which has been floating before our eyes builds upon itself to reconstruct the Garden of Eden I had first viewed late yesterday afternoon. For with the mountains now fanning back to a distance of a half to three-quarters of a mile, the Lake of Learning, with its five thousand acres of water wonderland, takes center stage, amplifying the omnipresent Rhapsody of Scenic Splendor into a full-fledged Symphony. As fully encircled by a thick bank of old-growth trees and flowering shrubs, Leane's violins now sing the siren's song underneath a sky that has grown impossibly blue while harboring powder-puff clouds – caressing with charm one's every nerve ending, carving yet another mesmerizing memory inside one's heart, and spiriting impulse to shout loud and long: "Killarney, you are the Kingdom of Camelot!"

I don't, simply because my vocal chords are as frozen in awe as the rest of me. Instead, I just sit, shaking my head in disbelief over how one small island could possibly hold so much treasure. And awakening from my daze only when I hear Brian's salient summary that "some dreams do come true," my return of a wide smile soon transforms into hearty laughter when a series of waves slap against the sides of the boat, spraying us with a chilly mist. "You see," Brian chuckles, a gleam in his eye. "Ireland even baptizes those of the Hebrew persuasion." And after wiping my face with the sleeve of my jacket, my retort is a cheery, "That's okay, if it makes me part Irish!…"

The consensus is that it does. And now officially adopted, I turn my focus toward the island of Innisfallen, which now appears off to our right. Twenty-one acres in size, and heavily forested, as we draw closer to a narrow opening in the trees, I can faintly make out the ruins of the monastery which St. Fallen founded in the seventh century. Memory reminds that it flourished for a thousand years, and that it's believed that both Brian Boru, the great Irish chieftain, and St. Brendan the Navigator studied here. Moreover, adding further to its celebrated tradition of scholarship, the *Annals of Innisfallen*, a chronicle of early world and Irish history, was also crafted in this secluded spot by a succession of thirty-nine monastic scribes – in both Gaelic and Latin, no less. And as my eyes squint in order to more clearly see the sad remnants of yesteryear's academic glory, I suddenly wonder, Is this why Lough Leane is called the Lake of Learning?…

Well, it certainly makes sense to this newly minted Irishman, forms my conclusion, after thoughts of the Muckross Abbey also surface. From my nautical perch, I can't actually see it due to the density of the forest. But on the eastern shore, about a mile north of Innisfallen, also stand the ruins of a second learning center, this one established by Franciscan monks in the 1440s, and called the Friary. Legend has it that the courtyard is still home to an ancient yew tree, reputedly as old as the Abbey. And nearby lie the honored graves of Kerry's four famous Gaelic poets, also commemorated on the white-marble silhouette of Speir Bean. Ohhh, yeah…We've got some serious learning here, all right, I confirm as the boat motors on. And quite possibly, the most beautiful campus in the entire world, to boot. I mean, old St. Fallen and the Franciscans could've moonlighted as real estate agents, 'cause they most certainly understood location! location! location!

And speaking of which, how about this beauty for a waterfront site with a big-time view? trails my train of thought as our boat nears the landing dock beside Ross Castle. Constructed of light-brown stone, and probably built by the local O'Donoghue clan during the fifteenth century, this imposing structure's feudal personality is further enhanced by the fortified bawn that surrounds it, as well as its two circular towers. Once the home of Lord Kenmare, who built Killarney town, as the late-afternoon sunshine casts a golden hue across its sizable curtain walls, it glows like a princely palace in paradise, providing a sublime ending to a fairy-tale experience.

Only, it isn't. Unh-unh, no way. For the four friends, having grown unusually close during the short space of a single day, are not prepared to let go of the happy hours just passed, or of each other. And after busing back to the center of town, we immediately retreat to Hannigan's Pub for a pint in order to properly celebrate our shared good fortune. One round leads to two, and in turn to a dinner that features as much warm-hearted laughter as food. And still lingering together afterward over cognac and coffee, when eleven o'clock arrives, a unique friendship has been nourished into one which will last a collective lifetime, though this is not yet fully realized. What can be clearly observed, however, rising off the firm foundation of fellowship, is the exchange of addresses and telephone numbers, followed by a round of "all the best" farewells squeezed out between hugs.

On my stroll back to the McSweeney, my sense of satisfaction swells so thoroughly complete that several times I stop in my tracks to question whether the day's magic had actually occurred. Did I really see such wondrous beauty? floats the inquiry innocently. I mean, on top of the miracles already experienced? Huh?…Honest?…And is it possible that on top of those blessings, one gets the priceless bonus of finding such loveable friends? To be invited to visit Brian and Mary in Dublin, and Maivor in Stockholm?…It's like a waking dream, whispers acceptance, slowly sinking in. A sweet, sunshiny dream that arrives unexpectedly alive by grace of God, then grows sweeter and stronger each time it's nurtured and cherished.

And smiling knowingly as the hotel now slides into view, suddenly music sounds inside my memory, the soft silky strains of violins accompanying a chorus crooning a lullaby: "Don't let it be forgot/That once there was a spot/For one brief shining moment/That was known as Camelot!"

XIX

THE RING OF KERRY

S UNDAY BEGINS WITH TELEPHONE CALLS. "SEE YOU IN DUBLIN, IRISHER," says Brian, who with Mary is motoring north to their next vacation destination in half an hour. And the amiable sound of his voice is still smiling in my ear when Maivor checks in from the airport with, "I'll expect you in Stockholm soon, hear me?…"

I do. Both of them, loud and clear. And their warm wishes not only accompany me through breakfast, but along the entire route of my return to the Tourist Centre, where once again I board a bus, this time for a tour of the fabled "Ring." Aptly named for its one-hundred-and-ten-mile circuit of scenic wonders and spectacular views, unlike many other parts of Ireland, this paramount parade of nature does not host any great historical landmarks or famous museums, leaving the scenery alone to star as the central attraction. And –

What?…There's more? you cry out in absolute disbelief. You mean to tell me, that after the glories already gifted by the Land of Heart's Desire and the Connemara, then crowned by the Burren, the Cliffs of Moher, and the positively divine Lakes of Killarney, there's more?…Have you lost it, Hobman, old chum? Did guzzling all that Guinness with your new-found bosom buddies last evening wash away what's left of your twisted, tortured, and tangled mind?…I mean, you said Eire was an island, not a continent, didn't you?…

True…True…All true, dear Reader. But remember also my appraisal that the Godperson loves Ireland with a whole heart?…Well, then, never, not even for a single, solitary second, underestimate the size of the Lord's heart! Unh-unh, no way. Instead, try recalling the size of the universe, and when that little number sinks in, just sit back and leave the driving to Dennis, our guide, and the scenery to Heaven!…Which, after a brief legal discussion with the Professor about whether or not your query re the state of my mind assumes a fact not properly in evidence, is precisely what I do. No notes. No photographs. Instead, like our Deros Tour Bus, I simply slip my psyche into second gear and allow my eyes to wander casually over a steadily unfolding panorama of bogland, mountain, lakeside, and seacoast vistas, the enormous beauty now an accepted norm.

For several minutes, our path points west, following the lovely River Laune, before turning north to reach sleepy Killorglin, a small marketing town of thirteen hundred, a half hour later. At the fishing village of Glenbeigh, some thirty minutes further into our journey, we're treated to a breathtaking view of Dingle Bay, and stop to stretch our legs with a visit to Kerry Bog Village. Meticulously recreated to present exact replicas of dwellings used in rural Ireland in the early 1800s, the village also includes an equally authentic display of various tools and trappings in the thatched-roof homes of the blacksmith and dairy farmer. And while the former are quite interesting, it is the turf cutter's house that truly intrigues me. For it is here that one learns how it takes nature two thousand years to mix decaying trees and shrubs into one foot of peat, or turf as the locals call it. A source of fuel for heat when cut and dried, as well as fertilizer, peat bogs to an average depth of eight feet cover approximately fifteen percent of Ireland, a tribute to nature's patience that even captures the attention of the ageless sage who accompanies me.

"Good thing the government is regulating cutting," he nods out, fingering one of the rounded blades used during harvest. "'Cause that way, the peat moss export business still brings in the bucks, while the ecosystem is also protected, and a two-hundred-year supply is ensured to boot."

"Right…Three birds with one stone," I chirp cheerfully back at him. "Four, if you count the fact that burning turf releases no harmful emissions. Pretty good, huh?…the government being both practical and farsighted…"

No doubt about that, we agree. In fact, a national authority actively promoting sound ecological and economic policy side by side is not only a true wonderment, but one whose wisdom is still smiling at me ten minutes later when the bus stops again, this time to offer an even wider panorama of the Dingle Peninsula, complete with the Blaskett Islands lying in the Atlantic off its western tip. And as if that isn't treasure enough, there's a bonus. Just across the road from our viewing point, where the land slopes gently upward into the mountains, lies a sheep ranch. And after our party settles into a small set of bleachers, Ian, the ranch-owner, ably assisted by his band of border collies, treats us to a true "rural reality show" that is nothing short of amazing to us city folk. With several small flocks grazing about a half-mile up the nearest mountain, the intention is for Ian, aided only by a brass whistle, to direct the collies to collect the sheep and herd them down the mountainside and into an enclosure just off to our left. And following the subtly nuanced sounds from their master's whistle, for the better part of five minutes the dogs artfully dart left, then right, and so on, until their energy and expertise have safely guided the sheep inside the waiting pen, a hearty round of applause stamping an exclamation point on the accomplishment. Beginning at four months old, it takes two full years to completely train a collie, Ian explains afterward, and the accumulated affection between the clever canines and their owner is as obvious as their combined abilities. An endless supply of patience is also required, but as we learn, the net effect is that one shepherd, working alone, can easily maintain a herd of up to five hundred woolies. And as Ian then fields further questions from the group, my mind wanders back to Carrick-on-Shannon and my old friend, Jerry Mac, who I now envision in a like setting, with a much better understanding of how he goes about his business.

Once I have reboarded the bus, his smiling face slowly fades from my mind's eye, replaced instead by the renewed view of the sun sparkling on Dingle Bay as we pass through the villages of Kells and Cahersiveen, the latter containing the ruins of the house where Daniel O'Connell, the Great Liberator, was born. Then, turning south, as we approach the town of Waterville, the island of Valencia appears. Seven miles long, and one of the most westerly points in all of Europe, it was here that the remnants of the defeated Spanish Armada beached in 1588, with some sailors deciding to stay and marry pretty colleens, thus providing the term *Black Irish* for their mixed offspring.

Following history's hint, we also stay, stopping for lunch at the Scariff Inn, perched on a steep cliff overlooking the Atlantic. And while once again testing the patience of Father Matthew by forsaking food in favor of a large piece of chocolate cake, from the patio area I then share my sweet snack with a totally stellar view of the also visible Skellig Islands, sitting some eight miles out to sea. Then, after coffee and a pipeful for dessert, once again the strummings of Willie N's guitar sound, and our bus rolls onward. Almost immediately, we pass by the tiny hamlet of Caherdaniel, and approach Staigue Fort on the outskirts of Castlegrove. A large, stone, circular structure, it was built almost a thousand years before the arrival of the Celts by the Bilford Tribes in approximately 1500 B.C. And though once a symbol of warring factions, surrounded today by heavily foliated green fields, with the shimmering Atlantic lying just beyond, the ancient barricade now appears as peaceful as I feel – a condition that only gains weight, as our tour continues its circuitous route back to Killarney along a seascape that ceaselessly soothes the soul, mile after mile after mile.

At Sneem, a mere slip of a settlement located at the head of an inlet where the River Sneem meets its brothers, the Kenmare and Ardsheel-hane, we stop a final time to stretch our legs. And while savoring a homemade ice-cream cone from the Green Door General Store, I slowly stroll the mini municipality's main street – which, having taken its cue from the lovely stone church at one end of its three-block length, is per-forming a divinely inspired impression of a rainbow! With both its houses and commercial buildings painted vibrant shades of blue, pink, purple, yellow, and orange, and having added a smidgeon of green from its tiny twin parklets, Sneem is a living, breathing smile that not only prompts one's body, mind, and soul into instant imitation, but also engenders the desire for permanent residency! I mean, this happy haven is so cheerfully peaceful that the great Charles de Gaulle gave up France to retire here. And why not?...Only love and ice-cream cones are allowed inside the town limits! Frown, even once, and poof, you're gone. 'Cause it's simply the sugar inside sweet, the comfort inside contentment, and a wellstone of warmth to last a lifetime!...

Well, that is, it would if one didn't have to leave. And even then, even after we reboard and return to the highway, Sneem's gleam lights our way back to Killarney, twinkling like a silvery star as dusk descends over the MacGillycuddy Reeks when we reach Moll's Gap, and shining like the friendly lights of the cozy town awaiting us below. Ohhh, yes, County Kerry, you're a Kingdom all right, I muse contentedly as the bus slowly passes by Ladies' View, offering one final look at Lough Fada in the distance, flashing scenes from yesterday's glorious adventure with Brian, Mary, and Maivor, merging with the Ring's lush forests and spectacular seascape. In fact, your treasure can't even be totaled in only one visit, so I'll just have to come back, tantalizes my follow-up thought, my smile a silent promise as I snuggle restfully against the window.

XX

LUCY'S TOWN

THE NUMBER 9 HAS ALWAYS BEEN LUCKY FOR ME. BEGINNING WITH Grampy Max being born on February 9, the good fortune follows next with Grammy Esther arriving in September, and then trails steadily through my sixty-one years all the way to the appearance of my kidlets, with Amy saying hello on March 9, Matty on June 9, and Nicky at precisely 9:00 p.m., albeit on August 26th. And now, as I begin my third full week in Eire by saying so long to Room 108, the sudden realization that 1 and 8 add up to 9 once again slides a smile across my lips. It's a melancholy smile, though, as I don't want to leave the Kingdom, or Camelot, where I've experienced so much beauty, and have been further gifted with such special friendship. But with warp speed, however, it turns happier upon my brain's next announcement that this day promises a visit to Cork City, and dinner with Lucky Lucy. "Yeah, that's right," I whisper, my smile now brightening further as I flash on how fortunate I was to make friends with this transplanted young Irishwoman when she solicited me for insurance back home, and the absolutely incredible further stroke of luck that she had planned to visit her Mom and Dad on the exact date my itinerary brought me to her home town. "Well," I chuckle, "it's not s-o-o incredible, if you stop to consider that her full name, Lucy Walsh, is composed of 9 letters. In fact, old boy, your entire Irish experience is happening in the calendar's ninth month, so how about we put a damper on the nostalgia, and get on with enjoying this precious new day?" I tell myself as I make my way downstairs and take a final look around the lobby, before exiting and starting my stroll to the bus station.

A good idea. Logical, with a thick coating of common sense. But not so easy to totally adopt, if you're a mushpot like me. And it's only after Bus Eireann pulls out of Killarney at eight-thirty sharp, with my solemn pledge to return echoing over my shoulder, that I'm finally able to slip the magic of County Kerry inside a warm pocket of my heart for safekeeping, and allow the adventure lying ahead to fully occupy center stage. And a bright theatre it is too, with the sun rising steadily into an azure sky to spotlight the company of lime-green fields flowing flatly for miles, then clasping hands with the emerald-green forest that blankets the hilly horizon. I'm used to it by now, of course, being a veteran Irisher. But still, the size of nature's sweet smile is so great that one cannot help but warmly return it, as I spontaneously do, toasting the repeating miracle with a frosted mini-wheat as the bus rolls on eastward. At nine o'clock, we pass through the village of Balleyvourney, then stop fifteen minutes later in Macroon. A town of twenty-four hundred souls, it does its absolute best to ensure I'm fully awake by featuring an assortment of brightly colored buildings that even a citizen of Sneem would admire. Our visit is only for several short minutes, but long enough to count blue, red, yellow, and purple, pink, orange, and mustard as friendly faces – the cheer emanating from this home-grown kaleidoscope then coinciding with my sudden awareness that today is Rosh Hashanah, the New Year, to raise the simple celebration of color to a hopeful consecration of new beginnings, featuring a silent but high-spirited prayer for peace.

Less than an hour later, the Cathedral of Countryside Greenery gives way to the stone edifices of University College Cork as our bus sweeps up College Road, then slides eastward to the banks of the River Lee and Central Bus Station. Once outside, for a slow minute my eyes meander over the smooth surface of the blue-gray water to the multi-colored buildings comprising Cork City's skyline, before settling onto the map I've pulled from my backpack in order to refresh my recollection of the directions to the Hotel Metropole Ryan. No problem, my red-inked notation says it's north of the bus station on MacCurtain Street. However, the next moment promptly presents the day's first difficulty: On which side of the river is MacCurtain, as the bus station is conspicuously absent from the map, leaving me without a starting point. I mean, I know where I am, and that's nice for openers. But searching the maze of wavy lines serving as streets – some named, others not – for some indication of north-south, east-west, I come up empty. And after a minute or two devoted to doubling, tripling, and quadrupling my search, all without panic, mind you, I finally manage to ascertain why. Because my trusty guide doesn't contain one, that's why! Thus, I conclude after further contemplation, as I don't have a compass, and my legendary lack of even a rudimentary instinct for direction precludes the proverbial "educated guess," we have a little problem on our hands. Call it a challenge, for those of you wishing to remain positive. And in that this most fervently includes me, after an additional ten to fifteen seconds of heavy thought that conjures up a vision of Einstein on the verge of forming his Theory of Relativity, I finally manage to postulate that the odds of locating MacCurtain Street on my left or my right are approximately fifty-fifty. And armed with this pearl of navigational wisdom, I pick left on account of the fact that politically I naturally lean that way, then slowly shuffle off toward the next corner.

Wrong move. Dead wrong, as it turns out. As even though I'm momentarily comforted by reaching Oliver Plunkett Street Lower, solely because I recognize that it's named after the poet who participated in the famed Easter Rising, this solitary second of security quickly proves transitory, as upon second thought, the renowned bard was named Joseph, prompting a distant voice to then ask with considerable consternation: So who's Oliver?…And moreover, continues the insidious inquiry: What direction does Lower bear to Upper, in that no designation for the latter appears on my map, not to forget dear old MacCurtain, which shares a like status amongst the morass of scriggly black lines providing their impression of a group of worms dancing the boogaloo! You call this a map? seeps emerging anger. How about instead, we call it a masochistically inspired piece of modern artwork? You know, Mysteries of the Veiled Street, by Mystical Modigliani? flows my fuming indictment, joining the confusion boiling in my gut as well as my beleaguered brain.

Most fortunately, however, at this precise moment of rapidly parlaying pain, Adonai, in honor of my late but solemn recognition of Rosh Hashanah, sends forth an Angel of Mercy in the form of a lovely, seventy-plus-year-old lady who is so kind as to inquire if she might be of assistance. And after I explain my desire to locate the Hotel Metropole Ryan, and she graciously informs me that "it's recently changed its name to the Metropole Gresham, you see?" she then leads me back to the front of the bus station and points to the bridge I'm to cross to reach MacCurtain, just one block further north.

"Well, you had a fifty-fifty chance, and you muffed it!" chuckles out my chastisement through a sheepish smile after I've thanked my savior profusely, then set out over the Brian Boru Bridge, my smile brightening further at the flashing recollection of my high school English teacher, whose favorite reprimand I'd just invoked. "God bless you, Eunice," follows my petition. "Right after He-She directs the winning lottery numbers to my Good Samaritan!" I add, reaching the north bank and heading uphill toward the street of my recent dreams. Uh-huh, for sure, hastens a confirming thought. And wasn't she nice, so sweet and helpful?...And sprightly, too, I muse, recalling her quick, hard-to-keep-up-with gait as I plod along. Wonder how she knew I was having trouble?...

"Well, it certainly wasn't your sweet Irish face!" cracks the Professor, leaking sarcasm. "More like the same way Balboa just had a hunch that the Pacific Ocean wasn't some small lake he happened to stumble onto. Does that strike a chord of clarity perhaps?..."

"Uh-huh...Sure, Mr. Smart-Ass," I chuckle back at him. "And so does that!" concludes my retort, gaining strength after I turn left at the corner and with considerable relief point to the gold letters spelling out Hotel Metropole Gresham over the entrance.

Four stories high, half a block wide, with a red-brick facade, the Metropole stands proudly like a well-dressed Victorian lady surveying life on MacCurtain Street through a bevy of bay windows. And the lobby, with its molded ceilings, chandeliers, and broad staircase, serves well to cement its image of a grand dame presiding over an elegant but warmly intimate salon. My room, number 307, is also a gracious hostess, offering pastel-painted walls, a matching bedspread on my king-size bed with wooden headboard, and two large windows gifting a wide view of the shops and offices encased in similar Victorian-styled structures across the street. In fact, the only sour note in this Symphony of Welcome is a memo from the concierge that Lucy had called to say, "Sorry, but due to 9-11, my flight has been cancelled, so obviously we can't meet. But enjoy! enjoy! enjoy!" For a moment or two, memory lets me listen to her Irish lilt, while watching her winning smile, disappointment nagging at me. "Well, that certainly knocks the cherry off the sundae," I shrug, dropping the note onto the bed and picking up my backpack. "But maybe we can add an extra scoop of ice cream, or some more fudge – So let's go see," I tack on, heading for the door, my spirits rollercoastering upward once again.

Retracing my steps back across the Brian Boru Bridge, I stop near the center to take in a fuller view of the River Lee and the buildings lining the quays along both banks. Looking west toward St. Patrick's Bridge, I'm instantly reminded of Dublin, albeit on a much smaller scale. That makes sense, of course, I remind myself, in that Cork, Eire's second largest city, is home to a hundred and sixty thousand souls, not a million plus. Still, even at first blush, it appears larger than Limerick City and Galway – most definitely a city of some size, but with an equally certain aura of warmth and charm flowing from its river setting and the multi-colored facades of the edifices nestled close to the Lee. Not the least of which, I notice, is my new home away from home, as the rear segment of the Metropole faces squarely onto St. Patrick's Quay, in bright lemon-yellow, no less – a friendly beacon I carefully store in my memory bank for purposes of finding my way home. In fact, to ensure against repeat cartographical chaos, I decide to make the Tourist Centre my first stop, in order to purchase a new and improved map. You know, one which even a navigational nincompoop can read. An overwhelmingly comforting con-cept, it engenders a total mind-and-body smile as I move on.

Upon my arrival back at the corner of Brian Boru Street and Oliver Plunkett Lower, I am pleased to report that two previous mysteries are quickly cleared up via a brief consultation with my guide book. First, *Oliver* Plunkett, whom I mistook for Joseph, the poet of Easter Rising fame, is actually a revered archbishop who was martyred at the hands of Cromwell in 1681, and whose embalmed head can be observed in Drogheda's Catholic Church north of Dublin, should someone have a morbid curiosity in need of exercise. And secondly, while *Lower* does logically imply an *Upper*, such is not the case with Oliver's street. No, when one turns west toward the Tourist Centre, what should be Oliver Plunkett Upper turns out to be simply Oliver Plunkett. So, after apolo-gizing to Ollie twice for my twin transgressions, I then set out to traverse the ten blocks or so of his street that lead to a juncture with Grand Parade Avenue and my desired objective. Almost immediately, I notice that the late Archbishop's thoroughfare is both colorful and a beehive of activity. As lined by a mixture of brick and brightly painted frame-and-stucco edifices housing a wide variety of shops with offices overhead, it's also home to a steady flow of shoppers and two-way vehicular traffic. In short, Ollie's street is quite busy, but without being either noisy or frenzied, I note, nodding my approval. I mean, the cars are moving right along, but without any jams accompanied by short tempers and heavy-handed honks. And the smartly dressed citizenry, while most definitely active, is nevertheless moving at a civilized pace, smiles and chatter in evidence everywhere my head swivels. Nice, I muse. Very nice. We've got attractive architecture, and flowers and trees, right along with a wide diversity of shopping opportunities and an energetic but relaxed populace – all joining together to say: "Welcome! It's comfortable here, so c'mon and enjoy!"

At the intersection with Cook Street, where I stop to admire a striking blue-green building, housing a restaurant-bar with outside seating beneath a matching striped awning, I spy the familiar name of Bewley's just three doors north. And lo and behold, right smack in the center of its glass-enclosed pastry counter is a tray of Chocolate Bars that look lovingly like those of Sligo's Gourmet Parlour fame. Well, I enthuse through a rushing smile, it is noontime, and we were looking for some extra fudge to ease the pain of losing Lucy for dinner. Hell, we'll buy one for her too, she'd like that! I assure myself, then share the good news with the bright-eyed, sweet-faced colleen who asks kindly: "Anything further?..." Oh, sure, fantasy flashes. In that I'm unexpectedly free for dinner, wanna slip on thirty years like a new dress, and join me?...

A good idea. Inspired, innocent, and hopeful. But like many of its sisters that I've enjoyed for a fleeting second or two since I landed in Eire's enchanting environs, it too succumbs to the harsh rigidities of reality at the same speed with which it was born. Most fortunately, however, Miss, Ms, or Mrs. Chocolate Bar ride to the rescue. Uh-huh...that's right. I bought a third one to quash my sorrow over losing the lovely young lass to that Grand Miser, Father Time, and a large coffee for good measure. Never mind Father Matthew and his School of Abstinence, I tell myself as I proceed on toward the Tourist Centre. After all, it is the New Year, and a time to celebrate. We can repent on Yom Kippur, two weeks down the road. And even though my confectionary treat is a full notch below the Gourmet Parlour's standard of Masterpiece, still, a nine on a scale of ten is cause for celebration itself!

And party, I do, royally enjoying Choco Bar II after exiting the Tourist Centre, armed with an equally divine map. I mean, this colorful cartographical gem, complete with the River Lee in blue, the streets and avenues in white and pink, and points of interest circled and numbered in red, is as sweet as the sugar melting on my tongue. Ohhh-kay, Lucy's Town, sings the anthem inside my brain. Here...I...come! And as if to second the motion, the sun slides out from behind a bank of puffy white clouds to smile in a paint-blue sky, a light breeze stirring to freshen the Fall air, whispering, "Isn't it great to be alive and free to explore Cork City?..." You just betch'um, Red Ryder! answers enthusiasm, adding bounce to my step as I head further west to meet the National Monument.

Dedicated to all the Irish patriots who died between 1798 and 1867, and located at the junction of Grand Parade and South Mall, two of Cork City's main arteries, this milky-white stone memorial instantly reminds one of the Campanile at Dublin's Trinity College, with its triple-tiered body, enchanting spires, and intricately carved figurines on the corner posts that pay homage to Eire's fallen heroes. And for a full five minutes, I slowly circle round it, admiring the beauty of its symmetry, and scanning the long list of revered names chiseled into the tablets adorning the walls of the base. Then, after nodding my head in silent salute, I ramble onward onto nearby French Quay, where I renew my appreciative gaze from a distance, while also stealing glances of the south channel of the River Lee.

In turn, French Quay leads me onto Bishop Street, home to St. Finbarr's Cathedral, the very spot where Cork City was born. No historical marker exists, no plaque or signpost. But as my eyes fill full with the illustrious French-Gothic edifice built in 1867, its massive cone-shaped spires appearing to touch the clouds overhead, I recall that it stands on the very site of the monastic settlement which St. Finbarr founded around 650, thereby giving birth to Cork City in the process. In fact, within a short time, during the eighth and ninth centuries, this burgeoning colony was a focal point throughout Ireland's period as "the isle of saints and scholars," when students from all over Europe gathered here to immerse themselves in Christian scholarship. Thereafter, as the community continued to grow in size and importance, like other parts of Eire, Cork also experienced long periods of domination under the Vikings and the English. Right, I muse, pulling my eyes down from the smaller spires which edge the roofline and turning them back in the direction of the National Monument. Now I see why it's so close by. 'Cause during Eire's long struggle for independence, it was usually the

Corkonians who led the way in exhibiting self-reliance and spunk, thus earning the title *Rebel Cork* for both the City and the County. Yeahhh, rumbles my follow-up thought. Where better to place the memorial than in the heart of the City? "Hell," I muster out loud, the words now pushed by the emotional rush of Eire's painful history, "it was crafty and courageous Corkmen who paid the price to be at the forefront of Ireland's modern political formation, from local heroes Thomas MacCurtain and Terence MacSwiney to the legendary Michael Collins. Rebel Cork?…For sure. And damn proud of it!" I conclude, smiling and reaching for my pipe. Then, as smoke curls upward, I say so long to St. Finbarr's and saunter back to the head of South Mall.

A broad street – really an avenue or boulevard – that runs east-west for a mile or so, South Mall is the fiscal center of Cork City, which is not only an important seaport, but equally well established as a manufacturing center. And as I amble along, puffing on my Peterson, I am soon enveloped by the charm and beauty of the thoroughfare, with its many well-preserved Georgian-brick and stone buildings, judiciously set back from the tree-lined sidewalks. As my eyes pass from one distinguished-looking edifice to another, now occupied by banks, stockbrokers, and other financial institutions, I can't help but wonder what St. Finbarr would think of his little settlement now. I mean, Cork's name comes from the Gaelic word Corcaigh, which means "marsh." So do you think that we could convince him that over a thousand years later, his fellow Corkonians filled in the marsh and constructed this absolutely lovely street? He was very religious, you know, so his belief in miracles might help. "And speaking of same," escapes a whisper as I reach Lapp's Quay and spot the City Hall: "How about that for an eye-opener?…" As puffed out with appropriate importance for three quarters of a block along the Lee's southern bank, the graceful classical structure with a turquoise-domed cupola over the columned entryway further polishes the neighborhood's persona of *impressive* by saying authoritatively: "Cork's come a long way, so please take note!"

I do. As undoubtedly St. Finbarr does also, from his perch atop the closest of the elephantine white clouds floating lazily overhead. In fact, on the walk back to the National Monument, he further joins in my appreciation of the imposing architectural attributes of the AIG building, a massive light-gray stone structure of three stories, with large wood-framed windows separated by ornate columns across its facade. "Now, Mr. Saint," I suggest. "If that paragon of safety and security doesn't make you want to open a savings account, then you're as hopeless as Father Matthew marks me." He readily agrees, of course, adding his own suggestion that we push onward, so that I can burn off some of the sugar circulating through my bloodstream before it coagulates into a stroke. And after the Professor then adds an unctuously toned "Amen!" the merry trio ambles westward past multi-colored office buildings intermixed with brick and stone brothers and sisters, stopping only when an estate agent's sign catches my eye just beyond the lemon-yellow facade of the Imperial Hotel. "O'Mahony Walsh & Associates" reads its white letters on the blue glass window, instantly triggering Lucy's pretty face into view, her wink warming my smile.

At the National Monument, South Mall gently curves into the Grand Parade, an even wider thoroughfare that blends the remains of the Old City walls and eighteenth-century bow-fronted houses with modern offices and shops. Once again, color smiles back at me from the cheerful red, lime-green, and gold-freckled faces of the stone and stucco structures lining both sides of the avenue's six sumptuous blocks. And as I slowly stroll north on the extra-wide sidewalks, my feeling of being at home continues to grow. As completing my recovery from the early-morning navigational upset, Cork's warmth and beauty has now sufficiently infiltrated my psyche so as to place me fully at ease. Confusion has faded away. Strangeness has transformed into familiarity. And homeyness is now in ascendancy as north-south and east-west make sense, and I can actually *feel* where the River Lee is, and how South Mall leads to Grand Parade, and up past my old friend Oliver Plunkett to St. Patrick's Street just ahead. Not bad, for only three hours, I boast proudly to myself while returning the nods from a young couple pushing their daughter in a stroller. And when at the Parade's halfway point, I reach a welcoming patch of greenery known as Bishop Lucey Park, my sense of belonging ratchets upward one more full notch. "Hey, it may not be spelled the same," I whisper to my friend back in Portland. "But it's your park all the same, and quite lovely too, just like you. In fact, Lucy, your whole city is special," ricochets my swelling tide of attachment as I enter the grounds through a wrought-iron gate. "It's beautiful, and friendly – and I love its rebel history. And you know what?" I chuckle softly, shuffling toward a bench. "Even though it's pretty large compared to Limerick or Galway, it's still walkable, and really homey when you get to know it a bit. Hell, it's a damn shame we can't share dinner, and I won't get to meet your folks. But we'll do a raincheck for sometime soon, okay?…"

After she smiles her agreement from the vicinity of the water fountain, I leave my bench to pat the wall lining the park's southern perimeter, a well-preserved remnant of the medieval walls that once enclosed Cork. Then, after paying my respects to the local prelate for whom the park is actually named, I stroll further north to Washington Street, where I turn left to pay a brief visit to County Courthouse. Occupying a half-block, and composed of light-beige stone, with tall slender windows carved into its facade, its austere aura leaves little doubt that serious business is transacted here. "Wanna step inside, counselor, and defend yourself against the charge of Navigational Numskullery in the First Degree?" tease-taunts the Professor just as I start to leave.

"No, you old troublemaker, I've retired!" rockets back my reply. "And besides, since I gotta real map, and developed both a feel and an affection for charming Cork, I've been doing just fine, thank you very much! Not to forget, Mr. Cranky-Ass, that the minuscule-minded, insipidly intolerant would-be Prosecutor has been deported to an isolated island of undefined location. You know, your old hometown!…"

Silence. As after my heart-warming defense has stunned him into a muted, "Well, I'll agree that you're doing a lot better in Cork than Chicago, where you'd have already drowned in Lake Michigan," he falls stock-still, freeing me to then follow the crowing echo of my decisive victory until it finally fades out during the curvature of Grand Parade into St. Patrick Street, only to be quickly replaced by a lingering "Wow!…" For appearing even wider than its streetmate, *Pana*, as the locals call it, is Cork City's main avenue, and unabashedly a shopping street, with its great variety of department stores and specialty shops. Multi-colored building facades are once again prominent, intermixed with stone and brick companions, with one in particular, Roche's Store, capturing my attention. As a half-block square, and dressed in lemon yellow, with a turquoise dome for a hat, and a huge arched window beneath it that in turn spawns smaller columnar-shaped sisters and brothers across its wide fascia, all wood-framed in white enamel, "I am a class act!" is the message flowing forth loud and clear.

Uh-huh…I hear ya, answers my VISA card. But unfortunately for Cork's GDP, Mr. Time-Is-of-the-Essence will not permit an expedition into the merchandise-laden interior, as other sights also beg for attention, and there is even more to meet on several of the side streets. For instance, on Paul Street, once Cork's Huguenot Quarter, the cobbled streets and tiny storefronts formerly occupied by French Protestant merchants are still in service, now supporting a solid block of craft, fashion, and souvenir enterprises. And even more noteworthy, to those of a literary bent, the street is also a veritable *bookshop row*, with the international Waterstone's, and locals such as Mainly Murder, Mercier Press, and French Church Street well represented. Due solely to the fact that sugar is not involved, I manage to summon forth my otherwise steely discipline in order to push on to Paul's Lane, Cork's *antique row*, and thereafter, Paul's Place, where I bump into St. Peter and Paul's Church, a red-brick and stone edifice with intricately carved conical spires, just special enough to warrant the sponsorship of two such heavy-duty saints.

Upon returning to Patrick Street – I mean, Pana, as after four hours there's no doubt in my mind that I'm a local, though the Professor argues for just plain loco – I pause to light up my pipe before ambling onward to Princes Street. There, I find one of Cork's great institutions, the Old English Market, more popularly known as the City Market, a huge indoor marketplace dating back to 1610, that's stocked full with colorful stands brimming with fresh vegetables, fish, and fruit, as well as traditional Cork foods. Most fortuitously, my rapid review fails to spot a single confection for sale, as several blocks later, just after I pass my old friend Cook Street, of Chocolate Bar fame, who should I suddenly come face to face with but a large statue of Father Matthew located at the junction of Pana and Patrick Bridge. "Hi, there, Father Matt. How ya doing?" gallops my greeting in an effort to head-off a scathing indictment of indeterminate length, the sincerity of my tone as thick as the sugar-coated plaque lining my arteries. "Very nice likeness of you, sir. And really quite respectful of all these fun-loving Corkonians to place you in such a prominent spot here at the central point of the whole city, what eh?…"

Silence is the only answer. Bronzed silence, in fact. But in the corners of his mouth, I detect just the slightest inkling of a smile, and that's all I need. "Now listen, Father," oozes my plea, like maple syrup over buttery pancakes. "I know I've been bad, as in horrible plus. But you gotta understand, it's not easy overcoming a sixty-one-year addiction. No way. In fact, I've been trying really hard. For instance, it's true I bought three Chocolate Bars at Bewley's, but I'm only a visitor here, you know, just trying to help out the local economy a little bit. Besides, I only ate two, so you see, I *am* abstaining – I mean, kinda, at least for me. And you know what?" aims my knockout punch, my tone as promising as pecan pie a la mode. "The next two destinations on my tour are both churches, and I intend to pray for strength at each one. Not only that, but did I mention that St. Finbarr's a friend of mine?...Well he is, so don't give up on me, not completely, okay?..."

His smile, the inkling that is, doesn't widen. But it doesn't shrink either, so after a candy-coated "Thanks. Nice visiting with you," I hastily stride off along Lapp's Quay, and after concluding with relief that the Sugar Police are not in hot pursuit, then cross over the Lee on the bridge leading to John Street Upper. Well, this will penitently work off a few calories, forms my first thought upon sighting Upper John's forty-five degree upward slope, ironic justice also sliding into view. And after pausing to pocket my trusty Peterson, I slowly but steadily trudge northward toward John Redmond Street, three devilishly long and steep blocks ahead. When I reach it, and turn left, I'm promptly rewarded with a fabulous full-face view of St. Anne's Shandon Church, standing tall and proud a half block away. And a uniquely vertical view it is, too, with the slim shaft of its tower rising impressively from its only slightly larger base into the deep blue sky from its perch at the end of John Redmond's narrow configuration. Built in 1722, this Church of Ireland edifice is synonymous with Cork City's skyline. As from almost anywhere downtown, you can see the landmark tower, a giant pepperpot steeple, two sides of which are made of limestone and two of sandstone, with a top crowned by a gilt ball, on top of which appears an eleven-foot, gold-toned, salmon-shaped weathervane. And just to ensure that its presence is known, eight melodious bells sing out on the hour to serenade Corkonians, and remind them to synchronize their watches with the large, gold, Roman numerals on the black-faced clock which appears on each side of the revered steeple. In fact, Corkonian that I have become, I immediately adjust my faithful Timex Digital by two minutes when four o'clock sounds sweetly over my admiring gaze.

For a musical minute, the chorus continues, so I simply stand and listen, perfectly content to rest, and smiling at the thought of how joyful and triumphant the bells must have sounded to Rebel Cork on Independence Day. Then, after visiting Shandon's interior, which is surprisingly small – and of course, murmuring the promised prayer – I nod so long, and continue farther northward through an intricate series of alleys and short streets in search of the North Cathedral. Realizing that the risk of recreating my early-morning cascade of confusion was considerably better than the odds of winning the lottery, still, buoyed by my flawless performance ever since the Debacle of Ollie's Street, and basking underneath the warmth of the late-afternoon sun, I continue swerving left, then right, and so on, until magically, some fifteen minutes of interpolation later, I suddenly emerge from the mysterious maze onto Cathedral Avenue to claim my prize.

A massive red-brick structure occupying the better part of a block, with a sizable square tower of its own, and large arched windows softening its fascia, the North Cathedral is not nearly as famous as its landmark sister. But no matter. After my fifteen-minute meander in the blind, I am so pleased just to have found this lordly looking house of worship, that Promised Prayer Number Two flows from my happy heart as easily as a Chocolate Bar melts on the tongue. Ooops, wrong analogy. Sorry, Father Matthew. But I did keep my promise, and I haven't eaten anything with sugar for over two hours, so that should count for something, right?... gallops my gleeful gibe through a victorious grin.

Silence. Again, silence. But listening carefully, inside it I can hear a faint echo grow louder. "If you can't do great things," it counsels, "then do small things in a great way!" And heeding its wisdom, I decide that to further celebrate my small spiritual accomplishment, albeit with sizable nutritional and navigational overtones, I will allow myself to wander farther north, just to see what's there. What I find are houses with well-kept yards, an elementary school, and a view. But then I do have a well-recognized facility for understatement, don't I? I mean, did I say *a* view?... Well, how about we change that to *the* view. For there, atop the northernmost reaches of Upper John Street, my eyes feast upon a southerly sweep of Cork City that places a capital P in panoramic. I mean, even the Professor is impressed. And as for St. Finbarr, well, suffice it to say, that he's currently thriving amidst the throes of religious ecstasy!

Me?...I'm close behind. For as I look out over the North Cathedral to the Shandon, then farther south all the way to the majestic spires rising over Cork City's birthplace and the green hillocks beyond the River Lee, the moment fills with serene satisfaction. The sun has begun its descent into the western sky, and as I light up my pipe, my mind's eye smiles too at the shadows gently falling on South Mall, Grand Parade, and Pana, no longer strangers, but now old friends, all in the space of one precious day. Uh-huh…ab-so-lutely amazing, I muse lazily, my mind's eye then wandering off Pana onto Emmet Place and Cork's leading art venue, where I plan to have dinner in its first-floor Crawford Gallery Café. Yeahhh, murmurs anticipation. And not only do they promise real *Cork County cooking* such as chicken pie, Scotch eggs, and stuffed filet of pork, but also the chance to view the Opera House right next door, before returning to Paul Street to browse bookshop row. It won't be the same without Lucy of course. But you know what?…By the time you get back to the Metropole, she'll be at work, and you can call and tell her just how terrific Lucy's Town is. Not to forget, old buddy, what you've got stored in your backpack for a late-night snack, ends my sunset soliloquy as I grab a final glance, then begin my return to City Centre.

"Uh-huh…for sure, and then some!" I chuckle in affirmation. "Sorry, Father Matt. But terrific *must* be celebrated! Not to worry, though. I'll be extra good tomorrow, or the next day. You'll see…"

XXI

HARBOR OF THE SUN

When I finally returned to the Metropole late last evening, after dinner, scouting out Cork's Opera House, and browsing bookshop row, Nuala was waiting for me. Now, I don't want to say she was jealous exactly, feeling neglected is closer to the truth. But in any event, accusations were forthcoming, accompanied by tears, and after some discussion, I had to admit the lady had a case, at least prima facie. I mean, due to my full schedule in Limerick City and Killarney, I hadn't spent much time with her. And now, on top of that, here I was with two new books clutched in my hot little hands. "Now, is that any way to treat a faithful bedtime companion?" she cried out. "Especially an Irishwoman, in Eire?…"

I tell you, I needed a defense. And quickly, as in "HELP!" Temporary insanity jumped into mind. Hell, the Professor would testify on behalf of permanent, with Father Matthew in full support. And even St. Finbarr could be counted on for a few sympathetic words, not to forget that kind old lady who'd verify how lost I'd been, and harboring a near monopoly on confusion to boot. Uh-huh, the makings of a solid defense existed, all right. But as I stood there, studying the hurt etched into Nuala's pretty face, it had entered my mind that sometimes, in truly delicate situations such as these, honesty is the best policy. And acting on this irrational but highly practical proposition, I had simply confessed that first of all, she was too good for me, being so beautiful and successful. Then, I quickly followed up with the fact that it wasn't my fault that Ireland's extraordinary uniqueness and charm had kidnapped my attention. And when I concluded by telling her that she was

186

by far my favorite Irish lady, especially since she was age appropriate, she forgave me, and all was well once again. We had climbed into bed, snuggled underneath the covers, and she had shared with me the interesting friends and acquaintances she had made during her rising journalistic career, such as the poet Philip Larkin, and the short-story writer Alice Munro.

In fact, as I shave this morning, Nuala's lifelong struggle to shed the insecurities fostered by a dysfunctional Irish-Catholic family, and her uphill battle to make a place in the world and find love, are still very much on my mind. Listen, she's just trying to find home too, runs my reasoning as the blade cuts through the foamy lather. "And as you know, old Hobman, it ain't easy," I grumble back at myself, reaching over the trite but true colloquialism for a sip from my coffee cup. "Nooo…For sure," adds experience, before flashes of today's agenda force me to temporarily tuck Nuala into a rear compartment of my mind. "Hey, we've got Waterford to look forward to!" I chirp more cheerfully, my suddenly brightening mood propelling my tone louder. "So get a move on, Buster Brown. Ya hear?…"

I do. I listen, and I hear. And at eight-forty-five, when Bus Eireann pulls out of Cork City, I'm firmly ensconced in my seat, and silently saying so long to Lucy's Town. I'll be back, purrs my promise. As surely as today's the eighteenth, it concludes, the one and the eight then adding together to form nine and slip a fresh smile across my face. It turns into a full-fledged grin, when bolstered by the realization that not only is it a double nine, this being September, but also the sixty-first birthday of my oldest friend Noel. "Happy B-Day, pal, and all the best!" I whisper, spiriting my wish all the way to San Diego, our meeting in the third grade flashing into mind for the trillionth time.

As always, the Eternal Green Blanket soon finds my eyes from its customary position of flowing past my window. And settling back in my seat, I share with it the remaining half of my Chocolate Bar. Uh-huh, that's right, I actually abstained from eating it all as a midnight snack, on account of I was totally stuffed from dinner, and then became too absorbed with Nuala to finish it. I did, however, manage to sneak in a call to Lucy at her desk in Portland. She was as pleased as she was surprised to hear from me. And after we had commiserated over our sabotaged dinner, a festive substitute was planned for the week after my return, albeit with the definite understanding that this was only to be a pacifier until a Cork City Special can be rearranged. Boy, are you lucky to have found such a wonderful friend, or what? I muse contentedly as the bus rumbles onward along Highway N-25.

And the good fortune also applies to the scenic Cinerama playing on an extra-wide screen outside my window. For while the panoply of soft green fields and gently rolling hills maintains its ubiquitous presence on my left, on my right and closest to me, the Celtic Sea now makes a cameo appearance, pinpoints of light sparkling like diamonds beneath the bright sun. And though it's hard to believe, the golden globe's smile widens even further when we reach Youghal, and even more broadly when the town of Dungarvan slides into view, spread out along the banks of its even larger and prettier harbor, the Monavullagh Mountains hugging the far horizon. As having begun our journey by traveling east, now, the full addition of the soothing Celtic seascape serves as a rich reward for our having reached the coast and turned due north toward Waterford. And totally relaxed and carefree, I am not only easily mesmerized, but happily remain so for the sixty-minute duration of our trip.

Emerging reluctantly, only when our driver announces, "Waterford," followed closely by "Plunkett Station!" I am further summoned from my cozy cocoon and into wide-awake consciousness by the suddenly surfacing need to locate my hotel. No problem, however. Not this time. For when I promptly examine my map after exiting the bus, bingo, the pink letters spelling bus station streak to my eyes like the Hobman homing in on a bakery. And to further complement this momentous discovery, when my eyes then lift from the divine designation to trail southward across the street, there, in all its two-hundred-year-old glory, stands the Granville Hotel. As in *my* hotel, sings the song sweetly, accompanied by strains of Handel's "Hallelujah Chorus"!

A full half-block wide, and four stories high, with an orangish-red facade that is home to columns of white, wood-framed windows, the Granville incorporates several buildings that were once private Georgian-era residences, including the birthplace of Waterford patriot Thomas Francis Meagher. In fact, to the left of the entrance, a brass plaque commemorates the 1823 birth of this principal member of Young Ireland, with highlights of his life duly noted. Arrested for fomenting an uprising against English Rule, then banished to Tasmania in 1848, this rebel first-class later escaped to the United States, where he commanded the Irish Brigade during the Civil War, and thereafter served as acting Governor of Montana. "Now how's that, for a colorful two-country career?" I mutter as I enter into the traditionally furnished lobby, noting that it's appropriately fitted with a Waterford crystal chandelier. Room 109 not only incorporates my special number but also follows the traditional line of interior design, outfitted as it is with pale-gold wallpaper that softly sets the scene for matching red-gold-and-green-striped draperies and bedspread. Watercolor prints and a mirror decorate the walls, and to complete the warm and homey feel, next to the window which overlooks the Suir, there's a small mahogany table and two padded chairs. "Comfycozy, for sure," I beam, pleased-plus with the newest of my homes away from home. "Now, let's go get to know Waterford!"

Upon my return outside, one question nags for attention: Is Plunkett Station named for James or Oliver?...My guide book is totally silent on this historically significant issue, so once again I'm on my own. And though a bit uncomfortable, after deep concentration and heated thought lasting for several seconds, I opt for James, giving major weight to his valiant role in the Easter Rising, and feeling that Ollie was already well represented in Cork City and Drogheda, what with his head on display and all. That settled, I turn my attention to Waterford's main feature, known simply as The Quay. Which, most conveniently, is where I happen to be standing, courtesy of the Granville's central location. Actually, The Quay is a series of four quays named Gratton, Merchant's, Meagher, and Parade, which stretch for ten blocks along the south bank of the River Suir, connecting to numerous side streets, and housing a wide variety of shops, restaurants, and pubs, along with several points of historical interest.

On Meagher Quay, just past the Tourist Centre, which is housed in a mixed stone-and-brick building, I garner a clear view of the Edmund Ignatius Rice Bridge. Named after Waterford's spiritual hero, its generous span is a fitting tribute to this eighteenth-century local who became quite wealthy as a merchant, then sold all his possessions in order to help the poor. "Okay, let's hear it Big Time for major unselfishness!" salutes my admiration as my eyes scan the considerable width of the river, noting a string of good-sized barges which remind that Waterford is the main seaport for Ireland's southeast coast. Uh-huh, that's right, memory rolls out. The City's not only famous for its world-class glass-making, but in addition, hosts the traditional industries of meat-processing, brewing, and iron-founding, along with newer trades such as the making of pharmaceuticals, optical products, electronics, and aerospace components. And once unleashed, like in sports, momentum-fueled memory-rushes are hard to stop. Right again, Mr. Recall continues to instruct, me nodding my head to show I'm following along. And while you may think that Waterford is small because of its homey feel, just remember that it's Eire's fifth largest city, and home to fifty thousand fun-loving yet also industrious souls.

Okay…No problem, I acknowledge, now heading back toward the Granville. Before reaching it, however, where Meagher Quay junctions Gladstone Street, I venture up the narrow thoroughfare to meet the Port of Waterford Building, a massive four-story edifice that houses both the Chamber of Commerce and the Harbor Commission. Sporting ornate wooden frames around each of its numerous windows, as well as four chimneys atop the peak of its slanted roof, both its impressive size and aura of importance further attest to Waterford's bustling economic life. Neither Galway nor Limerick City showcased their business community in such grand fashion, I note, as my feet carry me back to Meagher Quay, where I then continue my eastward path. No, finishes the thought, in the Big W, the business of business is easier to get a handle on.

Two minutes, and a short block past the Granville, bring me to the Clock Tower, one of the locale's favorite landmarks. Built in 1861 of cut-stone, this Victorian-Gothic styled tower, with ornately encased clocks surrounding a steepled top crowned with a weathervane, most certainly has eye appeal. And while no longer helping local sea captains keep their ships on schedule, it still serves as a handsome reminder of the recent past, as well as allowing the citizenry to emulate their brothers and sisters in Cork City and keep their watches timed up to the minute.

What? you say. How can a hundred-and-fifty-year-old yesteryear be termed the *recent* past?…Well, the concept of historical time, which employs *feel*, as well as its precise measurement, is relative. So, while the era in which the Clock Tower originated may seem far away, recent yesteryear soon proves to be as accurate as the hands on its four clocks. For just five blocks farther east stands Reginald's Tower, a proud stone fortress whose birth dates back to 1003. And now, we're not only talking *serious* age, but if a major historical landmark, with uniqueness written all over it, causes your curiosity to tingle, we're talking Total Treasure! Uh-huh, that's right, a bonanza of historical authenticity, standing right before your astonished eyes on the eastern tip of Parade Quay!

Okay, to begin at the beginning, like numerous Irish cities, Waterford was founded by the Vikings around 850. The Danes named their settlement Vadrefjord, replacing its earlier Gaelic title of Cuan na Greine, which means "harbor of the sun." Then, to cement their control, as well as to fortify against attacks launched from the River Suir, in 1003, a Viking governor named Reginald built the tower-fortress which still bears his name. And when I use the term tower, once again my gift for understatement springs into action. I mean, this tower is a TOWER! As in fifty feet tall, seventy feet around, and with walls that are ten feet thick! Not to forget either, its huge conical roof. Fortress?...Hell's bells, you just better believe it, all right. Old Reggie wasn't kidding around. Unh-unh...No way, fortification fans. This fella was serious, with a capital S!

Which is precisely the change of clothes my mood has slipped into, as I stand awe-struck, staring at the weather-worn, white-flecked, grayish-brown edifice from a thousand years ago. I mean, my studies had yielded but a scant paragraph about this marvel, leaving my overwhelm to scream "Just look at it, wouldja," and thereby jump-start my imagination in the process. What was Reginald like? it asks. How old was he? Was he single, or did he marry a local colleen like Strongbow would later on? It was probably the latter, huh? 'Cause Eire absorbed the Vikings, remember? adds reason to the boiling pot. Meanwhile, what enemies was he worried about, that he built such thick walls? And what was daily life like a millennium ago?...

Some of the answers lie inside. The arched doorway is only six inches taller than my five-foot-six, so the Vikings harbored no candidates for the NBA. And the stone stairwell leading to the second floor is so narrow and cramped that NFL scouts were also absent. Once I wriggle my way upward, however, the amenities are actually quite nice: wood-planked floors, large archways, the circular, open-space interior, with narrow slits for windows, and enormous wooden beams for a ceiling. No bathroom facilities existed, of course. But as on the first floor, there is a gigantic fireplace for heat and cooking, with the thickness of the walls holding the warmth in. Sleeping arrangements consisted of some straw on the floor, and bathing facilities remained outdoors, weather permitting. All in all, quite livable for the year one thousand, I observe. And the view of the River Suir from the third and fourth floors is nothing short of sensational!

Upon my return outside, I retreat to a small bench near the river for a smoke and additional reflection. Inside, at the admittance counter, I'd learned that the Tower is the oldest urban civic building in Eire, and quite possibly the oldest tower of mortared stone in all of Europe. "And for being so special, all you get is one stinking little paragraph?" I mutter disdainfully. "Why it deserves – "

"Hey, hey, Little Boy Lover of the Ancient, ease up," interrupts the Professor, smiling kindly for a change.

"Uh-huh, I hear ya. But it's a wonder, an absolute wonder!" flows my admiration through the smoke billowing from my Peterson, "I mean, we think it's great, just to be alive at the birth of a millennium. Hell, Reggie's Place has lived *through* one!"

"Yeahhh, I know, it's special, all right. And you've certainly given it a lot of love and attention….So just sit back and enjoy, Reggie'd be pleased."

"He would? I mean, you knew him?…"

"Uh-huh. And he was a pretty nice fella, for a Viking. You know, a little obsessive-compulsive like you, but sorta nice and hospitable all the same. So relax, and finish your smoke. Then maybe it'd be a good idea if you explored some more of Waterford, don't ya think?…"

Actually, the idea is sparkling. Both of them, in fact. And after I've enjoyed a full five minutes more with my adopted tower, I pat it so long, then walk with the Vikings round its circular shape one final time and onto The Mall. Waterford's wide ceremonial street, The Mall instantly greets its visitors with an array of warm-colored storefronts, trees, and flowers. At the southern entrance, a life-size statue of Luke Wadding welcomes you from his perch amidst a triangularly shaped flower bed brimming with pink and white impatiens, saying: "Enjoy!" A local from yesteryear who spent most of his life in Rome as a Franciscan priest and scholar, Mr. Luke is distinguished for being the only Irishman ever to be considered for the Papacy. And when I confide in him that I'm an inti-mate of both Father Matthew and St. Finbarr, his bronze likeness appears most soberly impressed. As am I, though much more happily so, with the avenue over which he presides. It's really quite lovely, with its red, yellow, aqua, and pink facaded buildings, many of which are four stories tall, the sidewalks crowded with peaceful but purposeful pedestrians, and the vehicular traffic sliding along at an unhurried pace. Just a block or so farther south sits the City Hall, an impressive stone structure with large arched windows that was designed by the Waterford-born architect John Roberts. And for company, right next door stands the Theatre Royal, home to music as well as the dramatic arts.

Stopping to scribble a note on what's playing this evening, just in case time permits, my innocent effort at long-range planning somehow causes a charming housewife named Ann to mistake me for a City official about to issue her a parking citation. And when I quickly inform her that I'm simply a visitor who finds Waterford rather wonderful, she's so relieved that she chats with me for several minutes, finally stamping her seal of full Irish approval on me by confiding the name of her family's favorite restaurant for dinner. "You see," I chuckle as she drives off. "You're so Irish, that you've now achieved governmental status, along with access to local secrets." Then, still smiling from the warmth of the unexpected sharing, I push on across the street, off The Mall, and onto Cathedral Lane.

There, I meet Waterford's version of Christ Church Cathedral. And though not nearly as large or magisterial as the Strongbow-sponsored masterpiece in Dublin, it is nonetheless quite impressive in its own right. Also designed by native son John Roberts, it features a classically columned entryway topped by a pediment, along with a towering steeple, and occupies the site of a former Viking cathedral and its medieval successor, which lasted until 1770. Though it still holds a Middle-Aged crypt and tombs from the fifteenth and sixteenth centuries, I pass on the opportunity to view them in favor of wandering onto the adjoining Lady Lane, a narrow passageway that is Waterford's best surviving medieval street. Now home to a host of small shops, some with colored awnings, amidst this charming commercial district also stands the City Library, a large cut-stone structure that was a gift from Andrew Carnegie. And after a much needed bathroom break inside its warm and cozy confines, I also add my heartfelt thanks to the steel magnate-philanthropist for his educationally valuable and equally practical contribution to Waterford's welfare.

Another long block westward, and Lady Lane forms a juncture with Michael Street, once the headquarters for Waterford's guild of weavers, and now, like its sister, home to a wide variety of shopping opportunities, most notably William Gear Confectioners. Now, c'mon. You didn't think I'd miss it, did ya? I mean even partially reformed sugar addicts require some sucrose sustenance. One doesn't just go cold turkey. It could cause heart failure, at least psychologically, and put an untimely end to our shared experience. Now, you wouldn't want that, would ya?...Aaah, good. I didn't think so. Not after we've become such dear friends. So that being the case then, let us return to Michael Street and the Tale of Two Pastries. Uh-huh...With heartfelt apologies to Charles Dickens, the fact remains that I purchased two, and a Triple Play Lottery Ticket to boot. The latter was a two-pound charitable contribution to the disabled. And if a nutritionally incapacitated dude like me fails to show some sympathy, then who will?...

Ohhhkay...Alllright. My brainwaves may have been momentarily mesmerized by my newfound sugar-high, but fortunately not my feet. And as 3:30 approaches, they are hard at work climbing Patrick Street, which I located off Broad after departing the munificent Michael. It's not nearly the workout Upper John presented in Cork City. But when I reach the summit some twenty minutes later, I am treated to a similarly spectacular panorama of Waterford below, with Christ Church's steeple and the kelly-green hillocks beyond the Suir occupaying center stage. And in like fashion to my sojourn atop Cork City, I pull out my trusty Peterson and allow myself the luxury of a full half hour of dreamy enjoyment: just sitting, and looking, and feeling good about the day and its timeless treasures.

When the sun begins to set, I return to City Centre past St. Patrick's Gate, stopping briefly to pat the wall which was once the chief entryway to medieval Waterford. Then, when I reach High Street, I complete my tour of the Middle Ages with a visit to the ruins of the Grey Friars Abbey, which was founded by Franciscan Monks in 1240. Roofless, but with its one-hundred-foot tower still intact, it still feels quite *real* to me, courtesy of an imagination that's fueled by a strangely innate connection to yesteryear. And though also no longer in use, the burial ground still holds numerous centuries-old tombs, including that of Waterford's esteemed architect, John Roberts. I stop by to tell him how much I admire his work with the City Hall and Christ Church Cathedral, then take leave to meet his most famous work of art, a block farther west on Barronstrand Street.

Regally entitled the Cathedral of the Most Holy Trinity, when I reach it, slivers of gold are still slanting across its austere, Ionic-columned façade, creating a soft glow that gently floats my eyes upward to study the religious figures carved into the light-colored stone pediment high over the entryway. Noting further the five life-sized stone likenesses of pilgrims spaced out along a balustrade behind the pediment, before dropping my gaze past the rectangular windows to the large arched doorways, I feel a thin smile curl across my lips in recognition of how handsome plain and simple can be. In stark contrast, however, the Trinity's interior is both rich and decorative, with a high vaulted ceiling, Corinthian pillars, a carved oak pulpit, and most appropriately, a magnificent set of Waterford crystal chandeliers which were donated when the two-hundred-year-old Cathedral was renovated in 1979.

"Well, you're not that old," I murmur through a wider grin after emerging back outside. "But you're special, all the same." And speaking of special, interjects a sudden, hunger-driven idea, time to try out Ann's recommendation for dinner, okay?…Okay, indeed. For once serendipity's secret is actually shared, The City Arms Bistro proves to be a true treasure! The salad is crisp, and dressed in a sweet vinaigrette. The Chicken Kiev needs no knife, and oozes a boatload of butter into the accompanying wild rice with mushrooms. And the chocolate mousse finishes a close second only to the Gourmet Parlour's Chocolate Bar.

Afterward, as I stroll slowly through the settling dusk back to the Granville, I am one happy human. It has grown surprisingly chilly by the time I reach the Quay, and when the wind whips off the Suir and swirls round the twinkling lights dotting the waterfront, chilly changes to downright cold. I don't feel it fully however, as I'm still warm inside from the cabernet that celebrated the Chicken Kiev – and the day's many adventures, already celebrating their own coronation into cherished memories, add an additional layer of warmth over my heart. "Harbor of the Sun?…" I chuckle suddenly, watching the lights sparkle and glitter. "Ohhh, yeah. For sure. 'Cause there's all kinds of warm, and Waterford's got most of them!" answers experience, my head nodding knowingly as the Granville slides into view, coffee and a visit with Nuala waiting.

XXII

IRELAND'S GARDEN

JUST LIKE MY FIRST FULL DAY IN DUBLIN, THURSDAY OPENS CRYSTAL clear, with the sun smiling out of a cobalt-blue sky. And just like sixteen days ago, I make coffee in Room 322 of the Hotel Central, then part the curtains so as to look out on Exchequer Street.

What's different is that this time the street looks familiar, not foreign, amazing me yet again with the strangeness of how quickly the unfamiliar can become like an old friend. In fact, yesterday, when the bus from Waterford had entered Dublin, all of the streets had seemed like bosom buddies. I didn't even feel the need to stay on board all the way to the station, hopping off instead at an unscheduled hotel stop on Abbey Street Lower because I *knew* without thinking that the spot was a half mile closer to home base. Hell, I hear my unconscious reasoning repeat as a smile now finds my face, I know where I am, and where to go. This is Dublin, and I'm part Dubliner. And pulling Big Blue along behind me, I had easily steered a course up Abbey onto O'Connell, then scooted across the Liffey to College Green, Grafton, Wicklow, and finally Exchequer, whose Georgian buildings had smiled a warm welcome then, just as they do now – my eyes happily returning the grin as they wander anew over the weathered brick facades, before dropping to street level in search of fellow Dubliners walking to work.

I'd done a little walking myself, I recall, after having checked back into Hotel Central. Originally, I'd planned to explore Howth, a northern suburb of Dublin, upon my return. But after the journey's Eternal Green Blanket had once again mesmerized me into a state of total relaxation, villages and towns such as Ballyhale and Carlow slipping quaintly by my window, once back beside the Liffey, I had opted instead to leisurely revisit several of my favorite friends. And a happy homecoming it was, too. Beginning at Trinity College, where I sat on the steps in Parliament Square and felt like an alumnus, I had then strolled through Temple Bar to Edward Street where I greeted the Lord Mayor in City Hall and waved hello to Dublin Castle, making sure the Irish flag was still flying overhead. Next, I'd meandered over to Christ Church Cathedral to see how Strongbow was faring and share thoughts of John Roberts and his architecture down in Waterford. A short while later, my old buddy Joe had found me back on my bench in front of St. Patrick's Cathedral. And after we'd chuckled over my admiring "It's still here," and his tongue-in-cheek "Yeah, has been for eight hundred years," I'd then wandered over to St. Stephen's Green, where I'd read the *Irish Times* and people-watched for a full hour, before finally drifting down Grafton Street to Bewley's for dinner. I had wanted to call Brian and Mary, of course, and invite them to join me, but they were still on holiday. Nonetheless, however, the afternoon had remained a pure delight: rich and rewarding, while unhurried, unplanned, and carefree. In fact, the only complication preventing total success was the sad fact that I was also beginning to say good-bye, which caused more than an ounce or two of wistfulness to intermittently creep in, especially when I telephoned to confirm my return flight at day's end.

"But not yet," I suddenly urge, snapping myself out of reverie and back to the present. "Unh-unh, no way. There's a whole twenty-four hours to go, and one eagerly anticipated adventure still to be enjoyed. So how about we stop feeling sorry for ourself, go grab a shower, and get with the program?..."

A good idea. Slip in a hearty breakfast, followed by a good smoke as I wend my way down Wicklow to Suffolk Street and the Tourist Centre, and it turns positively "brilliant," as we Irish say. And once perceived, then settled fully into mind and heart, like a self-fulfilling prophecy, brilliant also serves to accurately describe both the color of the unfolding day, and the host for the natural and spiritual experiences waiting patiently to be shared.

First, however, there is humor. As when the Wild Tour Bus arrives promptly at nine o'clock, one is warmly welcomed aboard by Dave Kearns, a young Jack Nicholson look-alike performing a remarkably good imitation of the venerated star, complete with matching voice tones and arched eyebrows. In fact, it is "Jack" who ensures that each of us is properly introduced to him and every one of our fellow sojourners, before Dave then puts *Mercedes* in motion and we're off. Uh-huh, that's right. Our mini-bus is manufactured by none other than Mercedes-Benz, and though less than half the size of a regular tour bus, comes specially equipped with a super powerful engine, plush seats, an intercom with grade-A speakers, and extra-large windows. And while the nineteen of us are still chuckling over Jack-Dave's opening barrage of commentary, under his skillful guidance it heads south out of Dublin through the suburb of Ballsbridge, a very exclusive part of the City which is home to many wealthy residents, as well as several embassies, including that of the United States. Housed in a circular-shaped, honey-hued stone edifice, as we pass, a bittersweet smile curls across my lips upon sighting the long line of Dubliners waiting to show their sympathy for the 9-11 tragedy by laying flowers on each side of the massive entry gates. For an added moment, I flash on last evening's news report that the Taliban was stalling about handing over Osama Bin Laden, while the U.S. was gearing up to attack Afghanistan. And though unquestionably as real as the hand cupping my chin, the scary prospect of war somehow seems light-years away from the leafy streets and lovely Georgian mansions now flowing past my window, so after whisking a prayer heavenward, I manage to squeeze the ugly subject out of mind.

Five minutes later, we pass Booterstown, a civically constructed bird sanctuary in the form of two blocks of watery fields that "flopped" according to Dave, "because even the birds found it too ugly." Next up is Blackrock College, a private and prestigious institution from which Eire's first president, De Valera graduated, followed shortly afterward by James Joyce's house on Temple Street, a simple, brown-brick structure that breezes by faster than one of his stream-of-consciousness sentences. And with my eyes darting to and fro to take it all in, I'm still smiling from Dave's continuing editorial on the social and political complexities involved in the proper selection of bird habitat, when a minute or two later we reach Dún Laoghaire Harbor on the coast and find ourselves staring out at Wales dotting the distant horizon some ninety miles across the Irish Sea. The view is hampered a bit by early morning cloud cover, so I can't make out any of Catherine Zeta-Jones' countrywomen to invite over for dinner. But after we turn south along the sea, such is not the case when ten minutes' further travel brings us to the famed Martello Tower, standing proudly on a rocky promontory above the village of Sandycove. No, here I have a crystal-clear view of the honey-colored column in which the young James Joyce once lived briefly as a guest of our old friend Oliver St. Gogarty, and which serves as the setting for the opening chapter of his revered novel *Ulysses*. Following up on his earlier theme, Dave adds that the tower is actually one of fifteen built between Dublin and Bray in 1804 to withstand a threatened invasion by Napoleon. "But in that it failed to materialize," he concludes with a chuckle, "it was up to famous old James to rescue this civic boondoggle – though it's highly questionable that even his eloquence and mystique could turn Booterstown to profit."

The quaint little village of Dalkey appears next, dating back to medieval 1358. And while its main street is lined with an array of handsome Regency and Victorian homes, it is just south of the tiny town that a true eye-opener awaits, courtesy of the sublime beauty of Killiney Bay. Nicknamed Eire's Bay of Naples because of its striking resemblance to its Italian counterpart, the view is so simply magnificent that even when Dave slips in the ritzy fact that houses overlooking it from nearby Serrento Terrace cost from one to five million pounds, pricey but worth it! is the aesthetic valuation that continues to filter back from my celebrating eyes.

And though nature's party is indeed dazzling, the beauteous bay soon proves to be only a warm-up for the majestic, almost mystical experience lying ahead. For when eleven o'clock arrives, our tiny transport passes through Loughlinstown, the last village in Dublin County, and enters the wonderland of Wicklow. Called The Garden of Ireland, because one can count forty shades of green, my first thought is that the namegivers had borrowed my gift for understatement. Green?…Uh-huh. Just a tad. As in: Does the Mona Lisa have a mysterious smile? Is Babe Ruth synonymous with baseball? And is Infinity a wee bit further than the tip of your nose? Ohhh, yeah, we've got green all right. More even than Bill Gates when the Dow Jones breaks new ground. We've got blue-green, gray-green, and yellow-green. We've got sap green, spinach-green, avocado, kelly, and emerald. We've even got greens the counters have no names for, but they're different all the same, say your eyes. And dabbed across a gigantic canvas of mountains and valleys, with a complexity that almost defies the complementary pattern, this painting leaves little doubt as to who the painter is, while lifting the lucky observer one short step beyond awestruck, a helpless "Wowww!" trickling off the tongue.

There's more, however. Much more. For nestled into a cozy corner just inside this heavenly Gallery of Green sits sleepy Glendalough, one of Eire's greatest treasures. Translating to The Valley of Two Lakes, Glendalough was founded as a monastic settlement in the sixth century by St. Kevin, and over time became one of the greatest learning centers in all of Europe. In fact, the eminent historian Thomas Cahill observes that through monasteries such as Glendalough and the one founded at Cork by our old friend St. Finbarr, "the Irish saved civilization."

What? you say. How can that be?

Well, as Professor Cahill teaches, just as the Roman Empire was collapsing and transforming from peace to chaos in the fifth century, Ireland was rushing even more rapidly from chaos to peace, courtesy of St. Patrick and his Christian Mission. Totally unique, in its introduction of Christianity without bloodshed, the result was that Eire produced no "red" martyrs. But not wanting to be left out of the Martyrs Club, the Irish, struck by sparks of genius, created the "Green Martyrdom," with Green Martyrs being those who left the comforts and pleasures of ordinary human society to retreat to the woods or a lonely island in order to study scripture and commune with God. And from this religious study, there developed and steadily grew a love of learning for all subjects – a desire for education so equally devout that it led St. Kevin and his monks to build on a plain to the east of the Lower Lake what would become in time a kind of "university city," attended by thousands of hopeful students from all over Ireland, then from England, and eventually from all over Europe. Then, as the centuries slowly passed, these students, spearheaded by emigrating Irish monks, spread the Irish monastic tradition far beyond Eire. Known now as the "White" Martyrs, for following the white sky of morning to unknown places, these self-sacrificing descendants of Sts. Kevin and Finbarr founded monasteries all across Europe, bringing with them their great love of learning and their happy obsession for copying books – a fateful process, whose dual purposes directly resulted in the saving of civilization. For when the Dark Ages descended upon Europe, these scholars and educators not only reestablished literacy and preserved the great works of Greek and Roman philosophers upon which western life is built, but in addition breathed new life into all the habits of mind that encourage thought.

"Well, how's that for a little contribution in the crucial category," seeps my admiration softly after the rush of history into mind has subsided. Then, emerging from the bus to congregate with our group before two massive brown-stone arches which once served as the Gatehouse entryway into the Monastic City, for over a minute I just stand and stare, letting the importance of this special spot sink in, before slowly following St. Kevin's footsteps inside.

The "Worry Stone" is the first object of interest to greet us. Located just past the second archway, the large, gray-white, rectangularly shaped stone is fully surrounded by a darker cut-stone wall to our right, so that it appears embedded. "Touch it," Dave instructs, "and worry goes away or is solved within twenty-four hours," a captivating concept with which I strike an immediate rapport. "Hell, you should downright hug it," adds the Professor after I gently pat it several times, a parade of concerns marching through my mind in sync. Not a bad idea, really, smiles my response as we meander farther up the gravel pathway past the cemetery housing several decorated Celtic Crosses, then emerge into the large clearing that is home to the main body of buildings which once formed the core of the monastery. Approximately a half mile across, and twice as long, the plain is surrounded by lush green hills that appear soft as they slope toward the taller Wicklow Mountains, and the aura instantly communicated is one of total peace and tranquility, the ruins now standing silent in mute testimony to the glory that was Glendalough during the Golden Age of Saints and Scholars.

It lasted for a thousand years, until King Henry VIII's edict dissolved the monasteries in 1539, I recall as I wander over for a closer look at the Round Tower. Constructed of stone, its waist is not nearly as sizable as that of Reginald's. But spiriting upwards to a height of a hundred and ten feet, and crowned with a short steeple that appears to touch a puffy white cloud floating in the turquoise-blue sky, it easily maintains its own remarkableness, especially when one considers that it has been standing sentry for fourteen hundred years. That's four hundred more than the Viking Wonder, trips my next thought in amazement, the latter state only growing greater when I further note that incredibly it's in near perfect condition.

Not so, unfortunately, with the nearby church named St. Mary's. All that remains now of this once proud edifice are the walls, patiently awaiting for someone to kindly restore the roof and the long vanished altar. Standing inside, I note that there are large arched windows on the east-west walls, then nestle into a deserted corner and sit down on the stone floor for a minute to try to feel the presence of St. Kevin and his fellowship of dutiful monks. I can't. Not as fully as I'd hoped. But in the pure peacefulness that surrounds me, I am able to whisper to him my thanks. "Hey, the roof may be off," murmurs my heart. "But your goals of loving learning and spreading wisdom are alive and well. I mean, we still don't have the love and peace part down pat, that's for sure. But you'd still be very proud, I'll bet, of all our schools and universities, and the countless books now in the world – not to forget, of course, the scientific and technological advances which knowledge made possible...No, Mr. Saint, your sacrifices didn't end up in ruins, they're honored every day. So rest easy, ya hear? 'Cause you did your job, Big Time!" I conclude, smiling broadly at the afterthought that it's no accident that such a small island had produced such an enormous pool of literary talent, including four winners of the Nobel Prize for Literature. Unh-unh, I muse happily. Enscript literacy as a religious act, then foster a love of learning, while nurturing books, books, and more books, and you'll live in the hearts and minds of a grateful mankind forever!

Our return to the entrance also permits a short sidestep for a brief visit to St. Kevin's Kitchen, a small oratory with a steeply pitched stone roof, which gets its name from its chimney-esque belfry. In stark contrast to St. Mary's, this chapel, which was erected six hundred years later, is in almost perfect condition, as is St. Kevin's Cross, which we meet soon thereafter upon re-reaching the cemetery. Less ornate than other nearby Celtic Crosses, at twelve feet tall, its pale-gold granite body most certainly catches your eye. And when Dave then drops the tantalizing tidbit that if one makes a wish for another while hugging it, the wish will come true within a year, I readily comply, giving it one tight squeeze for each of my three kidlets once I'm finally able to fasten my arms around its considerable girth.

For good measure, I also lay a hug on the Worry Stone as we return through the entryway, winking smugly at the Professor upon completing my hopeful task. Then, after one last look back at the steeple atop the

Round Tower, it's *lake-time*, our bus rolling slowly past the small but lovely Lower Lake before stopping on the shores of its much larger brother less than a mile away. Surrounded by the same lush hills that flank the Monastic City, with their dense foliage reflecting green hues onto the stone-still water, the bucolic scene simply aches with beauty, capturing, then almost refusing to release one's attention. History, however, also lives in this luminous location, and after a minute or two of gentle nudging, successfully shifts center stage to a spot on our left, where, maybe two hundred feet up the hillside, and surrounded by bushy trees, appears the entrance to a small cave. Just four feet wide, by seven feet deep, and only three feet high, legend holds that this is where St. Kevin actually lived in his old age, from 104 to 110. And after Dave passes out plastic glasses, which he then fills with a spot of Jameson's Irish Whiskey, a communal toast is raised to this courageous and innovative scholar, followed by a prayer for a world peace to match the pure serenity of the surrounding setting.

I'm not sure if our aperitif awakened our appetites, or it was the simple fact that two o'clock was fast approaching, but as we wave so long to unforgettable Glendalough, hunger suddenly centers itself in our collective field of attention. Most fortunately, our able guide knows just how to cure the problem, stopping our trusty transport in the nearby village of Laragh, a lovely little hamlet of fifteen hundred souls oozing charm from the cluster of small ivy-covered shops inhabiting its three-block long central street. For some strange reason, however, known but to the Godperson, the Hobman is the only member of our party who isn't hungry, not even for sugar. I don't know why, maybe it's the lingering fallout from the contemplative mood that Glendalough so powerfully generates? Or maybe it's the fact that as this special day slowly turns toward its end, the knowledge that I must leave Eire tomorrow seeps in to tie a knot or two inside my chest? But appetite is totally absent. So, perfectly content to just sit in the sunshine at a small table in the tiny park across from Lynman's Pub where I purchased coffee, and reflect on the cardinal contribution made by St. Kevin and his faithful descendants, the nagging uneasiness which has been rubbing at the edges of my sense of satisfaction soon subsides, then ceases upon the arrival of my fellow sojourner Simon. For while sharing his orange, along with a hearty conversation that ranges from Glendalough, to life in his native

Tel Aviv, to the events of 9-11, before returning full circle to St. Kevin and what a fanatical genius he was, the sneaky snippets of anxiety finally disappear, and once again I'm wearing a wide smile when we reboard the bus an hour later.

Our direction is now north, back toward Dublin. The sun has reached its apogee, and streams from the true blue sky as we steadily climb into the heart of the Wicklow Mountains. When we reach their zenith, some thirty minutes into our ascent through the Sally Gap, and nine hundred feet above sea level, we stop to enjoy a view, which once again ensures that the Godperson was in an especially good mood when He-She made Ireland. For in all directions, as far as the eye can see, are mountains, broken only by unspoiled valleys, and to the immediate west, the shimmering surface of Lough Tay. Infinity is the concept that muscles into mind as my eyes struggle to grasp, then hold the totality of the enormous beauty which surrounds, as one feels as though it's possible to see forever while trailing the endless path of the mountains. And when I wander off from the group some fifty yards or so, I am further surrounded by silence. A silence which is so soundless, that you are tricked into thinking you can actually hear it. A whisper would sound like thunder, and without conscious thought, I hold my breath so as to not disturb such absolute perfection. Then, after a frozen minute, when I finally thaw and lower my eyes to the valley below my perch, they're further entertained by a patchwork quilt of oak, birch, and rowan enthusiastically turning Fall colors, with heather clinging to the last of its bloom, the pale purple flowers weaving into the lemony gorse.

It is indeed a portrait of perfection, and the perfect end-view for my last day in Ireland – a divine exclamation point, stamping its heavenly seal of approval on the lordly landscape, from the Land of Heart's Desire, to the Connemara, the Burren, the Cliffs of Moher, and the Lakes of Killarney. And if any further proof of perfection was needed, when we stop next in the village of Enniskerry for ice-cream bars, any and all doubt is happily removed. Permanently, and forever, the cold sweet sugar spilling over my tongue like the stream of memories smiling into mind.

Smiling. And smiling. And smiling.

XXIII
TRUTHS

DECEMBER.

2001.

I'VE BEEN HOME IN PORTLAND NOW FOR SOME NINETY DAYS, THE HOLI-
days fast approaching. And though Ireland is once again six thousand miles away, its magic remains active on a daily basis inside both my
mind and heart. For like the River Poddle, which flows underground,
the gentle ache of separation trickles into the background, then stealthily
seeps back inside the smiling Liffey-like current of Sligo, Galway, and
Limerick City, Killarney, Cork, and Waterford as they glide before my
eyes, Dublin, dear, dear Dublin, pushing, then pulling the tide's ebb and
flow.

When I wake, Eire joins me for breakfast, where I check the tem-
peratures on Exchequer Street in Dublin inside the weather section of the
Oregonian. And when it's time for bed, I slip into sleep beside the silvery
surface of Lough Gill, or the majestic Cliffs of Moher, Sneem's serene
wheel of color and Glendalough's Round Tower of Hope also dreaming
into view. In between, during quiet moments of serious reflection, as
well as spontaneous eruptions in the unlikeliest of places such as the
tennis court, the process of evaluation begun shortly after liftoff from
Dublin Airport continues. A fresh adventure, seeking to somehow make
cohesive sense out of all I'd seen and heard, to try to weave each separate
thread into a whole fabric which can be more comprehensively observed
and carefully listened to, then more wisely understood, at times it seems
like I'm back in Cork on the corner of Brian Boru and Plunkett Street
Lower, lost and confused. For to paraphrase the Professor's old friend

Plato, permission having been granted by petition: *Truth is tricky!* As shadowed by cultural differences, then time-weathered by age and its varying perspectives, and clouded further by the arguments of individual preference and conflicting self-interests, color it continuously changing shades of gray, and hope for the best. Which is precisely what I do, the Professor knowingly winking "Good luck," as I manufacture patience one minute at a time.

The journey began, memory reminds, with a thought, followed in short order by desire, idea and need then merging into a mysteriously romantic dream. And even allowing for the sad nonappearance of Rachel, one clear and certain conclusion is that the reality of Ireland bettered the dream. Big Time, and then some! For living, waking Eire is a land of extraordinary enchantment, a country whose verdant landscape, melancholy history, and vivacious citizenry have combined to produce a truly unique cultural blend of yesteryear and today – one which, even amidst the prevailing skepticism and cynicism of the twenty-first century, has somehow managed to maintain some semblance of *innocence*. And like a shy smile composed from memory and shared experience, along with humor and irony and even absurdity, it warmly welcomes all who step inside its aura, then captures your heart with the magnetic authenticity of its inclusiveness.

But what about secrets, the implied revelation of truths? asks a distant voice as I rattle around in my kitchen late at night, its tone soft, but inquisitorial nonetheless.

Well, Eire's landscape is certainly not a secret, forms my answer slowly. No, the lyrical grandeur of nature's green blanket is unmistakable to anyone with eyes, creating a geographical poetry that is greater than Yeats, Shaw, and Joyce combined. But, however, while *green* is the color of *natural and balanced*, and founds a society of like personality, to ensure that simplicity and innocence survive in an increasingly complicated world, the Godperson played a trick: In this land of enormous beauty, He-She left out natural resources of great commercial value. The land provides sustenance and a slow and serene way of life, but there is no coal, no iron, no oil. And as a result, no industrialized society, such as exists in the United States, Great Britain, or Germany.

True, I recall, reaching for my pipe, technology has most surely discovered the Emerald Isle, with its young and highly educated populace.

But even allowing for this increased prosperity, which the citizenry eagerly welcomes, Eire nevertheless remains in large part an *intact rural civilization*, a society still in touch with nature, and one that protects its treasured landscape, and honors its farmers, its elders, and the traditions of its country life. Change, the cardinal rule of the universe, is of course, inevitable, and modern advancements have most certainly entered Irish culture. However, while the computer is welcome indeed, and higher-paying jobs greeted with open arms, nonetheless, roots to the land that run three thousand years deep still mandate an overriding simplicity in the service of values deeply felt. That is why the air is clean, the lakes and rivers clear, restrictions exist to preserve the supply of turf, and for every tree cut down, two are planted. That is why the *Consumer Society* mantra of more, more, always more, does not dominate. And that is why in Eire, the notions of a full appointment book, designated quality time, and death by stress are still in large part alien notions, with most people applying instead different rules of time, having learned a crucial secret of human happiness: "that's it's better to do a few things slowly, than a lot of things fast!"

"You got that right," I suddenly blurt out through a smoke ring, smiling sourly at the bleeding ulcer I'd earned at thirty-three, my instinctive identification with Eire swelling back up inside me, the picture of lost-little-boy-me, high up in the backyard avocado tree pondering and dreaming of where he fits in, also resurrecting itself in a corner of my eye. "Hellll," meanders my murmur, "I sure learned that lesson the hard way. We need to get next to ourselves, and listen to our inner voice, like the Irish do so naturally..." Then, in the silence that instantly returns to surround me, I listen once again to the lilting accent of the people, and their laughter which seemingly flows so easily, the centuries-long struggle for freedom flooding into mind, accompanied by a wailing ballad that somehow holds all the pain from the Battle of the Boyne to the Easter Rising. Is that why they laugh so much and so heartily, to keep from crying, as Lincoln said? springs a sudden query. Is Mark Twain right in his observation that the secret source of humor is not joy but sorrow? Is that the mask of melancholy that sometimes edges round their cheery faces and clouds the twinkle in their eyes, a distant but never forgotten reminder that the hill is steeper for the underdog, and that once even there was a terrible famine? And is that why, Mr. Public Defender, you so readily identify, and why Eire, with its rootedness and balance, and non-Protestant Work Ethic, makes you feel so at home?...

"I...I...don't know," stumbles out my initial response hesitantly, the sudden onslaught puzzling me back into silence. What is *home* anyway? Is it a place, a town or city or neighborhood where you were born, or grew up, or lived a long time? Geography that is fragrant with memory and desire, the place to which the compass always points, or you visit in nightly dreams, or always aim to return to, no matter how far the ship drifts off course?...Or is home simply a special spot inside the heart where it makes lakes of love? A safe harbor of unifying emotion, within which you are known, and accepted, and belong? Or even, maybe...is it both? I mean, part of each? Or could we have more than one?...

I don't know. I just...don't...know, echoes my earlier response, my mind still grappling with the complex concept, pictures of my childhood home flashing into those of the house on Aldbury Court where Patty and I had brought the boys home from the hospital, then merging into the brick Tudor where I now stand, my eyes suddenly searching the darkness outside the window for assistance in the form of my beloved fir trees and the pond lying beyond.

Seems to me, picks up my thorny trail of thought after several seconds' hiatus, that it's a combo, and there can be more than one. And that means, also, that sometimes home can *change*, change so much that it isn't home anymore, that one no longer belongs there. I mean, that's why part of my love for the old comes from my hostility to the new, I nod, finally beginning to see through the morass of my jumbled thoughts and feelings. Because today, change comes faster and faster and faster, the eye-blurring speed dislocating one from his roots. And that's what's happened to America since World War II! shouts a sighting from out of the shadows. We've changed so much, so fast, that we've lost touch with our roots in the land, with rules of time that allowed for knowing our neighbors, for stopping long enough to truly appreciate what we have, to focus on what's really important! That's why, in our adolescent society of bigger is better, more is never enough, and I want it now, home for many is the house or apartment in which one sleeps, as if American life were an exhausting tour of duty, and home is a mere rest stop on the Interstate of Personal Advancement. 'Cause we no longer try to see today through the prism of yesterday. And we've lost sight of the fact that we are who we are, because of what others before us thought and did, and that to have only contemporary values is to have no values! chugs the thought-train into the station, a faint smile curling out of the corners of my mouth as I retrace the tracks of discovery.

"Uh-huh…that's it all right," I affirm, growing excitement now pushing my musings off my tongue. "And that's why I'm so comfortable in Eire. 'Cause they haven't forgotten where they came from, or how better to walk into tomorrow. In fact, in an increasingly fragmented and unstable world, Eire's lesson on how to fix ourselves on the map of our pasts, and our world, and our personal histories, is truly an extraordinary gift. As in Big Time, plus, plus, plus!" marches my enthusiasm, my grin now widening full.

But in the renewing silence, once again the distant voice pokes me squarely in a vulnerable spot between the ribs, "How can you be so sure?" it asks, then waits patiently for a reply.

Well…I can't be, of course, compels honesty, my mind probing anew. For Truth is tricky indeed, and one must find it inside oneself for oneself. Hell, I know that Eire's not perfect, 'cause people are at the controls. Just as I realize that I never actually lived there, only visited. However, in the same breath, I know also that Eire suspends geometry, for it is more than the sum of its parts, its geographical wonderland mixing with its historical struggle for freedom, its art and architecture, and ancient love for the written word, to create a way of life that changes yet remains the same, and whose safeguarding simplicity, welcoming warmth, and stead-fast courage absorbed the Celts, the Vikings, the Anglo-Normans, and little old me in an eye-blink – implanting a sizable segment of Irish soul squarely inside the center core of its American counterpart.

"And you know what?" I suddenly smile out, catching sight of St. Rita, the patroness of Impossible Dreams. "It's no problem that I don't have all the answers, it just means that my Irish Experience isn't over, that's all, that I'll be going back. That maybe next time, I will meet Rachel, or at least wangle an introduction to Nuala, with whom I have so much in common. I mean, no way is it over, not by a long shot," sounds my rushing glee as I reach over Father Matthew's flashing image for a cookie to help celebrate my newest discovery, "It's only the end of the beginning!"

ACKNOWLEDGMENTS

No BOOK IS CREATED, THEN BORN INTO PUBLIC LIFE SOLELY DUE TO the author's efforts. Instead, the final result requires a *community* of contributions, and I wish to express my heartfelt gratitude to the following individuals.

To Annie Forshaw, who initiated the idea of AIE, and served as sounding board and proofreader during the first draft. To Victoria Arrelaño for lovingly believing in me for over thirty years. To Ken Hinsvark, who counseled that "betting on yourself is the best bet you'll ever make." To Leon Vahn, for gently nudging me toward publication.

And also, to Nuala O'Faolain, esteemed author and special friend, for her kind and generous encouragement. To Brian and Mary Arrigan, for adopting me so that I have an Irish family. To David Long, Ciarán Ganter, and John Flynn, for guiding me to Eire's extra-special places, sharing their insights, and becoming good friends.

Finally, to the entire staff of Inkwater Press for their tireless efforts and steadfast support, and especially to Lindsay Burt, Acquisitions Editor; Jo Ristow, Director of Author Services; Michelle Madison, Publicity and Marketing Manager; Masha Shubin, Director of Design; Linda Weinerman, Editor-in-Chief; and Jeremy Solomon, Publisher.

HUGE THANKS to each of you for your generous gifts!

ABOUT THE AUTHOR

Howard G. Franklin received his B.S. from U.S.C. and his J.D. from the University of California, Berkeley, and currently lives outside Portland, Oregon.

His short stories and poetry have appeared in *A Different Drummer, Razem, The Lake Oswego Review, The Sandwich Generation, Silver, Quill, Nomad's Choir, Single Vision, Poets at Work, Grit, Eureka Literary Journal, PoetSpeak Portland Anthology,* and *Verseweavers*, the Oregon State Poetry Association Anthology.

He has also appeared as a guest poet in PoetSpeak's Reading Series at Portland State University, and in the Northwest Poetry Coalition's celebration of National Poetry Month in Vancouver, Washington.